Another day in Paradise..?

Another day in Paradise..?

THE REAL CLUB MED STORY

Patrick Blednick

Macmillan of Canada
A Division of Canada Publishing Corporation
Toronto, Ontario, Canada

Canadian Cataloguing in Publication Data

Blednick, Patrick.
    Another day in paradise

ISBN 0-7715-9282-5

1. Club Méditerranée. 2. Resorts – History.
I. Title.

TX941.C48B58 1988   647'.94   C88-093191-4

Design by Falcom Design & Communications Inc.
Printed in Canada

For Cathy and Joan,
who were always there

ACKNOWLEDGEMENTS

A book of this nature is never a solitary effort. I would especially like to thank a number of people who helped make it happen. They are:

Larry Dent, my agent and friend, who undoubtedly knows more about Club Med than he ever would have dreamed possible;

Linda McKnight, my publisher, who believed in the idea;

Brigitte Cavanagh, who tirelessly worked with me on innumerable aspects;

Helen Mercer, a brilliant researcher who provided many of the details;

Bruce Homer, another friend who helped in any way he could.

I would also like to thank Jane Rowland, Kyle and Dawn Baumanis, Jill Sexsmith, Ted DiBiase, Maurice Coombs, and everyone at the Copy Factory, for their special efforts and generosity. Similarly, I express my gratitude to the Ontario Arts Council.

Finally, I would like to offer a word of appreciation to those who consented to interviews for the book, a task that wasn't always easy.

CONTENTS

Just Another Day in Paradise

"Along the rugged coast of western Mexico, wild horses once roamed free. And men with passions just as wild crossed the mountains to join Zapata. Today it welcomes a band of high spirited sophisticates who appreciate its rare beauty."

Club Méditerranée, 1984

August 25, 1985. Costa de Careyes, Mexico. It is just another day in paradise. Or so it seems. A scorching tropical sun is beating down, and the secluded Playa Blanca village, Club Méditerranée's oldest operating resort in Mexico, is throbbing with activity.

Late August is always hot and humid in Playa Blanca, but despite the frequent showers that occur at this time of the year, most of the 290 pueblo-style, adobe-brick rooms are occupied.

The beaches, bars, and restaurants are crowded. Men ogle scantily dressed women. Sunbathers are bronzing. Ivan Lendl look-alikes head for the tennis courts. California cowboys ride off into the jungle. Windsurfers sail the sparkling waters of Chamela Bay. Beefy men, anchored with gold like sunken Spanish galleons, patrol the beach. The lazy reflect on the lapping waves. Christopher Cross and Jimmy Buffet play softly in the background. The hedonistic scent of coconut oil, Bill Blass cologne, and strong Jalisco marijuana fills the heavy air.

Then suddenly, five gunmen, brandishing rifles, shotguns, and pistols, their faces hidden by improvised balaclavas, attack the Club Med village. It's a robbery, and the vulnerable Playa Blanca resort, situated a distant 94 miles south of Puerto Vallarta and 63 miles north of Manzanillo, is a perfect target.

Tom Barnette, owner of Voyager Travel in Brooksville, Florida, and president of Euro-American Programs, a European tour operator, was an eyewitness to the robbery.

"My wife and I were in the excursion office arranging an optional trip," Barnette explained to *Travel Weekly*, the leading travel trade publication in the United States. "About six or seven other guests were in the room as well as two office workers. One of the employees called out that we were having a hold-up. Everyone got on the floor or crouched behind chairs and tables.

"Then the telephone rang. One of the bandits ran into our room with a shotgun and started yelling to the woman holding the phone, 'No, No, No,' meaning to put the phone down. The bandit kept standing in the doorway while the other four finished taking things out of the safe."

After ransacking the safe, the bandits seized two Club Med staffers as hostages just in case the Mexican army or the much-feared Federales, Mexico's national police, intervened in the assault. At last the gang and their hostages, who were subsequently released unharmed, fled into the dense jungle.

The amount stolen in the Playa Blanca heist was considerable. Vincent Hovanec, an official with the American embassy in Mexico City, estimated the total losses at more than $73,000 in cash as well as undisclosed amounts of jewellery, cameras, credit cards, passports, and other valuables. It was reported that up to 500 guests were vacationing at Playa Blanca at the time.

As for the Barnettes, they suffered losses of $560 in cash, $100 in travellers' cheques, and a pearl necklace worth $450. In addition, the Florida couple lost 13 credit cards and their passports.

The August 25 robbery was not the first incident of this kind at Playa Blanca. In fact, it was the second hold-up in 1985 and at least the third since Club Méditerranée opened the vacation village in 1974.

The first reported robbery occurred on August 13, 1977. In retrospect, it was a comical, almost slapstick affair. The bandits were only interested in cash and stole about $25,000 in bills, mostly in American currency. They casually and inexplicably discarded thousands of dollars' worth of travellers' cheques and jewellery by the side of the road.

The next incident took place on a balmy Tuesday evening on January 29, 1985, just as the GMs (*gentils membres*, or gracious members, Club Med's term for guests) were preparing for a night of fun and frivolity. A gang of machine-gun-wielding desperadoes hijacked a taxi in a nearby town and roared over to the Playa Blanca resort. They stormed the Club Med office and forced frightened employees to open the safe. As in the August 1985 robbery, which happened less than seven months later, the loot included thousands of dollars in cash and travellers' cheques, large numbers of credit cards, passports, and other valuable items. Approximately 300 American, Canadian, French, Argentinian, and Mexican GMs were victimized in the raid. Amazingly, no one was hurt, a miracle considering the deadly weaponry carried by the bandits.

Playa Blanca's employees were not anxious to discuss the details of the robbery with the media. When reporters from the *Toronto Star*, Canada's largest newspaper, telephoned the Club Med village following the raid and requested more information, their efforts were in vain. "An attempt to talk to some of the Toronto victims was thwarted when a female employee denied there were any Canadians there, refused to give her name and banged down the phone," said the *Star*.

However, Norbert J. Gibson, the Canadian consul in Mazatlán, another Mexican resort located several hundred miles north of Playa Blanca, contradicted the Club Med staffer. He confirmed that 123 Canadians, 28 from Toronto, were robbed in the Playa Blanca attack.

Officials at Club Méditerranée's North American headquarters in New York were also more candid. Edwina Arnold, a spokesperson for the company, admitted that the robbery had taken place and gave details of how the gunmen had forced the Playa Blanca employees to open the safe. She added that the company intended to reimburse the victims as soon as their losses could be verified.

According to the rarely read fine print on the company brochure, Club Méditerranée automatically insures GMs against such incidents. "The policy will provide you with up to $2,000 coverage for lost baggage and personal effects," the brochure states. (All dollar figures in this book refer to U.S. dollars, unless otherwise noted.) There is a $400 limit on any one item and $25 is deductible for each individual claim. Credit cards and airline tickets are covered to a maximum of $500, and cameras are insured for only $250, not much when one considers the high cost of good photographic equipment. But the policy is still no guarantee that the company will honour all claims. "While Club Med takes pleasure in making this insurance available as part of your membership, we, of course, can assume no responsibility or liability respecting it," asserts the French vacation company.

Club Méditerranée announced plans for improved security after the second robbery at Playa Blanca in 1985. "We are in the process of installing individual safes at many facilities in the Western Hemisphere," Jacques Ganin, president of Club Med sales in New York, told *Travel Weekly*, spelling out a new company policy designed to prevent any more embarrassing raids by Mexican outlaws. The old policy, whereby GMs voluntarily placed their cash and valuables in a purportedly secure, central resort locale, was, quite simply, too convenient for robbery. The new measures were long overdue. In the bad old days, machine-gun-toting cutthroats had not had to waste precious minutes frisking hundreds of holidayers for their belongings. Instead, the company had inadvertently collected the booty for them. Robbery was simply a matter of visiting the Club Med office, issuing a few ultimatums, plundering the safe, and heading for the jungle before the Federales arrived.

Ganin, who explained that robberies were rare at Club Med villages, also said that GMs would be encouraged to deposit their valuables because there were usually no locks on room doors at company resorts. But the crucial question of the wisdom of Club Méditerranée's policy of operating hotels in remote, risky areas, like the Playa Blanca village in Mexico's rugged Pacific coast state of Jalisco, was not addressed.

Questions of that nature would have to be answered in Paris, the home of Club Méditerranée's international headquarters and of Gilbert Trigano, the company's legendary chairman of the board.

CHAPTER ONE

Kingdom in the Sun

"The days of senseless sunbathing are over!"
Gilbert Trigano, 1985

Gilbert Trigano, a grocer's son and former member of the French Communist Party, is not the kind of person one expects to find in charge of Club Méditerranée, the world's largest recreational vacation resort company.

In appearance, he bears a passing resemblance to Peter Sellers. Short and unathletic with metal frame glasses, slightly bulbous nose, drooping shoulders, and carefully groomed greying hair, he looks more like a banker or a lawyer than a holiday tycoon.

"His baggy trousers and slightly crumpled shirt are in contrast to the immaculately dressed French staff who surround him," observed the respected Australian *Financial Review* after a 1984 interview. But as the publication wryly noted, this reflects Trigano's "image as a modest hardworking person."

Trigano, an energetic shirtsleeves executive, is a brilliant mathematician and the most notorious pen thief in the office. Befitting his position as head of a vacation company, his manner is relaxed and informal. He likes to be addressed simply as Gilbert by his minions and uses the more affectionate "tu" rather than the formal "vous" when talking to people.

Trigano's demeanour and casual dress have nothing to do with his business accomplishments, of course. And at 67, an age

1

when most high-flying entrepreneurs have settled into a comfortable and less active retirement, he remains a workaholic who spends endless hours monitoring the progress of the company.

As chairman of the board and managing director of Club Méditerranée, Trigano enthusiastically rules his kingdom from a rejuvenated building on Avenue Hoche, just a short distance from the Arc de Triomphe and the fashionable Champs-Elysées.

Inside, Trigano's office is decorated with Pop Art — an immense painting of a Cadillac's chrome fender, a squashed beer can sculpture, buxom red and green chairs, a black plastic conference table, and an eye-catching purple neon trident, the corporate symbol of the company. This unusual office setting is indicative of Trigano's flair for creativity and innovation, two key factors in Club Méditerranée's rise to prominence in the competitive and complex vacation industry.

Trigano's empire, like other prosperous multinational enterprises, is a vast network of hundreds of component companies, ranging from the popular Club Med villages to mysterious offshore holding firms. Club Méditerranée and its subsidiaries generated close to FF6 billion in revenue in 1985 (about US$1 billion). The company employs up to 18,600 people annually and caters to over 1.25 million guests.

"Arguably it is the most original and creative large-scale holiday venture the world has yet seen," remarks John Ardagh, author of *France in the 1980s*, summing up the significance of Club Méditerranée. "This is the Great French Dream made reality."

What is Gilbert Trigano's "Kingdom in the Sun"?

First and foremost, it is the Club Med villages, a world-wide chain of resorts that at last count numbered 96 resorts in 33 different countries. Then there are Clubhotel-Maeva and Utoring-Maeva — 63 apartment buildings, mostly on the French Riviera, that are available for short-term holiday rental or time-sharing purchase. Another 14 Club Med–like resorts are operated by Valtur Vacanze, an Italian vacation company that is 45 per cent owned by Club Méditerranée. Add the Hôtel de

Neuilly, a four-star, 670-bed establishment in a suburb of Paris, and the five Archeological Inns that are managed by the company, and you have the 11th-largest hotel chain in the world, according to the American trade publication *Hotels and Restaurants International*.

Trigano's realm also includes a sizeable number of sales offices, management subsidiaries, and representative agencies to keep the tidal wave of GMs continually rolling in. These offices are located in France, Great Britain, the United States, Canada, Mexico, Australia, Japan, Singapore, South Africa, and a host of other countries.

Trigano has also established companies in various Caribbean tax havens. The offshore firms, like Club Med Inc. in the Cayman Islands, Club Med Holding in the Netherlands Antilles, and Club Méditerranée Bahamas Ltd., have vaguely defined functions. As documents submitted to the Securities and Exchange Commission (SEC) in Washington clearly explain, firms such as Club Méditerranée Bahamas Ltd. provide "certain management services to certain villages" or they might "from time to time make loans to other subsidiaries of the company."

Club Méditerranée is a public company with shares currently being offered on the Paris, Brussels, Luxembourg, and New York stock exchanges. But the fact that it is listed on a major exchange, especially in the tightly regulated and disclosure-minded United States, is no guarantee that the company will eagerly divulge all its corporate secrets.

Take the example of Club Med Inc., the Cayman Islands corporation that is currently traded on the New York Stock Exchange. If shareholders want to find out the names of their fellow investors or check on the propriety of their investment by examining company records, they are out of luck. As the company bluntly states, shareholders "have no general right to inspect or obtain copies of the list of shareholders or corporate records of the company."

To oversee the company and presumably offer the occasional bit of advice, Trigano has assembled a blue-ribbon 10-member board of directors that must be the envy of every multinational corporation. Composed of scions of international business, both private-sector and French government–controlled, these influential and powerful financiers are some of the wealthiest men in the world or acting as nominees for those tycoons.

Heading the list of directors is Baron Edmond de Rothschild, chairman of the French holding company La Compagnie Financière and reputedly the richest member of the fabled Rothschild family. Another is Ghaith Pharaon, the elusive Saudi Arabian billionaire with extensive interests in the United States, Great Britain, France, the Middle East, and the Far East and anywhere else that lusts for an injection of petrodollars. Then there is Gianluigi Gabetti of the Istituto Finanziario Industriale Internazionale (IFINT), a Luxembourg holding company controlled by the charismatic Giovanni Agnelli, chairman of the board of Fiat and reigning Croesus in Italy.

The other directors, while not in the same league as Rothschild, Pharaon, and Agnelli, include Christian de Fels, president of the executive committee of the Banque de Gestion Privée, a Paris bank, and Wolfgang Graebner, managing partner of the Berliner Handels und Frankfurter Bank, a West German financial institution.

The French government, through its nationalization of the country's largest banks, insurance companies, and other economic organizations, is represented by Jean-Yves Haberer, chairman of Banque Paribas, one of France's biggest investment banks; Yvette Chassagne, chairman of the Union des Assurances de Paris, a huge insurance group; Michel Gallot, director general of Crédit Lyonnais, France's second-largest commercial bank; and Robert Lion, managing director of the Caisse des Dépôts et Consignations, the most important French government financing institution. Not surprisingly, Club Méditerranée's directors are also the major shareholders of the company.

According to the 1983/84 and 1984/85 annual reports, Rothschild, Pharaon, and Agnelli's IFINT, as well as the French government proprietaries, collectively own about 25 per cent of Club Méditerranée's capital stock. (This figure contrasts with those disclosed in a 1984 prospectus issued in the United States, prior to the launching of Club Med Inc. on the New York Stock Exchange. This document states that the same group of shareholders control about 30 per cent of the capital stock.) The remaining shares are held by approximately 2,000 other investors.

Gilbert Trigano is not himself a big shareholder in Club Méditerranée. As he confided to the *New York Times* in July 1985, the company has not made him personally wealthy. He estimated his investment at only $100,000, not much when one considers the lifelong commitment he has given the company. But as he also confessed, he does earn a "high salary" for serving as the company's CEO.

In 1981 Trigano, like a Parisian butcher slicing goose liver pâté, began carving up the company into four distinct administrative sections called zones. He realized that Club Méditerranée had to become more streamlined and efficient if it was to compete for a larger share of the vacation market. The restructuring was a calculated move designed to make the company more available to the hearts, minds, homes, and wallets of the GMs.

The four zones, which include all of the company's resort villages and sales offices around the world, are loosely defined on a continental basis — Europe, Africa, and the Middle East; South America; America; and Asia.

The most important zone is Europe, Africa, and the Middle East, a huge territory with 70 villages that account for 70.6 per cent of Club Méditerranée's total bed capacity. The zone's villages, which attracted 577,300 guests, or 64.6 per cent of all guests in 1985, appeal mainly to a European clientele — 512,300 of the guests came from France, Italy, Belgium, Switzerland, or West Germany.

In contrast to the popularity of this sector, the South American zone is a virtual holiday wasteland. In fact, the zone has just one resort, Itaparica in Brazil. The lone Itaparica outpost, situated across the bay from the colourful and Carnival-crazed city of Salvador de Bahia, generates only a paltry 3.3 per cent of the company's total number of guests. But the South American

5

balance sheet is expected to blossom when another Brazilian village — at Rio das Pedras, about 45 miles south of Rio de Janeiro — opens in 1987 or 1988. Speculation is also rife that Club Méditerranée may open resorts in Colombia and Argentina.

The American zone, which includes Club Med resorts and facilities in the United States, Mexico, and the Caribbean, is the one in which Trigano anticipates significant growth for the company. Currently the American zone accounts for 26.5 per cent of all guests and represents 22.7 per cent of Club Méditerranée's capacity. However, these figures are certain to increase when a host of new properties, especially in the United States and Mexico, join the Club Med fleet.

Similarly, the Asian zone, which encompasses the South Pacific, the Indian Ocean, and the Far East, is charted to become a major producer in the years to come. Although the Asian zone currently generates only 5.6 per cent of all guests and just 5 per cent of capacity, new developments in Japan, Thailand, Indonesia, and the People's Republic of China (where plans call for two villages to be operated on the grounds of Beijing's Imperial Palace) will ensure that this sector will become much more important to the company in the future.

From an administrative standpoint, the Europe, Africa, and the Middle East zone and the South American zone report to the international headquarters in Paris; the American and Asian zones are controlled by the New York offices of Club Med Inc., the Cayman Islands subsidiary, which is 73 per cent owned by Club Méditerranée in France. The remaining affiliates — Clubhotel-Maeva, Utoring-Maeva, and the Hôtel de Neuilly — are administered from Paris, while Valtur Vacanze is managed in Rome.

"Our company is extremely healthy and growing rapidly," explained Trigano in a 1986 letter to shareholders. "Our villages, our clientele, and our plans all combine to place us in an enviable position for the future."

If his ambitious plans succeed, and there isn't any reason to believe they won't, Club Méditerranée expects to be operating 250 villages and generating billions of dollars a year in revenue by 1995. To attain this increase in capacity and cash flow, the company plans to open four new resorts in each of the four zones every year.

Are there enough Club Med fanatics out there to fill all those new rooms? Trigano, who always thinks big, has already analyzed the possibilities. As he said to the French magazine *L'Express*, there are "350 million" vacationers around the world. Of that number, he estimates that Club Méditerranée's concept "corresponds to the needs of 15 per cent," or about 42.5 million potential GMs.

Who are Club Méditerranée's clients?

"Our guests, referred to as GMs, are well informed, sophisticated, and educated," explains the company. "They come from all walks of life — lawyers, doctors, business people, artists, teachers, nurses, secretaries, students — and encompass all age groups."

A recent survey conducted by Club Méditerranée of its American clientele revealed that the median income of U.S. members is "over $50,000." A more precise breakdown indicates that 22 per cent earn over $80,000 a year, 28 per cent earn between $50,000 and $80,000, 34 per cent earn between $30,000 and $50,000, and 16 per cent earn under $30,000.

Besides having a lot of money, Club Med's American clients are, on average, 37 years of age; over 50 per cent are married. They are also well educated: 77 per cent of the GMs are college graduates; 38 per cent have post-graduate degrees.

"Not exactly the kind of people you find hanging around singles bars," trumpets one of Club Med's advertisements.

Trigano attributes the success of the company to several factors. "First, there are our GOs [*gentils organisateurs*], who serve as hosts at each village," says Trigano, recognizing the contribution of the company's energetic hotel staff. He believes that the GOs' "ability and enthusiasm bring the Club Med concept to life as a warm and welcoming reality." Then, Trigano goes on, there is "a management team which, behind the *joie de vivre* of each resort, exercises strong, cost-effective controls over day-to-day operations." Long-range planning "is skilfully handled by the Club Med headquarters staff," while the company's effervescent marketing division "is constantly uncovering new avenues of growth."

What about Trigano's own role as master builder of the company? "After all, I'm not an idiot," Trigano told *Réalités*, downplaying his business achievements. "It's luck. Otherwise, with the way I look, I would be selling lucky bags in the Paris subway."

Which brings us to the mythical Club Med "concept," the main difference between Club Méditerranée and its competitors and the reason why so many people are attracted to — or turned off by — the company.

"A Club Med vacation is a ticket to a carefree world where spontaneity, relaxation, and good, simple fun abound," explains the company in its promotional literature. "The result is a stress-free experience, a true vacation from the pressures of everyday life.

"There are no arrangements to make, no timetables to follow, no budgets to watch, no tips to hand out," says Club Med, alluding to the all-inclusive nature of the package. "Everything is already paid for, except excursions and purchases from the bar and boutique." It all sounds enticing, especially when one adds in beautiful and exotic locales, tantalizing gourmet food, and hints of uninhibited sensuality to the vacation fantasy. So why are some people turned off by the Club Med concept?

The reactions of people who have stayed at Club Med resorts are varied. Susie Krantz, a 27-year-old construction worker from Hopkinton, New Hampshire, did not enjoy her vacation at Club Med's Buccaneer's Creek village in Martinique. She was offended by a pack of leering men who swarmed around her.

"It's a meat market," Krantz complained to the *New York Times*, put off by the high-pressure sexual shenanigans. "There's a bunch of guys after sex. Maybe if I was 19 and still in college I could deal with it better, but as it is, I don't think I'll ever come back."

Not all women have to spend their holidays beating off the lusty advances of men. Karen Hepburn, a single, 31-year-old

Toronto Sun reporter, had an enjoyable time when she stayed at Club Med's new resort in Bermuda.

"I had been worried about holidaying alone, fearing I might spend lonely hours behind a book on the beach," confessed Hepburn. "Yet I ended up in the company of fun-loving new friends and acquaintances. There was never a dull moment. Needless to say, I didn't get a lot of reading done."

Club Med claims that most of its guests have a terrific time and share Hepburn's sentiments. An in-house survey of the company's clients indicated that 35 per cent had previously vacationed at a Club Med village and that a staggering 94 per cent had enjoyed it so much that they say they would gladly return again, probably the highest approval rating in the hotel industry.

In 1984, to further bolster mainstream impressions and hammer away at the false images, Club Med ran a series of advertisements in the American media questioning the company's wild reputation.

The advertisements, headed "Club Med Properly Explained" and "Where Is It Written that You Have to Be Young, Swinging and Single to Enjoy Club Med?" and "Club Med Isn't All It's Cracked up to Be," extolled the virtues of yoga, tennis, golf, scuba diving, aerobics, archery, and other wholesome activities. However, the celibate promotional campaign wasn't entirely free of vice. Drunken chortling was encouraged in one ad in which readers were invited to "giggle your way through carafe after carafe of wine" if they weren't interested in water skiing.

"Club Med is the world's biggest vacation company," observes British-based travel entrepreneur Bruce Homer. "Whenever you are the most successful at anything, there are always going to be a lot of misconceptions. It's natural. It's human nature. But what the hell, I have difficulty believing that Club Med is overly concerned about it. After all, they're laughing all the way to the bank more frequently than anybody else in the vacation business."

Nevertheless, Gilbert Trigano is perplexed by Club Med's raunchy reputation. As he explained to *Time* magazine in 1986: "There is an extraordinary difference between the image people

9

have of a Club Med village and what it actually is. Paradoxically, we are almost trapped, caught between our image and the reality."

But Trigano's views of what goes on at a Club Med village are contradicted by a GO currently employed by the company, who related rumours of sizzling sexual escapades that persist at some resorts, especially Buccaneer's Creek in Martinique.

There, according to the GO, GMs who are tired of volleyball can allegedly participate in unauthorized games such as "the Blow Job Olympics," a recreational activity that is definitely not listed in any of the company's glossy brochures. When quizzed about the rules, the GO, a man in his early 20s, blushed and explained that he wasn't really sure because he'd never been to Martinique and that his report was really only hearsay. But, he added, he was looking forward to working there one day. As with most rumours, it is hard to find anyone who has actually participated in the events described.

Also conflicting with Trigano's remarks are reports of "Club Med dermatitis," a skin ailment detected and named by Wain White, a physician at the New York Medical Center. Dr. White first became aware of the bizarre condition when a tanned, 18-year-old Hispanic woman who had just returned from a Club Med vacation in the Caribbean visited him and complained of irritating red rashes on both her thighs.

"Linear, hyperpigmented patches with scalloped borders," diagnosed Dr. White, in a letter to the distinguished *New England Journal of Medicine*. The cause of the strange rash, which was common among citrus workers in the early 1900s, was a mystery to Dr. White until his patient disclosed that she had participated in a Club Med drinking game that involved male GMs sliding limes up and down her bare thighs with their chins.

After listening to her story, Dr. White concluded that the source of the disorder was furocoumarin, a natural chemical compound found in the oil of lime peels. He determined that the skin of the limes must have become "disrupted" during the game, thereby releasing the harmful agent that caused the rashes. Dr. White warned Club Méditerranée of the dangers of rolling limes over the sensitive parts of a person's body, and recommended substituting grapefruits for limes because they do not contain the offensive chemical.

It is mostly in North America that Club Méditerranée has had to cope with problems concerning its reputation as a haven for sex maniacs. In Europe, where the prevailing mores are different, the matter is hardly raised.

"Trigano is a visionary who has always known, before anybody, where he could go and where he wanted to go," proclaims *L'Express*, praising the chairman's ability to navigate his way through the subtleties and risks associated with the international vacation business.

Whether it be the rising tide of Islamic fundamentalism in Arab or Far Eastern countries, political upheaval in the Caribbean, or the deteriorating economic and social climate in Latin America — developments that can seriously affect Club Méditerranée operations — Trigano has always weathered the storms.

In the many years that he has been associated with Club Méditerranée, he has won countless battles, including a few in which the very survival of the company was at stake. But no matter how tough the fight, he has emerged intact and more eager than ever to carry forward his extravagant plans.

"We plan and manage our business strictly and conservatively," says Trigano. However, beneath the strait-laced pronouncements, he is a fascinating man who indulges in fantasy and poetry. "A dreamer of a concrete utopia," he calls himself. Whether Club Med is that concrete utopia, however, is another question altogether.

11

CHAPTER TWO

Genesis

"Happiness is so simple, why don't we bother to
live it?"

Gérard Blitz

G ilbert Trigano, despite his pervasive influence and long-
standing association with the company, was not the
founder of Club Méditeranée. Nor was he the creator
of the legendary Club Med concept. These historic achievements can be attributed exclusively to Gérard Blitz, whose contributions to the company are all but forgotten or unknown by
today's generation of GMs. "We are not pleased with the world
as it is," he once idealistically declared. "We are going to create
another one."*

Blitz, a large, muscular man with curly blond hair, was born
in Antwerp, Belgium, in 1912. His father, Maurice, a Flemish
Jew, was a prosperous diamond merchant and cutter. Gérard
acquired the precision craft while still in his early 20s. Although
he was raised in wealth and was to become one of Europe's
premier diamond-cutters, Blitz's main passion in life was sports,
especially those related to water. A champion water polo player
and a member of Belgium's Olympic team, he was always eager

---

*Unless otherwise noted, many of the stories concerning the early history of the com-
pany in the next three chapters are derived from Christiane Peyre's and Yves Raynouard's *History and Legends of Club Méditerranée*, published in France by Seuil in
1971.

12

to participate in swimming, snorkelling, fishing, and anything else of an aquatic nature, an element that was to weigh heavily in Club Méditerranée's future sun-and-sea formula for success.

Blitz was polished and charming and had a strong interest in the arts. He liked to surround himself with writers, painters, and theatre people, perhaps fulfilling a need to make up for his educational shortcomings. At 23, he married Denise Libbrecht, and the couple had four children in rapid succession: Gérard Jr., Maurice, Hélène, and Jean.

In the Second World War, he was a hero of the underground and was subsequently awarded the Resistance Medal and Military Cross by Belgium's King Baudouin. Additionally, France recognized his wartime achievements by decorating him with the Croix de Guerre, and he was made a Commander of the Order of the Veterans of Foreign Wars by the United States.

After the war, Blitz helped manage a government-sponsored rehabilitation complex for Belgian survivors of the Nazi concentration camps at Lac d'Annecy in France. There, amidst the quiet, pastoral beauty of the French countryside, the refugees thrived. "I think without it these people might have died," Blitz told *Newsweek* magazine, recalling the plentiful food, abundant sports, and relaxed atmosphere.

Following his experiences at Lac d'Annecy, Blitz met Claudine Coindeau, a beautiful Frenchwoman who had been living in far-off Tahiti. A free spirit and a hippie before her time, she was to change his life forever. Blitz was captivated by the exotic Claudine, who regaled him with colourful stories of a liberated life-style on a South Pacific paradise. Soon the couple became inseparable, although they didn't get married until March 27, 1959, more than a decade after they met. There is no question that her utopian philosophy had a profound impact on Blitz and the later development of the Club Med concept.

Meanwhile, Blitz's sister, Judith, whom everyone called "Didy," had married a fellow named Mario Lewis, who ran the bar at a simple and inexpensive 300-bed tent resort at Calvi, on the Mediterranean island of Corsica. Known as Club Olympique, it was one of the numerous predecessors to Club Méditerranée that had been gaining in popularity since Léon Blum,

France's first Socialist prime minister, had introduced mandatory paid holidays for French workers in 1936.

Club Olympique was created and organized by Dimitri "Dima" Philipoff, a White Russian exile who was one of the early pioneers of cheap tent vacations in France.

Philipoff, like Blitz, was also a world-class athlete, renowned for his accomplishments in swimming and water polo. Handsome, clever, hard-drinking, and a bit of a Bohemian, he earned a good living as a sports writer working for French publications like *L'Auto* and *Paris-Soir*.

He had been dabbling in the tent vacation business since 1935. That was the year he approached the University Sporting Club of France (SCUF) with an imaginative idea for a low-cost, all-inclusive resort that in some ways was modelled after a *vitiaz*, a French youth camp, where he and other children of White Russians had holidayed in earlier years. The staid SCUF politely listened to Philipoff's proposal and then dismissed it as foolhardy and impractical — a decision that made the flamboyant White Russian stomp out of the room, slamming the door behind him.

But Philipoff didn't give up. Instead, he and a few other White Russians who were living in Paris formed their own club, called L'Ours Blanc (the White Bear). And in the summer of 1935, just a few months after the SCUF had scuttled his scheme, the fledgling association managed to lure 250 French vacationers at a mere FF500 apiece to its informal retreat in Corsica.

To the surprise of Philipoff and his colleagues in L'Ours Blanc, who had committed themselves to the project more as a hobby than as a business, the Corsican resort turned a small profit in its first year. This windfall was an encouraging signal to Philipoff, who immediately set about expanding the operation.

Philipoff, who had always been nonchalant about money, borrowed heavily to finance the expansion. "To owe a lot of money is to be somebody and be respected," he theorized. With financing in hand, he was aggressive with the fresh infusion of capital. He increased the capacity in Corsica to several hundred beds. To fill them, he advertised on Paris radio stations and placed posters in the Métro. He also wrote glowing articles in *L'Auto* to promote the venture.

It was a success. Soon the Corsican resort was doing so much business that Philipoff and L'Ours Blanc were forced to refuse guests. However, the Second World War put everything in neutral.

Gérard Blitz and Dimitri Philipoff crossed paths in 1949 when Blitz joined his sister, Didy, who was working with her husband at Philipoff's new Club Olympique retreat at Calvi in Corsica. Philipoff's post-war enterprise was originally organized to take French sports enthusiasts to the Olympic Games in London in 1948.

Blitz, who had been living in Nice in the south of France, had gone to Corsica two weeks after receiving a telegram from Didy; as co-manager of the Calvi resort, she wanted her older brother to give her a hand. Blitz and Philipoff soon discovered that they had a lot in common. Besides their common love of water sports, both men shared the conviction that life should be lived to the fullest without compromise or conformity, the two irritants that were ruining the so-called civilized world.

Needless to say, the pair quickly became close friends. In no time, Blitz was happily functioning as an unpaid aquatics instructor, teaching Philipoff's guests how to snorkel and leading deep-sea fishing expeditions.

Blitz was also impressed by the casual, unpretentious ambience of Philipoff's operation. He thoroughly enjoyed the impromptu performances that were staged nightly by Club Olympique's enthusiastic and friendly staff — an idea, Philipoff gleefully boasted, that had been borrowed years before from L'Ours Blanc by Billy Butlin, the famous Canadian entrepreneur who was making a fortune running low-cost holiday centres in Great Britain.

So it came as no surprise when Blitz approached Philipoff with a proposal for a joint venture — Club Méditerranée, a name thought up by one of Blitz's children. Club Méditerranée was a project that he and Claudine had been considering for a long time. It would incorporate a relaxed and carefree atmosphere, water sports and recreational activities, spontaneous shows, and a spirit of camaraderie amongst the guests and staff.

Philipoff was initially interested in the Belgian's scheme, but his ardour temporarily waned when he couldn't persuade his sidekicks in Club Olympique to participate in the deal. In retrospect, their refusal to get involved may rank among the worst decisions in French business history.

With Philipoff out of the picture for the moment (he would join Club Méditerranée later, in 1951), Blitz was forced to search elsewhere for a partner. He selected Tony Hatot, a friend of Claudine's sister and a former French swimming champion. Because of the nationalistic restraints of French law, the Belgian-born Blitz found it necessary to list Hatot as president when Club Méditerranée was formally registered as a non-profit sports association on April 27, 1950. But Blitz remained the power behind the throne. The first Club Méditerranée village opened for business just over two months later.

Blitz didn't have a lot of time to prepare for the opening of the Alcudia resort in Majorca. And he ran into many snafus from the outset. First, the authorities in Majorca didn't want to give him a licence to operate, an unforeseen mess that was eventually cleared up through the efforts of Robert Baudin, Blitz's cousin, who, after lengthy negotiations, convinced the local powers to grant Club Méditerranée the necessary permit. Then there were the endless problems associated with the site at Alcudia, a picturesque but entirely inadequate spot on the northern end of the island. Not only was the site barely big enough to accommodate the 200 or so tents Blitz had envisioned, but it lacked the basic infrastructure for a holiday resort. A chronic shortage of fresh water for cleaning and bathing, primitive sanitation facilities, and limited electricity were just a few of the problems Blitz faced.

Alcudia was also extremely difficult to get to from Paris, the source of most of Club Méditerranée's clientele. In those days, before the era of the passenger jet, it was a laborious, two-day journey that began with a tedious train ride from Paris to

Barcelona, continued with a nightmarish boat ferry to Palma, Majorca's pretty capital, and concluded with a bone-rattling bus ride the rest of the way to Alcudia.

As for all those tents that were needed to accommodate Blitz's guests, they too would have to come from France, as there was no local supplier on Majorca big enough to handle a venture of this size. Enter Gilbert Trigano, who was earning a living in Paris by renting out surplus U.S. army tents.

Trigano, who was born on July 28, 1920, in Saint-Maurice on the outskirts of Paris, was a different kind of person from Gérard Blitz, although they did share the Jewish faith. Unlike the athletic and outgoing Belgian, he never excelled at sports and was shy by comparison, an insecurity brought on by his self-professed concern about his physical appearance, a look he regards as "ugly," according to *Elle* magazine.

Gilbert was one of six children. His father, Raymond, was a successful businessman who owned and operated three grocery stores in the early 1930s. Later he started a company that man-ufactured canvas covers for trucks and other vehicles, a business that young Gilbert was never really interested in.

A rowdy, undisciplined student who was always clowning around to amuse his friends, Trigano was an educational flop who left school at 15. Scrounging around Paris, he eked out a precarious existence as a struggling script-writer and part-time actor. He even gave serious consideration to becoming a comedian.

When Gilbert was 16, his father, who was not impressed with his theatrical pursuits, issued him a challenge. "I want you to prove to me what you can do," dared his father, outlining his proposal. "I am putting you in charge of a grocery store for six months. If after six months you have succeeded in increasing the turnover and profit, I will leave you alone and you can do whatever you want."

Trigano took the bait and went to work managing one of his father's grocery stores. To his father's delight, he exhibited a previously unknown talent for management. He flourished in the job, dramatically increasing the turnover and profits. Satisfied that he had proved himself to his father, he set out once again to establish a career in the theatre.

After the outbreak of the Second World War, Trigano's father, fearing Nazi persecution of the Jews, moved the family south to the Ariège region, in the Pyrenees. While there, Gilbert joined the Forces Unies aux Jeunesses Patriotiques (the United Forces of the Young Patriots), a Communist resistance group that operated in the region. For his wartime efforts, he was later named a Chevalier de la Légion d'Honneur by a grateful French government.

Following the liberation of Paris on August 25, 1944, Gilbert and his family returned to pick up the pieces. He had not severed his ties to the Communists and was fairly active, successfully organizing the First Night of the Young Communists, a partisan rally that attracted over 30,000 supporters.

When the war was over, Trigano went to work as a journalist writing for *L'Humanité*, the newspaper of France's powerful Communist Party, and *Avant-Garde*, an offshoot of *L'Humanité* and the official newspaper of the Young Communist Party.

His articles were neither dogmatic nor particularly anti-capitalist in tone. Generally, his work was just straight reporting, with the subject matter ranging from the difficulties of learning to fly a glider to the training of sports instructors.

On June 9, 1945, Trigano married Simone Sabah. Like Gérard Blitz and his wife, the Triganos had four children: three daughters, Sylvie, Lydie, and Brigitte, and a son, Serge, who is currently a big cheese at Club Méditerranée and heir apparent to his father (when Gilbert finally retires).

In the same year, Trigano reportedly dissociated himself from the Communist Party. "I realized I wasn't a Marxist," he explained to *L'Express*, pointing out that it was the Resistance that drove him to Communism in the first place and that he had quit because the narrowly focused party bosses wanted to censor his stories.

He elaborated in a 1975 interview with *Réalités*. "I became a Communist because of the era and because of my faith. I was

20 years old in 1940, and taking into account what I am [a Jew], I didn't have any choice.

"I didn't have any contact with the secret army," Trigano went on. "Later on, when I got involved with business, I borrowed ideas from one or the other. The image that people have of capitalism is passé and the image people have of Communism is passé; there is a need for new structures to be invented.

"One has to take into consideration how ideas evolve. What would Marx think and what would he write if, like me, he was breathing the spring air of Paris in 1975? Would he write *Das Kapital* the same way? Certainly not.

"I am not afraid of capitalism because I know it; I am sometimes afraid of sectarial Communism, but I am not afraid of the Communist doctrine because I believe I know and understand it . . . The end justifies the means according to who you are. That seems to me to be the most beautiful dogma in life that we can imagine . . . "

In 1946, Trigano became a capitalist and joined the family business, which was still making canvas accessories for trucking firms and other commercial enterprises. Although the company was making a reasonable profit, there was a lot more money to be made in the camping equipment field, an emerging business that couldn't help but grow as France slowly recovered from the ravages of the Second World War.

The shrewd Trigano recognized and understood the implications of this changing trend. So he and his brothers reorganized the company, turning it into a new firm that also specialized in supplying all kinds of equipment for campers. For bigger deals, Trigano also had a handle on surplus American armed forces gear, a resource that was in almost unlimited supply in France following the war.

Four years later, in the spring of 1950, Trigano received a telephone call from a worried Gérard Blitz, who was having a problem finding tents for his new Club Méditerranée resort in Majorca. After hearing the details, Trigano wasted no time coming to an agreement with Blitz. It was the beginning of a new era in vacation travel.

CHAPTER THREE

Once Upon a Time

> "FOR 15,000 FRANCS: HOLIDAYS IN THE BALEARIC ISLANDS WITH CLUB MEDITERRANEE ... Club Méditerranée offers you a new and friendly holiday program, a comfortable tent village, the most beautiful sites in the Mediterranean, a large and devoted staff (cooks, waiters, stewards ...), all the Mediterranean sports ... fast and comfortable journey ... quality entertainment ... "
>
> Club Méditerranée's first advertisement, 1950

Gérard Blitz was thrilled by the overwhelming response to Club Méditerranée. The 2,400 bookings for the inaugural season at Alcudia had far exceeded his expectations. Many of the Parisians who initially signed up for Blitz's 15-day Majorcan adventure were attracted by the low cost, about $48, or the equivalent of an unskilled French worker's monthly salary in 1950. Others had been swayed by the advertisement that Blitz and his helpers had distributed throughout Paris. The ad, which promised accommodations, transportation, meals, sports, entertainment, and an exotic locale for the princely sum of about $3 a day, seemed too good to be true. It was.

The conditions were atrocious when the first wave of guests, who numbered between 700 and 800, arrived at Alcudia in early

July. Exhausted and irritable from the arduous trip from Paris, many were shocked to discover that Blitz's paradise in the sun was not what they had pictured or been promised.

The enticing "comfortable tent village" was, in reality, nothing more than a hastily erected campsite with 200 tents packed tightly together, sometimes within a few feet of each other. Offering neither privacy nor comfort, the tents were spartan, each furnished with metal army cots, a two-shelf stand for clothes, and not much else. It was more like a prisoner-of-war camp than a vacation resort.

To make matters worse, Blitz had also overbooked Alcudia, severely overestimating the acceptable capacity for the resort. To accommodate all the extra people, the desperate Belgian was forced to segregate some of his guests on the basis of sex, men in some tents, women in others. The slapdash, sardines-in-a-can solution saw frustrated men and women being crowded three or four to a tent. A number of disgusted guests fled to the relative luxury of nearby Majorcan hotels.

But the most appalling aspect of life for those who decided to stick it out at Alcudia was the sanitation facilities. The toilet, a ramshackle four-hole outhouse, was so foul-smelling that more than a few of Blitz's guests felt nauseated and were left gasping for air if they happened to be downwind after morning coffee.

The showers were also a joke. There were only three of them in the entire resort, or about one nozzle for every 275 guests. This meant long line-ups and not enough hot water (when there was any water at all). Most guests simply gave up and bathed as best they could in the salty Mediterranean or chose to remain dirty for the duration of their holiday.

Blitz's problems were compounded by his father, Maurice, who had cajoled a bunch of people in Brussels to vacation at his son's new resort. Enthusiastic and excited about Gérard's venture, he had exaggerated the wonders of Club Méditerranée as only a proud father could do, telling his fellow Belgians that Alcudia was fully equipped with all the modern conveniences like washing machines and refrigerators. He also mistook the location of Gérard's vacation village, explaining that it was situated in the Canary Islands, another group of Spanish islands about 1,000 miles southwest of Majorca in the Atlantic Ocean.

The Belgians, many of them middle-aged and humourless, didn't react well to the delights of Club Méditerranée, undoubtedly feeling that they had been lied to by Maurice Blitz. "We've paid too much for this," they snarled at his son, who tried to appease them by promising to give them their money back.

The bad food didn't calm the testy Belgians either. The kitchen, which was under the culinary supervision of chef Jo Bouillon, was a primitive affair with only one wood-burning stove and a few pots and pans. The meals, what there were of them, usually consisted of reheated canned meats and vegetables, soup, bread, and whatever else the underfinanced and beleaguered chef could throw together, a diet that sent many hungry guests scurrying to nearby restaurants and hotel dining rooms.

Surprisingly, most of Club Méditerranée's guests were good-natured and understanding about all the problems at Alcudia, laughingly realizing that you get what you pay for. Many helped out as best they could, peeling potatoes, washing dishes, and generally trying to alleviate the discomfort.

Blitz, who was as disappointed as anyone about the way things were going, tried to make the best of a bad situation. He apologized to all within earshot and offered refunds to anyone who requested one. Although he had been besieged by a fair number of outraged holidayers, very few took him up on his offer.

In spite of the comedy of errors, Blitz was pleased by the feeling of communalism that had swept over Alcudia, an experience that seemed to make it all worthwhile. Appreciative of his guests' efforts to co-operate, he started referring to them as *gentils membres*, or gracious members, the origin of the term GMs, which is still in vogue in today's Club Méditerranée.

Amazingly, matters continued to deteriorate.

A few weeks later, a freak tornado struck Alcudia, wrecking the Club Méditerranée village. The storm, which caused only minor cuts and bruises to the guests and staff, scattered tents everywhere, demolished the resort's electrical system, tossed army cots high into the trees, and trapped one poor fellow under the rubble of the dreaded outhouse.

Blitz assessed the damage following the tornado. Although the camp was not completely devastated, he realized it might mean a premature end to the season at Alcudia. But to the Belgian's amazement, the long-suffering GMs, who had already endured so much, were soon busily helping his small staff reconstruct the village. It was this unselfish act, more than any other, that convinced Blitz he was on the right track with Club Méditerranée, knowing that if the GMs could survive the kinds of disasters that had plagued Alcudia since the opening, they could cope with anything.

So when the deeply religious local Spanish authorities started calling Blitz's GMs "children of Satan" because they were running around half-naked and holding riotous, non-stop parties, it only reinforced the "us against them" philosophy that was now the order of the day at Alcudia. Through adversity — the overcrowded accommodations, stinking toilets, grumbling Belgians, execrable food, tornadoes, and Spanish censure — they had learned to stick together, a loyal band of adventurers sharing triumph and tragedy, the stirrings of the Club Med myth.

During the fiascos, Claudine, Blitz's glamorous girlfriend, never lost her cool or her femininity. She paraded around the filth and stench of Alcudia like a Polynesian princess, wearing her favourite *pareu*, a colourful wraparound cloth that serves as a skirt in her beloved Tahiti. Her *pareu*, which is still the dress of choice in some Club Med villages, was a big hit with the GMs, who instantly began imitating her by draping towels or any other piece of brightly coloured material around their waists.

Claudine, like her boyfriend, loved the sense of community that had enveloped Alcudia. She too felt encouraged by all the positive developments, hypothesizing that the Club Méditerranée village had become a country unto itself, a tiny nation of Europeans joyously coexisting under the French flag.

Leon Mortaigne, a GM at Alcudia, summed up the feelings of most of those who attended the birth of Club Méditerranée

23

in Majorca. "Those of us who thought we were jaded redis-
covered emotion," he remembered many years after.

Twenty-six years later, in 1976, Gérard Blitz explained his
version of the first season at Alcudia. "The lodgings were horrible," he told *Newsweek*. "The equipment was disgusting, the
food was horrible, and we had one boat for water skiing whose
motor never worked."

When Blitz returned to Paris after the first crazy season at
Alcudia, he was surprised to learn that he wasn't the target of
some lynch mob hell-bent on getting even for all the foul-ups. In
fact, Club Méditerranée was the talk of the city, at least with
those who had been in Majorca and the dozens of others who
pretended they had been. So to keep the ball rolling and drum
up business for next year, he decided to stage a reunion for the
Alcudia GMs on November 4, 1950.

The party was held at the town hall of the 16th arrondisse-
ment, Paris's equivalent of a city district. It lasted long into the
night as hundreds of GMs swapped anecdotes, drank, danced,
and sang about their unforgettable experiences at Alcudia.
Many more who had not been in Majorca also joined the rev-
elry, and soon there were so many people at Blitz's bash that the
town hall became overcrowded. But no one cared and the cele-
bration spilled merrily into the streets.

After his bewilderingly successful reunion, Blitz started planning for next year's season. Determined to be better organized
than before, he opened a small office on Rue Buffault, which
rapidly turned into a clubhouse for the enthusiastic GMs. The
magnetic Blitz, who was now attracting followers like some
latter-day messiah, was soon bumping elbows and jostling for
space with the GMs who couldn't seem to get enough of Club
Méditerranée.

Blitz, who knew what was good for business, encouraged the
cult-like fervour. In December, he published the first issue of
Trident, an amateurish four-page newspaper carrying the Second Coming headline "Club Méditerranée Is Born." The GMs
loved the idea of *Trident*, so much so that they did a large part
of the work on it, writing articles and stories, helping with the
layout, telling jokes, and even inventing a Club Med language,

the company's very own Esperanto. But for Blitz, the publication served a dual purpose. Not only was it an inexpensive promotional vehicle for the company, detailing all the events and happenings, but it also provided a forum for the GMs to persuade themselves that they were effectively participating in the affairs of Club Méditerranée, an ongoing illusion that was maintained by Blitz, who was extremely secretive about the inner workings of his organization.

Later, the GMs were to get so serious about the contents of *Trident*, which they believed to be their newspaper as much as Blitz's, that they divided into two groups, militants and moderates, and fought an absurd battle for editorial control. The militants, who took the elitist view that Club Méditerranée should be a privileged, quasi-religious experience, and the moderates, who felt the company should be for everybody, argued back and forth for months until the militants finally prevailed. It was a victory the opportunistic Blitz didn't really agree with, but he refused to do anything about it for fear of being labelled dictatorial.

Meanwhile, Didy, Blitz's sister, had written a comedy about Alcudia, highlighting the cultural and materialistic differences between the French GMs and the appliance-loving Belgians. Called "Good Neighbours, Good Friends, But So Different," it satirized all the funny things that went on in Majorca. The play also gave birth to the term *gentils organisateurs*, gracious organizers or GOs, which Club Méditerranée still calls its hotel employees.

Gérard Blitz had every reason to feel optimistic as Club Méditerranée headed into its second season. What with *Trident* telling the GMs that a confirmed reservation for 1951 was comparable to a winning lottery ticket, and with an upscale advertisement in *Paris-Match* that attracted over 1,000 new devotees, advance bookings had skyrocketed to just about double those of the first year.

This left Blitz in the enviable position of having to expand his operation. He first thought of accommodating the GMs in a second tent village in Alcudia, but that idea was shot down by nervous Spanish officials who had been so affronted by Club Méditerranée in 1950 that they had no intention of giving him a second permit. One tent village was bad enough, they reasoned. Blitz was forced to look elsewhere.

To help with his search, he finally managed to recruit Dimitri Philipoff, who had decided to leave Club Olympique. Philipoff was slated to take charge of the second village. He was assigned the task of finding and establishing the new resort.

He didn't have much time. In fact, he had only two days to locate an alternative site because the Spaniards had dithered about for so long before rejecting Blitz's proposal, a development Blitz had not anticipated. But the resourceful Philipoff was up to the task, and he found precisely what he was looking for in Italy.

The site, on the shores of the Golfo di Baratti in Tuscany, was ideal for Club Méditerranée. Not only was it situated in a popular tourist region, close to the historic cities of Florence and Pisa, but it was also accessible by road, which meant that the hardier GMs could make the long drive from France, thus alleviating some of the transportation problems.

Although Golfo di Baratti was perfect for Philipoff's purposes, he still had to convince the landowner and the local Italian authorities that it was in their best interests to let Club Méditerranée operate, quite a job considering the short time he had available before the first group of GMs were scheduled to arrive.

He started with the landowner, realizing that the camp was a hopeless cause unless he could get a lease on the property. Initially, the landowner, a wealthy, ageing Italian aristocrat, was hesitant about getting involved. But Philipoff found an angle when the landowner disclosed that he was an old acquaintance of the czar's former ambassador to Italy. Naturally, the sly Philipoff wasted no time taking advantage of this revelation, telling the landowner of his own anti-Communist, White Russian background, surmising that this was the surefire method of gaining the old fellow's co-operation. The ploy worked and the landowner agreed to let Club Méditerranée use his property.

With the Golfo di Baratti site taken care of, all Philipoff needed was an operating licence. He dashed off to negotiate this matter with the local officials in Piombino, a small coastal town in Tuscany that was controlled by the Italian Communist Party. For this group, he adopted an entirely different political posture, explaining that he was a sympathizer from the Soviet Union, the cradle of Communism. Philipoff spoke of the need for solidarity and how the new resort would cater to exploited workers. The officials, convinced that they were dealing with a comrade, eliminated the red tape and issued the necessary permit in record time. A couple of days later, after quickly putting up the tents, building a makeshift kitchen, installing the showers, and countless other last-minute chores, Club Méditerranée opened its second village.

Despite Dimitri Philipoff's eleventh-hour heroics in establishing the Golfo di Baratti resort, Gérard Blitz still had his problems.

First he had to explain to some of the GMs who had confirmed reservations for Majorca that they were now going to be vacationing in Italy instead of Spain. This last-minute change in plans didn't upset the GMs, most of whom were expecting the unexpected and were thrilled about having a reservation in the first place, quite a status symbol in some Parisian social circles.

That settled, Blitz also had to deal with the important issue of his own credibility. In the pages of *Trident*, he had spent a large part of early 1951 boasting that everything was going to be much better and more efficient in the second season. He had promised vastly improved shower and bathroom facilities as well as five times more sports equipment and enough tackle and rods for 40 deep-sea fishermen, pledges that he knew he would have difficulty honouring in light of Club Méditerranée's shaky financial position and the uncertainty in Majorca regarding the second village. But that didn't stop him from carrying on about how the GMs might find the new arrangements too comfortable, even going so far as to suggest that they might not like it because it wasn't going to be rough enough.

Blitz was, in part, aggressively promoting the improved Club

Méditerranée as a smokescreen to cover up his introduction of mandatory membership fees for the GMs, an additional sum of money to be paid on top of the cost of the vacation, a unique method of raising money that is still employed by the company. While not intended to make him rich, the small membership fee, only FF300 (or a little more than $1.25) for the head of the household and FF100 more for any other family member, created a new influx of cash that was to become an important source of funding as the company grew in the years ahead.

Although there was no question that the money was needed, the additional surcharges seemed a strange, almost exploitive way for the Belgian to show his gratitude to the GMs, who had given him so much sympathy and support and had stood loyally behind him in his time of need in Majorca. However, he wasn't entirely heartless. After buttering up the Alcudia GMs in *Trident* by proclaiming them the "aristocracy" of Club Méditerranée, he generously recognized their contributions by giving them a 10-day "priority" notice on reservations for the 1951 season. The GMs, who were supposed to feel flattered just to be considered a part of the *crème de la crème*, weren't entirely impressed, but most didn't argue and sheepishly paid the extra costs.

Back in Italy, another disaster was in the making at Golfo di Baratti. The GMs, who neither knew nor cared about Philipoff's behind-the-scenes wheeling and dealing, were once again forced to cope with uncomfortable and barely habitable accommodations, squalid toilets and showers, and limited or nonexistent recreational activities.

Even the beach, a gooey mixture of black tar, bunker oil, and sand, provided no relief for the GMs, who had to spend hours scraping the sticky goo off their bodies. Typically, Blitz tried to paint an exotic picture of the resort's polluted coastline. "It reminds you of the volcanic beaches of the Pacific," he expained to the GMs.

Although Club Méditerranée's second season didn't run completely smoothly, it was nevertheless a very successful year for the company. It had attracted thousands of new GMs and generated more excitement than ever in Paris, and there were

28

also a number of developments that were to have a lasting impact on Gérard Blitz's vacation enterprise.

The foremost was the entry of the industrious Prince Dimitri Koulikovsky into the Club Med fold. Koulikovsky, an old and trusted acquaintance of Dimitri Philipoff, was an exiled White Russian aristocrat and one of the founding personalities of L'Ours Blanc, the group that had pioneered inexpensive tent vacations in France in the mid-1930s.

An articulate and engaging individual who later became Club Méditerranée's director of transportation, he first got interested in Blitz's venture after visiting Philipoff at Golfo di Baratti following the opening of the new resort. While there, he noticed that many of the GMs were getting restless baking in the hot Italian sun or frolicking on the tar-splattered beach. So to alleviate the boredom and also put much-needed lire in the till, he began supervising tours for the GMs to Rome, Pisa, Florence, Venice, and other sightseeing centres.

Philipoff wasn't pleased by his old colleague's excursions, which were run in typical chaotic fashion, with three or four GMs crammed into a usually dilapidated automobile. As head of Golfo di Baratti, he felt that Prince Koulikovsky's holiday-from-a-holiday detracted from the true spirit of Club Méditerranée; but the popularity of the tours with the GMs (many of whom had not had the chance to see much of Europe because of the Second World War) and his chronic shortage of cash made him temporarily forget his annoyance.

(The advent of the Club Med tours also foreshadowed the evolution of the stunning variety of adventure locations that are currently operated by the company. Spanning the globe, the trips, knows as *les découvertes* in Club Méditerranese, offer the contemporary GM a rare opportunity for in-depth travel to such diverse and intriguing locales as Bolivia, Nepal, and French Guiana. These exciting vacations are not widely promoted in North America, but they are very popular with the company's European clientele.)

Besides Prince Koulikovsky joining the company, the other key development in 1951 was that Didy, Blitz's sister, became a member of the Club Med family. Because Philipoff was busy in

Italy, she was brought in by her brother at the last minute to manage Alcudia 2, the sister village of the original Majorcan resort that Blitz had belatedly gotten a licence to operate. Alcudia 2, just a short distance from the first Club Med village, wasn't really a resort in any sense of the word. Rather it was a bizarre assortment of stone cottages, peasants' houses, fishing huts, and other rustic dwellings that somehow met the confusing guidelines of the Spanish tourist officials.

By the end of 1951, after what might have been a disastrous start, Club Méditerranée was firmly established and growing by leaps and bounds.

CHAPTER FOUR

"Mister Dough"

"Nothing is as powerful as an idea that comes
at the right time! Don't you think? It's fantastic!
It must be frustrating and even horrible to be
ahead of your time ... by the same token it
must be very sad to be too late."

Gilbert Trigano, 1975

Although his family's business was Club Méditerranée's
biggest supplier of camping equipment throughout the
early years, Gilbert Trigano didn't become a partner
until 1953, the company's fourth season. In fact, it is doubtful
that he ever would have been involved had Gérard Blitz listened
to his head more than his heart. But Club Méditerranée just
kept expanding — a large, 150-acre resort catering to 1,000
GMs on the Greek island of Corfu, and a quickie facility for the
Olympic Games in Helsinki, Finland, in 1952, and another
village in Montenegro, Yugoslavia, in 1953. And as the operational debts kept mounting, Blitz had little choice but to offer
his largest creditor a stake in the company, albeit an extremely
silent one in the beginning.

"My administration was disastrous," confessed Blitz in 1978,
summing up the topsy-turvy state of affairs in the early 1950s.
"I soon realized after several setbacks that my friends and I
were subsidizing up to 40 per cent of the guests."

Blitz, who relied heavily on the GMs' membership fees as a

31

source of revenue, was so desperate for funds to keep Club Méditerranée afloat that he resorted to childlike pleadings in *Trident*, the company's promotional publication.

"Did you pay your membership fee? Did he pay his membership fee? Did they pay their membership fees?" he quizzed the GMs. If that crude approach didn't produce the desired results, he would become even more blunt. "Do not forget every morning when you wake up to ask yourself this question: 'By the way, did I pay my membership fee?' . . . And don't forget, if you didn't, we will remind you."

Blitz's financial status left him two options, neither of which he wholeheartedly embraced. He could slow the pace of growth and tighten up on expenditures, a manoeuvre that would risk losing the hard-earned and vitally important momentum, or he could bring in a partner, which would mean selling some of his own interest in Club Méditerranée and losing personal control.

He chose the latter course after listening to the advice of his father, Maurice. "I know your company is doing well," he remembered his father telling him. "It has met with a lot of success, but I ask myself, 'How do you manage?' You should find yourself an associate who knows how to count."

There is long-standing speculation that it was not only Gilbert Trigano's mastery of numbers that led Blitz to offer his supplier a partnership in the company. It is believed that Club Méditerranée was so deeply in debt to Trigano's family business for past favours that there was no other route to follow if the company was going to be saved from insolvency.

To prevent that catastrophe, Blitz sought out Raymond Trigano, Gilbert's father, to pursue the matter. "I literally asked for his son's hand," he recalled, which raises the interesting question of who was really in charge of the Trigano family business. Regardless of who was calling the shots at the company, Raymond Trigano must have liked Blitz's sales pitch because a short time later the entire Trigano family became partners in Club Méditerranée for the bargain basement price of FF36,000. To keep an eye on the investment, Gilbert, then in his early 30s, was made a director of Club Méditerranée, while his younger brother, André, took his place at the family enterprise.

"I was brought in to give it some management," Trigano laughingly told the *New York Times* in 1976. "But I was more enthusiastic and eager even than Blitz."

The precise date of Trigano's marriage to Club Méditerranée is still somewhat confusing. The company's own documents only add to the muddle. Papers filed with the Securities and Exchange Commission (SEC) in the United States state that the year was 1953. This contrasts with Club Méditerranée's 1985 *dossier de presse* (media information kit), distributed subsequent to the SEC filing, which says that Trigano became associated with the company in 1954. Whatever the year, what is certain is that his emergence on the scene was not universally popular. His detractors, and there were plenty of them at the time, painted a very ugly picture of Trigano as a greedy, cold-blooded opportunist, a money-hungry vulture cleaning the bones of the saintly Gérard Blitz, whose only ambition was to make the world a better place.

This, of course, was utter nonsense. In reality, Blitz, a hardened and highly decorated Resistance leader in the Second World War, was hardly an innocent being exploited by a maniacally avaricious Trigano. Blitz needed someone like Trigano, a workaholic who would put in long hours handling all the details.

Trigano's detractors even criticized his looks. According to Christiane Peyre and former Club Med employee Yves Raynouard, authors of *History and Legends of Club Méditerranée*, Trigano "did not know how to dress" and had the "silhouette of a rat" and a "weasel head." These nasty remarks Peyre and Raynouard attributed to anonymous "admirers." Gilbert Trigano is probably glad that they didn't seek out his enemies to comment on his appearance.

As for the beleaguered Blitz, he was pleased that Trigano was joining his "camp of travelling acrobats" and taking some of the burden off his shoulders. He elaborated in a 1978 interview with a French business publication, *Le Nouvel Économiste*.

"Gilbert, who was my counterbalance, was so happy that he went in the same direction I was going," he explained, pointing out that there were still problems at Club Méditerranée after Trigano became associated with the company. "As a result, the development was accelerated ... along with the chaos. For years, I assure you, Gilbert was, with me, the worst of managers," he carried on, undermining Trigano's highly touted image as a superhuman administrator. "Of the both of us, I was the most serious, the most reasonable."

From 1953 to 1956, Trigano stayed mainly in the background at Club Méditerranée, no doubt concentrating on the financial intricacies of Blitz's vacation enterprise. He remained virtually unknown to the growing legions of GMs, who by now numbered well over 30,000. But it is evident that he began to play a decisive role as the company moved on to a new era.

There were several major developments in the period immediately after Trigano joined the company. The most significant was the introduction of more permanent, Polynesian-style huts to replace the tents at the big Club Med village in Corfu. Called *cases*, these thatched-roof structures were a radical departure from the tent villages of Alcudia and Golfo di Baratti and represented the first serious effort to operate a real resort.

The advent of the *cases* at a Mediterranean locale was a fantasy come true for Blitz and his common-law wife, Claudine, both of whom had dreamed for years of creating their very own slice of Tahiti in Europe. A prime mover in making it all happen was Blitz's sister Didy. She was one of the mainstays behind a contest held in late 1953, near the end of the holiday season. The competition, which involved employees from all five Club Med villages, was initiated to find a more comfortable and durable substitute for the tents, a spartan form of accommodation that had to go if the company was going to widen its clientele. The hands-down winner was Jean Mahut, a GO at Corfu, who designed and built an esthetically pleasing circular unit that was not only waterproof but also inexpensive to erect.

Once it was confirmed that Club Méditerranée was committed to an exciting new direction, Didy became just as enthusiastic about the *cases* as her brother. In August of the following year, she organized the delivery of tons of straw, the primary building material, to the Corfu village. Working tirelessly, day and night, she spearheaded the construction of 500 two-person huts, and Club Méditerranée's first, Polynesian-type village opened in time for the 1955 season.

The introduction of the *cases* was a success from day one. Thousands upon thousands of GMs, new and old, were captivated by the South Pacific theme, a testament to Gérard Blitz's creative perseverance and a shot in the arm for Club Méditerranée. But for Gilbert Trigano, the coming of the *cases* was a mixed blessing. Like Blitz, he knew that changes had to be made if the company was to prosper. He also realized that switching from tents to huts would be very costly to him personally because his family's business could no longer count on large revenues from Club Méditerranée, a weighty financial sacrifice often overlooked by Trigano's critics.

Today the *cases* are still very much in evidence at Club Méditerranée. There are currently 14 villages of this type: Ipsos Corfu (the original resort) and Aighion in Greece; Les Restanques and Santa Giulia in France; Caprera, Cefalu, and Donoratico in Italy; Pakostane and Sveti Marko in Yugoslavia; Korba and Djerba Fidele in Tunisia; Al Hoceima in Morocco; Cadaques in Spain; and Arziv in Israel. Less expensive and perhaps a little too rustic for the older crowd that prefers the newer resorts, these vintage Club Med villages are tremendously popular with younger European GMs who enjoy the relaxed atmosphere.

Besides converting the Corfu village, Club Méditerranée also expanded beyond Europe for the first time, opening a resort in Djerba, Tunisia, in 1954 and another the following year on Tahiti, the source of Gérard Blitz's live-and-let-live philosophy and the site of the most erotically notorious village in the company's history.

While operations at the Djerba resort in Tunisia were disrupted by a bloody civil war, it was a completely different story in Tahiti. There fornicating instead of fighting was the feature attraction. Its reputation was sufficiently enticing to prompt

GMs to make the arduous month-long journey by sea to get there.

The small, 250-GM village was located on the tropical island of Moorea. Because of the great expense and the months involved in travelling there and back, most of the GMs who made their way to Tahiti were an affluent, footloose lot. They quickly adapted to the perceived sexual mores of the native Polynesians, whom they believed to be highly promiscuous. Soon the picturesque South Pacific retreat, with its stunningly beautiful lagoon, romantic beaches, equatorial vegetation, and attractive local populace, developed a reputation as a sexual Garden of Eden.

Whether to escape lifeless marriages in Paris or simply to fulfil their sexual fantasies, the GMs and the staff were making love at an unprecedented pace. In those wild early days in the 1950s, it was not unusual for an individual to change sexual partners frequently, sometimes several times a day. In fact, it was more the rule than the exception.

Women who were reluctant to participate in the sexual hijinks were often dealt with indelicately. One unwilling female was presented with a platter of imitation male genitalia, while others were subjected to peer pressure that eventually forced them to get involved. Still others were made to play silly games that called for blindfolded male GMs to publicly disrobe a female by scissoring off her *pareu*. However, some women needed no coaxing. Instead, they chased after the Tahitian men — bronzed and muscular natives who were always milling about the entrance to the Club Med village.

Most of those who visited the Tahiti village in the mid-1950s did not consider their behaviour vulgar or outlandish. Rather, the GMs and the Club Med staff viewed themselves as a merry band of erotic adventurers in a faraway Polynesian paradise. If the rest of the world didn't like it, they reasoned, then to hell with the rest of the world.

Although he was well known behind the scenes at Club Méditerranée, Gilbert Trigano was not formally introduced to the GMs until a small notice appeared on the back page of the

January 1956 issue of *Trident*, which was now calling itself the publication of world-wide laziness.

Shortly after this modest announcement, Trigano and Blitz orchestrated the purchase of Villages-Magiques, an important French-owned competitor of Club Méditerranée that at one time was partly owned by *Elle*, a leading Paris fashion magazine. The acquisition, which substantially increased Club Méditerranée's capacity and position within the industry, raised a few eyebrows. Sceptics wondered about Trigano's role in the deal, smelling a possible conflict of interest, because it was widely known that Villages-Magiques had also been supplied by his family's business.

Paul Morihien, a director of Villages-Magiques and not a fan of Trigano, was demoted to the publicity department immediately after the take-over. As he explained to Christiane Peyre and Yves Raynouard, the downgrading took place the morning after the sale, when Morihien arrived for work promptly at 9:00, only to discover that Trigano and Blitz had been in the office for hours.

"But Paul, where do you come from?" Blitz asked him, putting his arm on his shoulder. "There is nothing more to do here. Gilbert and I have taken all the necessary decisions. We had a meeting at six o'clock in the morning. You will have to change your South American hours."

Trigano wasted no time asserting his authority over the enlarged managerial staff. A fanatic about cutting costs, he sometimes went overboard trying to get his point across. At a celebrated meeting in 1956, he lectured his befuddled executives on the theme *un sou c'est un sou*, or "a cent is a cent."

"The Club is a marvellous thing since I've known it. It hasn't ceased to enchant me," he told his managers before rebuking them for their spendthrift attitudes. "But my poor friends, you are headed for disaster by throwing money out the window. I repeat it, a cent is a cent. I will never tire of explaining it. And that's why I'm here, because from now on we won't let a cent go astray."

The stunned Club Méditerranée executives didn't know how to react to Trigano's comments. Behind his back, they ridiculed and insulted him and gave him the nickname "Monsieur Grisbi" or "Mister Dough," a sarcastic sobriquet that was soon adopted by everyone in the company, including Gérard Blitz.

Blitz and Trigano opened their first winter resort in Leysin, Switzerland, in 1956, much to the chagrin of some other Swiss hoteliers in the region. They complained that Club Med's appealing program, which included free skiing, was hurting their traditional revenue base.

The village, which was initially managed by Dimitri Philipoff, was an immediate success, as thousands of snow-loving GMs experienced the joys of Club Med in the colder months. More importantly, the opening of the Swiss resort enabled the company to cater to its clientele year-round, a very important fiscal consideration for Club Méditerranée.

The following year Philipoff, who had contributed so much to the growth of Club Méditerranée, resigned from the company after a final season of managing the Caprera village in Sicily, one of the holiday properties acquired in the Villages-Magiques deal. He had become fed up with the direction in which Club Méditerranée was going. He thought it was getting too big too fast. He also wasn't impressed by all the mythological fanfare.

"From the moment Gilbert Trigano joined the party, we were beginning to build villages far too big for my taste," commented Philipoff. "I realized that when a whole group of people [GMs] were leaving, and there were at least 60 per cent I couldn't recognize. And yet I was the *chef de village*. So I told my wife: 'You know, Françoise, it's finished!'"

"We can really say, in one sense, that Trigano founded the Club," he continued. "Gérard Blitz, with all his heart and charm, starts things he doesn't finish. And me, I am an empirical craftsman and I intend to stay that way. I am totally against giantism."

After leaving Club Méditerranée, Philipoff became a competitor of sorts, launching a small resort company called Les Chemins du Soleil (Paths to the Sun), which operated several holiday villages in Italy.

Philipoff's resignation wasn't Blitz and Trigano's only problem. In 1955, the French government passed laws that directly affected Club Méditerranée's standing as a non-profit sports association, an almost laughable designation that had allowed Club Méditerranée and its competitors to have up to 5,000 members before it altered their taxable status. The issue became heated when French travel agents argued that the non-profit sports associations were, in fact, full-blown businesses that were taking advantage of a tax loophole. In response, the major associations — Club Méditerranée, Touring Club of France, Club Olympique, and Villages-Magiques (before Blitz and Trigano engineered the take-over) — retaliated by suggesting that French travel agents were an unscrupulous lot who could never guarantee the security of a holidayer's money. To settle the matter and protect the consumers, the French government enacted laws that called for all travel entities to become licensed, a legislative act that preceded Club Méditerranée's becoming a limited liability company on October 10, 1957.

Before the incorporation of the company, Gérard Blitz had hit upon the novel idea of making Club Méditerranée's GMs co-owners of the company, exchanging shares for compulsory membership fees. He wrote a letter to the GMs, soliciting their support for the scheme.

"Dear GMs," wrote Blitz, "soon you will be co-proprietors of the Club. Until now, you have paid a membership fee of FF1,000 per year. From now on you will pay the same FF1,000, but this time you will receive one share of the company.

"Because we are constantly growing, we are obliged to reinforce our base by modifying our administration of the association to make it more accessible to the GMs," he went on. "As far as we know we are the first in France to offer a concrete and simple solution to a common problem — that of a large association with a commercial function."

For a while, Blitz referred to the GMs as GPs, which stood for *gentils propriétaires*, in an attempt to develop some enthusiasm for his idea. But like many of his brainstorms, it was not a scheme that met with an eager response and it was quickly and quietly forgotten.

Besides testing the waters with unusual financial schemes, Blitz had also begun to criticize some of the GMs, openly discussing getting rid of undesirable members because he thought they were "unclean physically and morally." These stern pronouncements were primarily aimed at an ebullient crowd of rabble-rousers who believed that a Club Med vacation was a no-holds-barred permit to do anything to anyone. Not that he was a prude, but he realized that the company wouldn't survive long if it took on the image of a whorehouse. "We must cherish our good reputation as well-behaved people. It is as precious as eyesight," Blitz wrote in *Trident*.

Many years later, Trigano expanded on Blitz's feelings in an address before a group of French manufacturers. "In 1955, we found ourselves in a dramatic situation," he told the assembled throng, rationalizing Club Méditerranée's shift away from the swingers. "We had holiday villages full of people who were looking for a licence for freedom. We were forced to separate ourselves from them or die because they would have paralyzed our development. So we chose to separate and appeal to couples and families. In the beginning," he summed up, "children were not admitted unless they were ten years old. Now we accept children under one year for free."

In spite of his ever-widening power and influence at Club Méditerranée, Gilbert Trigano was still largely unknown to the thousands of GMs in 1957. However, he was to become much better known in June of that year when Gérard Blitz penned a front-page story in *Trident* entitled "My Friend Gilbert Trigano." The article, published more than three years after Trigano became formally associated with the company, was designed to raise his profile with the GMs and combat some of the misunderstandings about his motives for getting involved with Club Méditerranée.

"We have had friendly relations since 1950. He has helped us unconditionally," wrote Blitz. "Then, taken over by the rhythm, success, and atmosphere of the Club, the supplier became a director.

"He was in favour of the *cases* [huts] without regretting his loss of business as a supplier. He is nice and he is loyal, he takes care of the dirty work. He is a financial expert, but he is of the same mind as we are.

"Mister Dough is enthusiastic and wise," he added, alluding to Trigano's penny-pinching ways. "He says no with a shy but firm little voice, although he would like to say yes. This fellow, to whom we owe so much, is still far too unknown to the GMs."

A year later, in 1958, Trigano's name was almost as synonymous with Club Méditerranée as that of Blitz, the sentimental founder of the company who was still adored by the diehard GMs of an earlier era. In 1958 the pair were operating ten Club Med villages — nine summer resorts as well as the highly successful winter village in Leysin, Switzerland.

The following year Blitz and Trigano brought the total number of villages up to an even dozen, opening a summer resort at Aighion in Greece and another winter village in the heart of the French Alps at Monnetier-les-Bains. They also converted the tent village of Santa Giulia, on the French island of Corsica, into a Polynesian-style resort along the lines of the original one in Corfu.

But the debts kept escalating. According to the French magazine *Réalités*, Blitz and Trigano had implemented a risky financial scheme to finance the expansion of the company, depending, in part, on the revenues from the GMs' membership fees to pay for the new villages. Their plan failed, and by 1961 the company was in debt for millions of francs, a formidable liability that would take Club Méditerranée to the brink of bankruptcy.

"We made a lot of mistakes," Trigano confessed many years later, explaining the economic conditions in the first decade of the company. "Three or four times we nearly collapsed because we didn't understand the difference between cash flow and investments, and used working capital to finance expansion."

In early 1961, Club Méditerranée's creditors notified Trigano that they were going to call the company debt on April 25, almost 11 years to the day from the founding of the company.

Realizing the desperate nature of the situation, Trigano fired off an urgent message to Blitz, who was in Tahiti. Blitz agreed to meet Trigano in Los Angeles to discuss the matter.

At the meeting, the partners decided to seek out fresh capital in a last-ditch effort to save the company. On the advice of a friend, they prepared a prospectus on Club Méditerranée and submitted it to one of the Rothschilds, France's wealthiest and best-known family. To their amazement, they received a response just a few days before the creditor's deadline. But it was not from the Rothschild they had initially approached. Instead, it was Baron Edmond de Rothschild, the 35-year-old president of La Compagnie Financière, a privately owned holding company in Paris, and reputedly the richest and cleverest member of the illustrious Rothschild clan.

Seizing the opportunity, Blitz and Trigano made an appointment to see Rothschild. "We went to conquer Baron Edmond de Rothschild," said Blitz, remembering how he and his partner were well received by the baron's two deputies, Messieurs Péreire and Meyer. "We sold them on the idea."

Blitz later explained how he persuaded Baron Edmond to invest in the company. "I told him, 'All your cousins have a specialty. Why not make yours vacations?' "

Rothschild, who had previously dabbled in the vacation business — developing the chic ski resort of Mégève in the French Alps and participating with his English cousin, Lord Rothschild, in the plush golfing resort of Caesarea in Israel — agreed to Blitz and Trigano's proposal. He reportedly invested $2 million in the company, a sum that cleared up the outstanding debts and kept the holiday enterprise afloat. For his timely investment, Rothschild was awarded a 34-per-cent interest in the company, making him the largest single shareholder in Club Méditerranée.

As a financial benefactor, Blitz and Trigano couldn't have found anyone better. Rothschild was ideal. A few years younger than his new partners, he brought not only a fresh infusion of capital to the company but also his much-needed business acumen. Rothschild changed little on the outside but entirely revamped the inner workings of Club Méditerranée, adding a state-of-the-art computer system and implementing modern management controls. More importantly, he treated Blitz and Trigano like responsible adults, not serfs. "It's you who are going to put this business back together," he told them at the time. "I am not giving you a chaperone."

Surprisingly, Rothschild had been aware of Club Méditerranée before he became an investor in the company. In fact, he had first visited the new Arziv village in Israel shortly after it opened in 1961. While there, Rothschild had a great time fooling around and behaving like any other GM, enjoying a festive dinner with his companions and even taking part in some of the Club Med games, one of which involved carrying women around on his back. Running out of his favourite cigarettes, Gauloises, he borrowed a few packages from the *chef de village*, Pierre Levrard, who was then offered an honorary membership in Rothschild's exclusive Caesarea Golf Club. "I really like your business," Levrard recalled the baron telling him. "I would like to meet your boss."

An early (1964) edition of Arthur Frommer's *Israel on 5 Dollars a Day* provides an interesting insight into what Rothschild found so appealing about Club Méditerranée when he dropped in at Arziv village, which is located north of Haifa just south of the war-ravaged Lebanese border.

"Here's the paradise for sophisticated bohemians who want to rough it 'in style,'" explains Frommer. "Striving for a kind of hedonistic Garden of Eden, the planners found an ideal site — a long golden beach in the shadows of an abandoned Arab village, framed by the sea on one side and crowned by tall date-palms and eucalyptus on the other. Sarongs [Claudine's famous *pareus*] and bikinis are the order of the day, and the management even helps you forget about money by providing strings of colored beads to wear around your neck — each bead being worth the price of an espresso, aperitif, or soda at the outdoor café on the sand.

"The vacationers live in weird hexagonal-shaped thatch huts (*cases*), with a hinged flap for entrance and another for ventilation. Guests are summoned to the dining room, a low flap-roofed shed under two palm trees, by a loudspeaker playing a

baroque march. French is the native tongue at this village —
because that's where most of the holiday-makers come from —
but a few Israelis also vacation here, as do some Italian and
English. The pace is relaxed, harmonious, but also very gay.

"There are several different price lists, each moderate and
designed for the types that go in for this offbeat kind of vacation," continued Frommer. "During the height of the season,
July-August, two weeks at Arziv will cost you $95, everything
included. [In 1986, the same vacation cost FF4,560, or about
$900.] However, in the slow months of May-June and Sep-
tember-October, you can take three weeks for the same price,
$95, about $4.50 a day.

"But the best buy is the package deal from Europe — which
is the way most of the vacationers make their arrangements
here. From Paris, round-trip plane tickets and three weeks at
the village run just $220."

CHAPTER FIVE

The Saviour

> "Life is a game, but the way to keep score is money."
>
> Ted Turner, 1978

I f money is indeed the measurement of life, as the flamboyant American tycoon Ted Turner suggests, then Baron Edmond de Rothschild, a man who is counted among the five wealthiest individuals in France and whose personal fortune was estimated at a mind-blowing $800 million in 1971, is an indisputable winner.

Born in Paris on September 30, 1926, the red-haired and bespectacled Rothschild initially came by his money the old-fashioned way — he inherited it, acquiring a vast fortune from his late father, Senator Maurice de Rothschild, who was a banker, a politician, and a noted rabble-rouser (in no particular order). But unlike some of his wilder fellow aristocrats, who were very good at squandering their inheritances on wine, women, and insane business deals, he proceeded to enlarge the family trust to an amount that can only be gauged in the billions.

Although he is not as well known as a few of his famous relatives, who are involved in everything from vintage wines to racehorses to banks and investment companies, Rothschild is, nevertheless, one of the western world's richest and most successful businesspeople. He is currently on record as chairman of at least eight major corporations and philanthropic organizations, and he is a director or investor in countless others.

At one time or another, his interests have spanned several continents and a wide array of businesses. La Compagnie Financière is a privately owned holding company in Paris that Rothschild calls "my main business den." La Compagnie du Nord, a huge Rothschild family enterprise that once owned the railways to Lille and Calais, is involved in large-scale projects like the world's biggest nickel mine, on the Pacific island of New Caledonia, and Penarroya, the world's leading producer of lead. Château Clarke is one of only five first-growth vineyards in Bordeaux, producing wines that are generally considered by oenophiles to be among the finest in the world. Rothschild also has an interest in Château Lafite, another of the five *premier cru* Bordeaux wines. And then there is Banque Privée, a privately owned bank in Geneva; De Beers Consolidated, the South African mining colussus that is the world's biggest producer of diamonds; Inter-Continental Hotels, a world-wide chain of first-class hotels originally established by Pan-American Airlines; Israeli General Bank, a financial institution in Tel Aviv; Bank Cal Tri-State, a California corporation that controls the San Francisco–based Bank of California; and Promotex, a Swiss holding company.

Other Rothschild investments have reportedly included an aviation service company in Ireland, residential developments in Paris, a bank in Italy, villas in Majorca, a pipeline company in Canada, industrial and commercial projects in Brazil, and upscale tourist resorts in Israel and France. And, of course, Club Méditerranée, which he has referred to in the past as his "favourite business interest."

Although he is a Rothschild born and bred, with relatives occupying all kinds of powerful positions within the upper echelons of global commerce, the baron is considered in some quarters to be a bit of a lone wolf in regard to his own investments. "He is regarded more as an independent investor," observed *Euromoney*, the influential London-based financial publication. "Whenever an investment turns sour, he is reputed to sell a painting from his collection of French Impressionists to pay for it." (Rothschild does have a fabulous art collection, much of it looted by the Nazis in the Second World War and secreted in Mad Ludwig's castle in Bavaria. After the capitulation of Hitler in Bavaria, James Rorimer, the Fine Arts Officer with the U.S. Seventh Army and later the director of the Metropolitan Museum of Art in New York, discovered a large part of Rothschild's father's collection, including Peter Paul Rubens's *Three Graces* and his substantial accumulation of Renaissance jewellery and 18th-century snuffboxes. Unfortunately, all the Rothschilds were a prime target of Hitler's art thieves; of the 22,000 major pieces stolen during the war, more than 4,000 belonged to the family.)

Baron Edmond de Rothschild, despite his lofty economic standing, is regarded as quite amiable; he is as down-to-earth and informal as men of his position get. For years he would attend Club Méditerranée's annual bash and be addressed simply as "Edmond" by company executives and lowly GOs alike.

Educated at the distinguished International School at the University of Geneva in Switzerland and at the Faculty of Law in Paris, he was awarded the Chevalier des Palmes for his academic achievements. A self-professed conservative who admits to being "hesitant" sometimes about all things modern, his pleasures are the traditional stuff of aristocrats — hunting and yachting.

Rothschild, who has been married twice, lives with his second wife, the Baroness Nadine, in a variety of fairy-tale residences ranging from Château Pregny outside Geneva to the warm and relatively intimate Château Clarke, which was designed by Alain Demarchy, one of France's leading interior decorators, on the grounds of his vineyard in Listrac. For getaways, the baron and his wife escape to the lush Caribbean island of St. Barthélémy in the French West Indies.

Baron Edmond de Rothschild's arrival on the scene in 1961 brought immediate stability to Club Méditerranée. Not only was the company on a much sounder financial footing — Gérard Blitz and Gilbert Trigano no longer had the ugly threat of bankruptcy looming over their heads — but there was also a new and more purposeful attitude added to the formula, an air of professionalism that would carry the vacation enterprise to unprecedented heights in the coming years.

CHAPTER SIX

Expansion

"Success is the analysis of mistakes."
Gilbert Trigano, 1976

B esides an extensive expansion program (four or five new villages, winter and summer, were opened every year), one of the key moves at the outset of the Rothschild era was the delicate reorganization of the company at the executive level. Trigano, a business bull who was well suited to cope with the changing complexities and demands of the travel industry, was a much more fitting candidate to head Club Méditerranée than Blitz, the legendary and charismatic founder whose management techniques were, at best, controversial. Younger, more aggressive, and endlessly energetic, Trigano was the right kind of person to provide the necessary drive and motivation to build the company into a holiday empire. But first Blitz, a sensitive and proud man, would have to be eased gently into other responsibilities. A classic compromise was reached when the two partners, along with Rothschild, agreed to alternate in the presidency of the company, changing places every two years. Because of his more senior and exalted status, it was decided that Blitz would become the chief executive officer for the initial two-year interval. In 1963, the ambitious Trigano would replace him, a position he has not relinquished to this day.

After his partner assumed the helm, Blitz briefly appeared to lose some of his enthusiasm for Club Méditerranée, taking time off to indulge in such diverse pastimes as astrology, astronomy, and science fiction. (He also became a devotee of Jiddu Krishnamurti, the East Indian philosopher who was much in vogue in the early 1960s. Krishnamurti, a renowned pacifist and author of *Commentaries on Living* and *The First and Last Freedoms*, was a staunch proponent of ridding the established world of isms — Catholicism, Protestantism, Communism, socialism, and so forth. Blitz, who at times seemed to be on a full-scale retreat from the civilized world, found comfort in Krishnamurti's teachings and adopted the proselytizing East Indian as his spiritual father.)

In 1965, the company opened its first year-round village in what is occasionally touted as the "Miami Beach" of Morocco — Agadir, the sunny Atlantic resort that had been completely shattered in the earthquake of 1960, a disaster that claimed more than 20,000 lives. The advent of the new hotel, a permanent, Moorish-style affair with a prime beachfront location, finally gave the company an opportunity to market well-constructed and comfortable accommodations to the long-suffering GMs, a welcome development far removed from the devil-may-care days of an earlier era.

"Hot water runs, cold water drinks, showers adjust and toilets flush. Hiltonesque almost," summed up American Hugh Moffett, waxing euphoric about the upscale Club Med village. "Here, be it noted also, members do not dwell in grass huts among varmints, but in clean cells called cottages."

Moffett, a *Life* magazine writer who had made the lengthy journey to Agadir from Casablanca aboard a rickety old DC-3, was also amused by one of the inhibition-loosening rub-and-grope games organized by the fun-loving village staff. "Members stand in a circle, boy alongside girl, facing inward," explained Moffett. "The organizers bind together all the ankles, boy and girl together. Now see whether, without tampering with bindings, you can rearrange so all toes point outward." Apparently the feverish thrashing about that ensues "softens everyone up for the writhing that follows to the guitars of the Sicilian quintet."

49

A year later, in 1966, Rothschild, Blitz, and Trigano converted Club Méditerranée from a privately owned business into a public corporation, issuing shares and trading stock on Paris's historic Bourse (stock exchange). Besides permitting the holiday venture to raise outside capital for expansion and other important matters, this milestone appeared to be the financial mechanism for Rothschild to recoup his original multimillion-dollar investment and a chance for his relatively impoverished partners, Blitz and Trigano, to cash in as well.

At the time of the initial listing on the Bourse in 1966 — the first offering of a hotel stock in the history of the French exchange — Club Méditerranée disclosed that it was operating 29 vacation villages, 18 summer and 11 winter resorts, and was grossing more than FF89 million in revenues annually. The company also detailed that it had more than 300,000 members who were collectively whooping it up at Club Med more than 2 million days a year.

But by far the most interesting revelation to come out of Club Méditerranée's switch from public to private ownership was the listing of some of the company's shareholders, with their percentage holdings. According to the French newspaper *L'Express*, La Compagnie Financière, Rothschild's Paris-based company, was the single biggest investor, with a reported 34.13 per cent of the company. Next were the *animateurs*, or prime movers behind Club Méditerranée, presumably Blitz and Trigano, who were cited as having 37.18 per cent of the shares. Then there was the 6.47 per cent controlled by Groupe Leven, a French consortium that owned Contrexéville, Charrier, and Perrier, the world-famous mineral water company. Finally, 11.87 per cent was held by the Union Panaméenne de Gestion et de Participation (Panamanian Society of Management and Organization), a mysterious financial entity.

Besides being listed on the Paris Bourse in 1966, the company also launched its assault on the lucrative American market by incorporating Club Med Sales, a Delaware-based subsidiary, to wholesale its vacations to travel agents throughout the United States. Headquarters for the new company was in New York, the past and present hub of the American travel industry. Soon after, another sales office was opened in Los Angeles and a similar marketing arm was started in Canada, a land of long, bitter winters with a large indigenous French-speaking population in the province of Quebec, a natural source of business for the company.

To boost sales and introduce the uninitiated North Americans to the delights of Club Méditerranée, Blitz and Trigano opened their first village in the western hemisphere, an attractive hotel and bungalow combination on the Caribbean island of Guadeloupe, in the French West Indies. Called Fort-Royal, the new village became an immediate success as thousands of American and Canadian GMs jumped on the Club Med bandwagon.

Half-way across the globe, in far-off tropical Tahiti, the company also reclassified its new Moorea resort, which had been opened in 1962, as the first English-speaking village, a firm commitment by Blitz and Trigano to chase the almighty dollar. An early visitor to the South Pacific retreat (which should not be confused with the fleshpot that was operating in the mid-1950s) was the travel editor of *Esquire* magazine, Richard Joseph.

"Nine out of ten GMs were Americans," observed Joseph. "The other ten percent were lean-looking French camping types and Polynesian dishes who, if not members, were probably working there or dressing up the landscape. The whole atmosphere was so loose and easy, it was hard to tell who was actually working there and who was there entirely to enjoy himself.

"The dress was pretty much what you'd expect," he continued. "The girls wore bikinis or *pareus* with blossoms in their hair or flower wreaths or crazy palm-leaf hats on their heads; the men wore swim trunks, shorts or cut-down jeans. They all wore strings of detachable beads — the club wampum."

Joseph, who observed whimsically that the GMs were being saluted into dinner accompanied by a stirring rendition of "Fanfare for the King's Supper" by de Lalande, asked a Club Med GO about the kinds of problems he encountered with the very un-French Americans.

"Exposed to our French cuisine three times a day, some of

our American members grow very fat," the GO indignantly explained. "And they complain to me. You would think the conversation and the friends-making would cut down on their eating, but no."

Not all the new Club Med ventures were successful, however. One of the most badly conceived and costly episodes in the colourful history of the company occurred when Trigano cast a greedy eye on the cruise business.

On paper, a floating Club Med village looked like an excellent, exciting idea. Cruise ships could visit all kinds of exotic ports. And holidayers also perceived them to be a luxurious experience, an important consideration now that Club Méditerranée was attracting an increasingly affluent clientele. Cruises were, the thinking went, a natural spin-off for the company, an innovation that would surely navigate Club Méditerranée to an unchallengeable position within the vacation industry. So with a great deal of fanfare and hoopla, the ill-fated Club Med cruises were launched, much like another fabulous idea from an earlier era — the *Titanic*.

The new venture got off to a shaky start in 1965 when Trigano signed a deal to charter a nondescript cruise ship from the Soviet Union, a grim 20,000-ton, 750-passenger vessel with the horror-movie name of *Ivan Franko*. Then, for reasons best known to himself, he scheduled the inaugural series of Club Med cruises — which were 8, 10, 12, and 15 days in duration and called on ports throughout the Mediterranean — for the winter season, from December 1965 to April 1966.

Trigano's decision to begin the Club Med cruises at the lowest part of the off-season was foolhardy. Not only was the weather unpredictable — it could be chilly, rainy, and quite miserable at this time of the year — but the Mediterranean Sea could also get rough, with the bigger swells easily reaching 15 to 20 feet, a roller-coaster-like condition that would cause a lot of seasickness among the landlubbing GMs and GOs.

To add to the nightmare, Club Méditerranée also planned a Franco-Russian menu for the cruise, completely oblivious to the fact that the heavier, more greasy Soviet-style food was the last thing anyone would want to eat to settle a queasy stomach, especially anyone who had been vomiting over the ship's rail all day in undulating seas.

"It was a flop," admitted Jean Lallement, formerly the president of Club Med in New York. "On the first voyage it poured for three days."

But none of this mattered to Trigano, who boldly upped the ante in 1966 by announcing that Club Méditerranée was chartering three cruise ships instead of one for the coming season. The *Ivan Franko* was scuttled from the Club Med holiday program and replaced with three French cruisers — the *Vietnam*, the *Louis-Lumière*, and the *Lyautery*.

Although Trigano appeared to be happy about his new trio of ships, which he had chartered from Messageries Maritimes and Paquet, he wasn't entirely satisfied with the names of two of the vessels. So the 440-passenger *Vietnam*, the largest of the three ships, was blandly rechristened the *Bateau-Blanc* (White Boat), and the 200- to 250-passenger *Lyautery* was changed to the much more romantic *L'Aventure* (Adventure).

In his second and final season in the cruise business, Trigano was in no mood to take chances. There would be no more disastrous schedulings of mid-winter cruises because it was, quite simply, costing the company too much money; the losses would eventually run into the millions of dollars.

To make amends, Trigano created an intriguing series of cruises for his expanded fleet. One of the more interesting itineraries he developed was for the *Bateau-Blanc*, which was selected to make a lengthy passage to the Far East. Departing the French port of Marseille, the ship was scheduled to make a 17-day voyage through the Suez Canal, down the Red Sea, calling in at Aden and Bombay before finally reaching the half-way point of Colombo, the capital city of the island then known as Ceylon. From Colombo, the cruise would continue for another couple of weeks to Yokohama, by way of Bangkok, Singapore, Manila, and Hong Kong.

The other ships, the *Louis-Lumière* and *L'Aventure*, were similarly assigned interesting destinations. For example, the intimate, 150-passenger *Louis-Lumière* was slotted to visit the sunny climes of South America via Lisbon, Montevideo, Buenos Aires, and Rio de Janeiro, while *L'Aventure* would explore the fabled waters of the eastern Mediterranean.

To make the cruises truly irresistible, Trigano also offered the GMs an affordable two-class system of pricing for the holidays. These remarkably inexpensive and virtually all-inclusive packages ranged from only FF4,500 (first class) to FF3,000 (tourist class) for the 26-day extravaganza to South America. The other cruises were also very cheap.

It was all to no avail as the GMs stayed away in droves. When Trigano finally pulled the plug on the cruises later in 1967, he had attracted only a few thousand GMs and had lost a staggering amount of money.

Several years later, Trigano talked about the problems of the cruises. "The market wasn't ready for it," he confessed. "To make it work, I needed 6,000 people. I only got 2,000. In our business, each missing person is a 100-per-cent loss. It's as stupid as that. So those 4,000 people that we were missing meant a loss of $2 million for two consecutive years. For a business that was making $3 million [Club Méditerranée's net profit], it was unacceptable to lose $2 million."

(Trigano has apparently never given up on the idea of Club Med cruises. In spring 1987 the company announced that it was once more getting into the cruise business. Plans call for the construction and operation of a new 1,000-passenger vessel, which will operate in the Caribbean and the Mediterranean beginning in December 1988.)

Despite losing millions of dollars and generating a lot of snickering in the French travel trade, the fiasco of the Club Med cruises had only a negligible impact on the company. Even though the losses had temporarily smudged the bottom line, the rest of the company was still performing very profitably, a factor that made Club Méditerranée attractive to outside investors.

In August 1968, Gérard Blitz, who had been spending a considerable amount of time in the United States promoting the company, convinced the travel and financial services giant

American Express to purchase approximately 15 per cent of Club Méditerranée for a reported $2.7 million.

Why did American Express want to get involved with Club Méditerranée? Besides being a sound investment (the company had grossed an estimated $30 million in 1968, and Club Med's stock on the Paris Bourse had skyrocketed from $88 to $120 a share in the months following the purchase), the link-up gave the American Express travel division a ready-made market of 17,000 GMs, the total number of North Americans that had thus far experienced a Club Med holiday. Finally, the American corporation also became the booking agent for the French company in the United States.

For Club Méditerranée, the deal was similarly attractive. Not only did it gain access to the much-vaunted computerized reservation system run by American Express, but it also acquired the use of a widespread sales organization in the all-important North American market. Summing up the new arrangement, a spokesman for American Express told *Time* magazine that the investment would help his company capture more of "the swingers market," a lucrative segment of the American travel industry in the late 1960s.

Throughout the 1960s, Club Méditerranée was expanding at a phenomenal pace. In Europe, the company was burying the competition by opening a host of resorts throughout the Continent and North Africa. And in December 1968, it celebrated another milestone by opening its first vacation village in the United States, a small, 140-bed resort in Bear Valley, in the Sierra Nevada mountains of northern California.

Unfortunately, the $1-million Bear Valley village, which had been used primarily as a weekend ski retreat by snow-starved San Franciscans before Club Méditerranée leased the property, had one major problem that doomed it from the beginning. It was simply not large enough to support a national advertising and promotion campaign. Consequently, it never really captured the imagination of the American masses and was closed rather unceremoniously after a few unimpressive seasons.

On a much grander scale, the company was also hard at work

in 1968 building a second Club Med village in the French West Indies, the now-famous Buccaneer's Creek resort on Guadeloupe's sister island of Martinique, a French possession since 1635.

At about this time, a crisis was developing. It centred on Gérard Blitz and was connected to the construction of the Martinique village, a project that was being spearheaded by Blitz.

The situation was so bleak — sloppy workmanship, long delays, and cost overruns being the order of the day — that Baron Edmond de Rothschild, who normally maintained a discreet distance from the management of the company, dispatched an emissary to get a first-hand appraisal of what was going on. Rothschild's representative reported back that the project was indeed in a mess and that Blitz was mainly to blame. A worried Gilbert Trigano, whose own management style was suddenly being questioned, got into the act and flew down to the Caribbean.

The problems culminated in Blitz's resignation from the company he had created in 1950. The end came one morning in 1969 when he arrived at the Paris office at nine instead of his usual six. He resigned, to the surprise and shock of many of the company's employees.

Blitz, who never appeared to feel comfortable with the growing size and decreasingly intimate style of Club Méditerranée, completed his exit by liquidating all his holdings in the company, a bitter gesture that indicated that he wanted to wash his hands of the experience forever. It was the end of the beginning for Club Méditerranée.

CHAPTER SEVEN

A Glass Eye and a Wooden Leg

"Club Med used to be the cushy answer to the
French Foreign Legion."

A former Club Med GO, 1986

In 1970, besides swallowing up the Club Européen du Tourisme (CET), a major French competitor, and generating revenues in excess of $56 million, Club Méditerranée hired Gilbert Trigano's talented 24-year-old son, Serge. The same year, another 24-year-old from Great Britain was recruited by the company. His name was Martin Harbury.

Harbury, a lean, dark-haired television producer now in his late 30s, was then a relatively sheltered young man living in London. Born and raised in the quiet Sussex community of Worthing, which Harbury remembers as "a living geriatric ward," he escaped by joining the British army. After serving as an officer in the Royal Artillery's Light Air Defence Regiment, a stint that took him from Wales to Singapore and back again, he left the army and found employment with a dreary British shipping company, where he languished as a junior manager earning a modest £25 a week. It wasn't what he had in mind.

"I was looking for adventure," says Harbury matter-of-factly, explaining that the primary reason he joined the shipping company was that he hoped to be transferred to the Caribbean one day. "But they put me in the South African department and told me that was the only place I was likely to go. I wasn't keen on that." He had even once considered a career with military intelligence to satisfy his thirst for adventure. "I had a couple of interviews with plainclothes officers."

However, his future as a cloak-and-dagger specialist was never resolved because a friend at the shipping company showed him an advertisement in the London *Times*. "The clipping said, 'If you like sailing and would like to spend 180 days in the Caribbean for free, we've got a job for you.' So I said to my friend: 'Do you mind if I apply too?' I knew nothing about Club Med. I hadn't heard of Club Med. It was just like that."

Harbury sent in an application to the Club Med office in London. A couple of weeks later, he received a telephone call from the French company telling him that the director of sports personnel in Paris was coming to London to conduct interviews. He met with the official a short time later.

The interview didn't go quite as Harbury expected. "Well, first of all the guy didn't speak a word of English," he recalls, chuckling at the memory of himself floundering around in his schoolboy French until the befuddled Club Med executive finally saved the situation by calling his bilingual wife, a woman of Swiss-English descent, into the interview.

"How much sailing have you done? Where did you learn? Have you taught sailing before? That sort of thing." Because he had never formally taught sailing and was concerned about his credentials, Harbury also went to the trouble of fudging a letter of recommendation with the help of an old friend in the British army. "I got him to write me a letter written exactly the way I wanted and I got him to temporarily upgrade himself from lieutenant to lieutenant-colonel. They swallowed that."

But Harbury's chicanery wasn't necessary. "Basically, they didn't give a damn," he observes in retrospect. "What they were looking for was personality."

Much to his surprise, Harbury received a letter from Club Med two weeks later offering him a job as a sailing instructor at the Martinique village, which was in its second season of operation. "I freaked because I never expected to get it," he remembers, adding that his starting salary was "the princely sum of $50 a month."

58

Despite the slave labour wages, which fortunately included accommodation, meals, and a few other small perks, Harbury immediately accepted Club Med's offer of employment. However, before departing for sunny Martinique, he and his friends had a boozy goodbye party in London. He recalls a close friend giving him some sage advice. "Don't worry!" his pal counselled him. "Even if you had a glass eye and a wooden leg, you couldn't miss."

Harbury has often thought about writing a book about his Club Med experiences and the salty expression has stuck with him over the years. " 'A Glass Eye and a Wooden Leg' has become the title of every version of the story I've tried to write," he says. "It's absolutely perfect."

A few days later, Harbury, with freshly trimmed hair and wearing the lightweight tropical suit he had had made in Singapore, was on his way. After catching an early flight to Paris, where he was to hook up with other Club Med GOs and GMs en route to the Caribbean, he hung around Orly airport all day, finally boarding a late-afternoon plane to Martinique.

Once aloft, he discovered that he was one of about ten new GOs who were heading to the Club Med village. Although he confesses to being a little naive at the time, he was surprised by the lusty enthusiasm of one of the other new GOs, a stocky Swiss fellow who was slated to be a diving instructor at the resort.

"He was telling me in his halting English that we were going to have a competition to see how many girls we could fuck," remembers Harbury. "I didn't know what he was talking about."

For the rest of the long transatlantic flight, Harbury wondered about what kind of place he was headed to. He first had to deal with the authorities at the Martinique airport after the plane landed, at nine-thirty that night.

"I sort of had working papers," he explains, pointing out that Great Britain in 1970 was not yet a member of the European Common Market, so his entry into the French colony was less than automatic. "I had a problem with customs and I was held up for a long time. But the Club is very strong politically."

Mike, the GO in charge of dive operations in Martinique, came to his rescue by bullying the customs officials to let him in. He was then led to the buses that would finally take him and the others to the Club Med village.

"There were yahoos in straw hats and *pareus*, with incredible suntans, shepherding people into four or five Mercedes buses." Shortly after, with all the GOs and GMs safely accounted for, the convoy of buses set out for the Club Med village. "We were driving like maniacs in these buses through the Martinique hills. We were careening around hairpin roads, really scary stuff. After about an hour's drive, we came to a guardhouse and went roaring in. We screeched to a halt and there were 50 million people dancing, waving, cheering, and drinking. It was chaos! I wanted to get back on the bus and go back.

"Have you ever heard of Butlin's?" he asks, mentioning the English resort company that features everything from gardening to professional wrestling to Freddie and the Dreamers concerts to attract its clientele. "That's what I thought I had arrived at."

One of the last to get off the buses, Harbury walked aimlessly around the Martinique village, uncertain of where to go and what to do. "I was overcome. Somebody shoved a rum punch in my hand. All I could do was wander around with my little letter of employment."

After stabilizing himself with another much-needed rum punch, he finally managed to locate another Club Med GO who spoke English. Harbury showed him his letter of employment. The other GO wasn't impressed.

"*You're* a GO?" he asked incredulously.

"Yes," Harbury said bravely. "I'm here to teach sailing."

Eventually Harbury was rescued by two more friendly and polite GOs, Peter and Madelaine, who helped him get organized. After getting him his room key, the couple took him down to Café du Port, the village's waterside bar, for yet another rum punch. Then they escorted him back to the main part of the resort, where it was Creole Night, a wild Club Med extravaganza that included everything from singing and dancing to colourful native costumes.

"Peter and Madelaine deliberately sat me at the edge of the dance floor and pointed me out," laughs Harbury. "At the very end, the girls came out and dragged me up on the dance floor. And there I was dancing the beguine [a frantic West Indian dance]. I felt like an absolute asshole."

Peter and Madelaine later introduced Harbury to Patrick, another sailing instructor at the village and the brother of the woman who had translated for him at the initial interview in London. Patrick took Harbury to the club's disco, located underneath the Café du Port. "He had been there a while," explains Harbury. "He knew everybody, and all these wonderful girls were coming up to him and kissing him. Patrick left me in the disco talking to a GM named John. We were standing at the bar and he passed me this bag. He said, 'Hold onto this for a second.' I opened it up and it had marijuana in it. I had never seen marijuana before in my life."

The next morning, after a short and restless sleep, Harbury blurrily awakened to the picturesque vista of the Buccaneer's Creek village in Martinique, a pretty, tropical setting that left him in awe.

"It was beautiful, really beautiful. I took photographs from my room that morning." His accommodations were spartan but comfortable. "I had my own double room. It was adobe-style, and it had a little balcony out the back. There were big shutters on the doors and windows. There was a table and a chair and a bathroom."

After a revitalizing breakfast, Harbury, a competent amateur yachtsman, headed for the dock to find out what his duties were as a sailing instructor. "Nobody asked me whether I could sail," he points out. "I was taken at face value."

It took Harbury about a month to settle in as an instructor, but it wasn't always easy. "There was a nice tradition in Martinique where the crew of the boat that capsized provided a bottle of Scotch for drinks at the end of the day," he fondly remembers. "My boat provided an awful lot of drinks at the end of the day."

Besides teaching sailing, Harbury also started chasing after girls, a not uncommon practice at Buccaneer's Creek in those days. "The first few women I went after turned me down flat," he confesses. "I had no self-confidence. I was as much out of water as they were, if not more so, because I was supposed to be competent and I wasn't. I didn't know my way around and I didn't even have a tan."

But this frustrating condition soon changed as Harbury began to feel more at ease in his surroundings. "Bit by bit, I got used to it. After about a month I realized I was dying because I was only getting two hours' sleep a night. I was fucking myself stupid."

There was no shortage of available females at the Buccaneer's Creek resort. "Some women would get off the plane and start fucking," he offers, confirming a lot of the wild stories about the Club Med village in Martinique.

The Swiss GO who had challenged him to a screwing contest on the flight down to Martinique was a case in point. "He came up to me and said, 'How many have you fucked?' I said, 'I don't know.' So he dragged me off to his room, and he had carved notches in his bedpost. I'm not sure, but he had something like 20 or 25 notches. And he was a fat, fairly obnoxious guy."

In deference to the all-pervasive party atmosphere at the Club Med village, all the GOs, like Harbury, were encouraged to have a good time with the GMs. "You were coached to think of yourself as a paid guest," says Harbury, explaining that the village's management preferred that the GOs socialized with the GMs rather than with the other staff members. "In essence, the Club looked on the GOs as prostitutes. Somebody said it once and we went on strike."

The "somebody" Harbury is referring to was his first *chef de village*, or manager, at Buccaneer's Creek, whom he remembers abusively lecturing the staff about their sexual obligations vis-à-vis the GMs. "You are here to keep the clients happy," the chef bluntly told the GOs. "If that means fucking them, then you'll fuck them!"

The GOs, disgusted by these comments, staged an impromptu strike to show their displeasure. "We basically got up and walked out." The GOs had a meeting in the resort's bar and collectively decided that they were not going to be treated that way. "From our point of view, it was an absolute moral issue. I don't want to think of myself that way."

The dispute was resolved when the chef apologized to the GOs for his remarks. To help everyone forget the ugliness of his outburst, he threw a party for the staff. Soon everything returned to normal (at least as normal as things ever get at Buccaneer's Creek).

"It didn't change a thing," Harbury laughs, gauging the disagreement as more of a tempest in a teapot than a full-scale labour war. "Let's face it, the type of young man they hire — it's a kid in a candy store."

Harbury was not disillusioned by Club Méditerranée. "It was the beginning of the rest of my life," he sums up, voicing a sentiment that is typical among the thousands who have worked for the company. "As far as I was concerned, it was a tremendous experience. There was a lot of growth."

And there were some truly invigorating moments. One was the time one of the world's most celebrated motor yachts, the *Ultima 2*, visited the Buccaneer's Creek village. "One Sunday, a ship hove into view ... and I mean a ship! It was probably about a 300-foot boat. We were sitting watching from the Café du Port and it anchored off the bay. We saw this tender being lowered over the side and after a while it came roaring towards the beach. It was a 30-foot launch with eight uniformed crew members on it and four people sitting on swivel armchairs in the cockpit. It came up to the dock. We strolled over and said: 'You can't land here!' "

The wealthy passengers were puzzled by the indifferent treatment they were getting. "This is Club Med?" one asked. "Can't we look around?"

As Harbury tells the story, "Two elderly men and two young blonde bimbos" were denied permission to wander freely around the resort. This was "because non-members are not allowed in. Period!" Finally, after a brief, escorted look around, the rich visitors returned to their seagoing palace. "They gave us their cards and one was Charles Revson [the Revlon cosmetics tycoon]. They said: 'If you're ever in New York, look us up.' Then they gave us 20 bucks and left."

Harbury observed an interesting characteristic of the richer GMs. "Generally, the more successful and wealthy, the more obnoxious they were. You put them in bathing suits, T-shirts, or *pareus* and give them beads. You give them no reason to carry around any trapping of wealth. They couldn't flash their opulence the way they were used to. It was really interesting to see how that kind of class barrier got broken down."

An unexpected natural disaster occurred in August, more than four months after Harbury arrived in the French West Indies. It was a powerful hurricane, a tropical storm with winds of more than 100 miles an hour, that wreaked havoc on the Buccaneer's Creek village and the entire island of Martinique.

"The whole island was cut off," Harbury remembers, telling how the airport was forced to shut, ships couldn't dock, and Fort-de-France, Martinique's picturesque capital, was under water. Besides flooding and wind damage, a major problem resulting from the hurricane was the contamination of the island's drinking water. But this was no problem for Club Med, which came up with an imaginative if heartless solution.

"We had fresh water," Harbury reveals. "The Club is in such an amazingly powerful political situation. They flew in a plane from Paris with bottles of Évian water. It was scheduled to arrive late at night so that the locals wouldn't see it."

Following the storm, Harbury was transferred to the Fort-Royal village on the neighbouring island of Guadeloupe. Shortly after, he left the direct employ of Club Méditerranée to become the skipper of his very own boat, a beautiful twin-masted schooner that was used by the company for charters and excursions and was featured, along with a suntanned Martin Harbury, in Club Med's 1973 North American brochure.

He even got a 50-per-cent raise as part of the new arrangement, going from a miserly $50 a month to an equally laughable $75 a month. But money was not the issue with Harbury, who, just a brief time before, could only have dreamed of living such an exotic life.

"It was stunning," he lovingly says of the yacht, which had been built in 1908 and had a length of 47 feet and bow width of 15 feet. "I sailed between St. Lucia and Antigua quite a bit. Sometimes I would have as many as 50 people on the boat."

As befits Club Med's style, there was never a shortage of liquor on board. "At all times I was required to have a case of white rum, a case of dark rum, and a case each of white, red, and rosé wines. If I ran out or was getting low, I just called the Club and got more."

For the first few months, Harbury immensely enjoyed being the captain of his own yacht. But his enthusiasm for the job started to fade as the monotony became apparent. "After a while, I became a bus driver," he says. He was also becoming aware that he might not have much of a future if he stayed on forever at Club Med. "I woke up from Never Never Land," he admits. He was forcibly reminded of the dangers of a prolonged stay at Club Med by the example of a fellow named Dimitri, a vulgar individual who used his position of authority to take sexual advantage of women and who was the antithesis of everything Harbury believed in.

"He was in charge of Air France reservations and ticket changes and that kind of thing. He was fat and in his mid-40s. He had curly black hair that he dyed every day. He would say to women who wanted to change their reservations: 'What's it worth?' And that's how he got fucked. I looked at Dimitri and I found him increasingly disgusting. He was everything I dreaded becoming at his age. I saw every potential to become fat, bloated, and unbelievably egotistical, and I saw myself in my mid-40s with nowhere to go and nothing in my pocket. I looked at that and realized I had two choices. Either I left or I stayed on and tried to have a career with the Club in management."

Harbury disagreed with the way things were run at Club Méditerranée. He decided that a career in management was not for him and quit. When he finally left Club Méditerranée seventeen months later, he was drained physically and emotionally. "It's exhausting," he remembers. "When I finally left I went home and slept for two weeks. I was fucked in every way.

"It's a hard thing to explain," he concludes, summing up his feelings about his time with Club Med. "The emotional stress of being in a place like that, having that many new people come in each week, forming emotional attachments and crying when they leave. And two hours later there was a whole new lot arriving. You're putting out, you're constantly putting out. And you almost never get anything back. There's a self-protective cynicism that sets in."

Although he has straightforwardly criticized some aspects of working for Club Méditerranée, Harbury today is not bitter about his experiences and is not against the company. He honestly believes it to be a fine organization that offers the consumer a unique vacation for the money. In fact, one has the sneaking suspicion that if the telephone rang and it was Club Med calling to offer him another job, he would seriously consider dropping everything to head off to wherever they wanted him. "It was the beginning of the rest of my life," he declares.

CHAPTER EIGHT

Consolidation

"God is dead! *Terminé*! Peace to his ashes. Is it good? Is it bad? I don't know. For me, it's a fact!"

Gilbert Trigano, 1975

T he absorption of the Club Européen du Tourisme (CET) in 1970 was a major coup for Club Méditerranée and Gilbert Trigano. Not only did the merger clearly establish Club Méditerranée as a colossus in the French vacation industry (the company was now the biggest holiday operator in France and one of the largest in Europe) but it also gave Trigano an unassailable base on which to expand. It would be difficult if not impossible for any rival vacation enterprise to compete with Club Méditerranée.

At the time of the acquisition, Club Méditerranée was catering annually to more than 215,000 GMs, 36 per cent non-French, in 31,100 beds in 51 holiday villages. All of this added up to a staggering 2,653,000 hotel nights and gross revenues in excess of FF209 million in 1970.

CET, which was founded in 1951, a year after Club Méditerranée, was about a quarter of the size of its new parent. For its part, CET brought to the deal 100,000 clients, 20 per cent non-French, 8,700 beds, and 13 vacation resorts. This translated into more than 700,000 hotel nights and revenues of about FF53 million.

"Experience proves that there are three different kinds of clients," said Trigano. "The one who likes to stay put, the one who likes to move about, and the one who likes a balance between the two. The association with the CET will allow us to better fill that latter need."

The merger had other benefits. CET, unlike Club Méditerranée, was primarily a tour operator, a travel company that organized and packaged vacations. With both companies annually selling more than 198,000 individual "charter" trips, the Club Méditerranée–CET combo would become one of the largest travel companies in Europe.

"The CET's activity was that of a pure tour operator," Trigano later explained. "From now on, we can use larger airplanes like a 747. When we have two villages in the same area, as in Turkey, we will be able to use a full 747 to transport the passengers. On the other hand, when we have only one village in one area, we will balance the load of the jumbo jets by using half of the capacity for the village and the other half for packaged holidays."

Besides generating increased revenues, Club Méditerranée's take-over of the CET also opened up new avenues of financing for the company. For example, Trigano approached the Banque de Paris et Pays-Bas (Paribas), one of France's biggest investment banks, to underwrite the purchase of the CET. Paribas agreed and became a 16-per-cent partner in the new arrangement. However, Baron Edmond de Rothschild remained the single biggest investor, with his interests declared at 33.5 per cent in 1970.

Meanwhile, in North America, Club Méditerranée was consolidating its position as well as offering some insights into the vacation requirements of Americans. "People here don't want the phoney, spoon-fed luxury of an expensive hotel," said the company's U.S. representative, John Youngman. "Those hotels have to add frills to justify their high room rates. It's a vicious circle. In a man's everyday life, he is part of a complicated pecking order. Our resorts have none of that. Everybody is equal. Our staff even eats with the guests, and of course tipping is prohibited."

Gilbert Trigano concurred. "We never wanted to use the principles of the American hotel chains. From one side of the continent to the other, they offer their clients the same room where the interiors are perfectly identical. To us, every project is a true prototype."

One "true prototype" that Trigano would probably like to forget was Club Méditerranée's first vacation village in Mexico. Opened in 1970, it was a slapdash conversion of the Majestic Hotel in Acapulco. Dismissed by observers as "old and uncomfortable" and "285 steps above the beach," the Acapulco Club Med village did not capture the imagination of North American GMs and was closed two years later.

In 1971, the American business magazine *Forbes* examined the reasons for Club Méditerranée's success. The influential publication surmised that it could not be attributed entirely to fairmindedness and unabashed creativity.

"Le Club's prefabricated rooms still cost only $13,000 to build, compared with $20,000 for a conventional resort," said *Forbes*. "The staff is still modest, too. While some luxury hotels employ three workers per guest, an average 600-room Club resort is run by a band of 200. With economies like that, it's easy for Le Club to throw in all the wine you can drink with meals, and sports ranging from scuba diving to horseback riding and skiing."

(Another reason for Club Méditerranée's success was Gilbert Trigano, whose ability as a negotiator was demonstrated that same year when he managed to get permission from Anwar Sadat's Egyptian government to operate Club Méditerranée tours between Egypt and Israel.)

In March 1972, Club Méditerranée announced a further economic restructuring of the company. Joining the ownership group were financial heavyweights Crédit Lyonnais (France's second-biggest commercial bank), the Union des Assurances de Paris (a big French insurance company), and CEMP Investments (the Canadian holding company for the billionaire Bronfman family of Seagram's fame, the world's largest distillery company). Each of the three new partners had an 11.4-per-cent interest.

There was also some shuffling with Club Méditerranée's remaining owners. American Express, which had initially held 15 per cent of the shares in 1968, reduced its interest to 11.4 per cent, while Paribas, which had a 16-per-cent interest following the CET merger, also lowered its holdings to 7.8 per cent. Baron Edmond de Rothschild similarly started to diminish his position in the company by reducing his interest to 26 per cent.

Of the new investors, CEMP Investments was the most interesting. CEMP — the acronym comprises the first initials of the first names of the four children (Charles, Edgar, Minda, and Phyllis) of the late chairman of Seagram's, the legendary Samuel "Mr. Sam" Bronfman — is controlled by one of the wealthiest families in North America. Called the "Rothschilds of the New World" and "certainly richer and without a doubt more secretive" by Canadian biographer Peter C. Newman, the Bronfmans became involved with Club Méditerranée through Minda's husband, Alain de Guinsbourg, a French aristocrat and distant relative of the Rothschild family.

As impressive as Club Méditerranée's new trio of stockholders were, their arrival earned Trigano more criticism than kudos. In an interview in 1973, he was accused of being a *danseuse*, or dancer, to the big-money boys behind the company. "Aren't the banks in it for the money?" asked one naive interrogator.

"I believe that when banks invest money in a business it is always to earn more," Trigano calmly explained. "But I believe that at the same time they are amused and passionate about the Club. In terms of great enterprises, the Club is a little thing. It is almost nothing to them."

"So you are their *danseuse*?" his inquisitor carried on, attempting to rattle Trigano.

But Club Méditerranée's clever president refused to be drawn. "Yes," he politely confessed. "We are their *danseuses* a little bit, part of their fantasy and dream. It happens that one becomes tired of *danseuses*. That's for sure."

Trigano, who also disclosed that his salary was a modest FF30,000 a month in 1973, was asked what he would like to do if, for some unforeseen reason, Club Méditerranée went out of business.

"Oh, là là! Two thousand things," he responded. "I would go and work in an African country, the Ivory Coast or Senegal, and I would bring with me a number of retired men and women. But from all trades. Plumbers, roofers, sheet metal workers, construction workers, teachers, engineers . . . and I would propose another form of co-operation to the Africans. I would tell them: 'We are not unhappy, we are retired. But we feel like living with you under the sun. So, we'll make you a proposition. You give us your sun and we will give you our knowledge.' Okay! And so we will teach our trades to the 20-year-old Ivoirians and young Senegalese as grandfathers and grandmothers would. I would really like to do that."

In 1973, Club Méditerranée ventured further afield by opening its first vacation village in the Indian Ocean, an exotic retreat on the volcanic island of Réunion. An overseas department of France, Réunion is about 500 miles east of Madagascar off the coast of East Africa.

A year later, in 1974, the French company opened another resort on Réunion's neighbouring island of Mauritius, a 787-square-mile island that was once a colony of France but is now a member of the British Commonwealth. Although the circumstances may have been different at the outset, the structure of the present ownership of the Mauritius village is a good example of the way Club Méditerranée operates in the Third World.

Typically, it is a complicated financial arrangement that allows the company to control the holiday property but also permits Club Med to claim that it is nothing more than a minority participant at the same time, an all-important condition that is sometimes very necessary in the often hostile and nationalistic Third World in which the company does a lot of business.

It works like this. A new company, the Compagnie des Villages de Vacances de l'Île-de-France (COVIFRA), was created to own the resort's buildings (rooms, restaurants, swimming pool, and so forth) on land leased from the tourist-hungry Mauritius government for 99 years. Club Méditerranée owns 43.77 per cent of COVIFRA. Another 6.8 per cent is held by a French company that owns Club Med's Le Lagon village on Réunion. Not surprisingly, Club Méditerranée owns 44.02 per cent of this company, thus collectively giving the French vacation giant a 46.76-per-cent indirect stake in the Mauritius village — a minority position.

The illusion of local control is maintained through the participation of the Mauritius government, which owns approximately 34 per cent of COVIFRA, and of other local investors who account for the remaining shares, a little over 15 per cent of the company. The numbers add up to about a 49-per-cent interest in COVIFRA, a figure greater than Club Méditerranée's 46.76-per-cent share but less than the magical 50 per cent necessary for outright majority control. Therefore, the likelihood of a take-over by a suddenly unfriendly government is diminished. In such a case, the citizens of Mauritius would be slitting their own throats, because they have a bigger stake in COVIFRA than Club Méditerranée.

Club Med's position is more powerful than it might seem, however. If one adds Club Méditerranée's direct 43.77-per-cent interest in COVIFRA to the 6.8 per cent held by the French company that owns the Réunion village (a company in which Club Méditerranée has a 44.02-per-cent stake and probably a substantial amount of power), the total is 50.57 per cent — a majority and controlling position.

While one can only speculate about how much influence the Mauritian interests have over the French company that owns the Réunion village, it is hard to believe that it would be greater than Club Méditerranée's. Of course, a problem could arise if all the other participants in COVIFRA in Mauritius, Réunion, and France got together and organized a united front against Club Méditerranée, but that is most unlikely because of the enormously complex jurisdictional and cultural differences.

Half-way across the globe in strife-torn Haiti, Club Méditerranée was laying the groundwork for its future Magic Isle village.

Although the 700-bed resort, which is located about 50 miles north of Port-au-Prince, Haiti's slum- and disease-ridden capital, would not greet its first guest until 1980, it was necessary to start working on the project years in advance. Besides coping with the effects of the country's poverty (Haiti is among the poorest countries in the world), the French vacation company also had to learn to live with the corrupt Haitian government headed by Jean-Claude "Baby Doc" Duvalier, the son of the bloodthirsty dictator François "Papa Doc" Duvalier, who terrorized the country from 1957 until his death in 1971.

Baron Edmond de Rothschild, Club Méditerranée's most important stockholder, was also reportedly investing in Haiti. In 1974, he was listed as a backer (along with Mick Jagger, Prince Egon von Furstenburg, George Plimpton, Roger Vadim, the Duke of Bedford, and other jet-set luminaries) of Habitacion Leclerc.

Habitacion Leclerc, said to be the former estate of Napoleon's nymphomaniacal sister Pauline, is a sybarite's delight, characterized by Frommer's 1980 *Guide to the Caribbean* as "the most decadent resort in the world." The tropical 30-acre setting seduces its clientele with "a botanical garden with ruins of statues, hidden paths, waterfalls, and a menagerie of wild birds."

And 1974 was also the year that Giovanni Agnelli, Italy's richest and most powerful industrialist, purchased an 8.62-percent interest in Club Méditerranée. Agnelli, who owns Fiat, one of Europe's largest automobile manufacturers, invested $8.53 million after American Express, citing the costly expense of management, decided to liquidate its holdings in the French company.

CHAPTER NINE

Croesus

> "Anybody can make a fortune. It takes a genius to hold onto one."
>
> Jay Gould, 1836–1892

I n 1983 he was identified as the wealthiest man in Italy. The year before, a survey in the Italian business weekly *Il Mondo* determined that he was more powerful than Pope John Paul II and the Mafia. He owns Italy's biggest company and largest automaker, Fiat, a $14-billion conglomerate that employs more than a quarter of a million Italians. He owns two of Italy's leading newspapers, Turin's *La Stampa* and the *Corriere della Sera* in Milan; in the past he has owned Bantam Books, the world's largest paperback publisher. His world-wide business associates have ranged from Muammar Gaddafi's Libyan government to David Rockefeller's Chase Manhattan Bank, where he is a member of that institution's prestigious International Advisory Committee. He lunches with President Ronald Reagan and meets privately with former President Jimmy Carter. He was a good friend of John F. Kennedy and his family. He discusses global issues with knowledgeable insiders like Henry Kissinger and Alexander Haig. For sport, he can cheer for his own soccer team, Juventus, the world's most illustrious squad. He has survived a life-threatening heart attack and is a prime target on any terrorist group's hit list. He is Giovanni

Agnelli, one of the world's most prominent industrialists and a key investor in Club Méditerranée.

It is hard to tell who benefited more from the infusion of funds — Agnelli himself or Club Méditerranée. In 1975 he was reportedly feeling "extremely satisfied" because his original 1974 investment of $8.53 million, made through the Agnelli-owned holding company Istituto Finanziaro Industriale Internazionale (IFINT), had quickly escalated to about $11 million the following year, a profit of almost $2.5 million on his initial investment.

Agnelli, who has a law degree from the University of Turin, was born in the industrial city of Turin on March 12, 1921. A handsome and celebrated pleasure-seeker in his younger days, he is now in his mid-60s, greying and distinguished in appearance and looking every bit the successful magnate that he is. He remains a larger-than-life figure in his homeland.

As a youth, he frequented the Scuola di Cavalleria (Cavalry School) in Pinerolo. At 20, he joined the Italian forces and took part in the Axis campaigns in Russia and North Africa in the Second World War. Following Italy's surrender in 1943, he participated in the liberation of the country with the Italian troops of the Allies' Fourth Army. For his contributions in the war, he was decorated with the Italian War Cross for Military Valour.

Besides providing reams of copy for the international business media, Agnelli has also served as a director of numerous other corporations and associations. These include SKF-Goteberg, a large industrial equipment company in Sweden; Mediobanco, a financial institution in Italy; the Italian Manufacturers Association; the Turin Industrial Association; and the International Industrial Conference in San Francisco. In addition, he is chairman of the family's Agnelli Foundation, a governor of the Atlantic Institute of International Affairs, a member of the executive committee of the Trilateral Commission in Paris, and a member of the Groupe des Présidents des Grandes Entreprises Européennes (the Group of Presidents of Large European Enterprises) in Brussels. Finally, he manages to find time to attend meetings of the Bilderberg, an influential organization established by Prince Bernhard of the Netherlands to give international political and economic leaders an opportunity to discuss the significant issues of the day in an informal fashion.

Agnelli has also been involved in a number of spectacular and sometimes controversial business deals over the years. In 1966, Fiat signed a $1.5-billion contract with the Soviet Union, then headed by Leonid Brezhnev, to construct a colossal automobile manufacturing plant that would turn out over 600,000 vehicles a year. The deal, which was one of the largest ever signed by a western company with an Iron Curtain country, would effectively triple car production in the Soviet Union.

Ten years later, in 1976, Agnelli planted the seeds of future problems by entangling Fiat with the regime of Libya's Muammar Gaddafi. This deal called for Gaddafi's government, through the Libyan Arab Foreign Investment Company, to invest $320 million in Fiat in exchange for 13 per cent of the common stock and 15 per cent of the preferred stock of the Italian auto-maker. In addition, two of Gaddafi's representatives were elected to Fiat's board of directors. At the time, Libya's money was needed to finance the modernization of Fiat's ageing plants. "We liked petrodollars. Everybody needed petrodollars," said Agnelli, justifying the arrangement.

Agnelli's business dealings with Libya were called into question following the American bombing of Tripoli on April 15, 1986. One month later, in May, the U.S. Pentagon cancelled a $7.9-million contract with Fiat for 178 bulldozers for the Marine Corps (a hypocritical action, in light of subsequent revelations that members of President Reagan's administration were already secretly selling arms to the anti-American regime in Iran).

For Agnelli, the message was loud and clear — either get rid of Gaddafi as an investor, or risk losing the valuable U.S. contracts, especially for the Strategic Defense Initiative (Star Wars) program, that Fiat had been pursuing.

Agnelli asked the Libyans to sell off their interest in Fiat. "Their answer was that they were not ready to sell and do not wish to sell," Agnelli told a news conference in June 1986. "If they sold the shares back, I would be very happy. But I am in no position to do any arm-twisting."

In August, the pressure on Gaddafi was increasing when a prosecutor in Milan ordered several Italian banks to freeze all Libyan government assets, about $23 million, under their control. This action was taken in response to the Libyan government debt of $928 million owed to more than 20 Italian firms. Perhaps fearing another Italian move to freeze the Libyan holdings in Fiat, they approached Agnelli in mid-August to work out a deal.

Finally, on September 23, 1986, Fiat announced that the Libyans had been bought out for approximately $3 billion. Two banks, the Deutsche Bank in West Germay and Mediobanco in Italy, purchased about two-thirds of the Libyan shares; the remaining one-third was bought by Agnelli's IFINT.

Agnelli couldn't explain why the Libyans had agreed to sell their holdings in Fiat. "I don't even want to imagine what it could be," he told the *Wall Street Journal* following the buyout. "I had always stated that if they would sell, I would buy." As for Fiat getting a piece of the Star Wars business from the American government, he expressed confidence. "Fiat is surely going to get a certain amount of contracts," he said.

In light of the fact that Rothschild, Agnelli's fellow investor in Club Méditerranée, is a staunch supporter of the Israeli state, the Libyan connection is particularly interesting.

CHAPTER TEN

Fatality and Irrationality

"The profit is vital."

Gilbert Trigano, 1985

By 1974, Club Méditerranée not only had established itself as a powerhouse in European financial circles, but it had also become a formidable force in the world-wide vacation industry. While some countries, like Italy, were suffering a heavy decline in tourism because of the fall-out from the Arab oil embargo, the French vacation company just kept on piling up the profits. This was true not only in Europe, where the company had become an institution, but also in the rapidly developing North American market, where Club Med's formula for success, the enticing four S's — sun, sea, sports, and sex — was proving to be just as seductive as on the Continent.

To keep the momentum going, Gilbert Trigano continued Club Méditerranée's expansion program. In 1974 the company opened the Playa Blanca village on Mexico's west coast. A much more attractive resort than the first Mexican Club Med village in Acapulco, it was an immediate hit with the GMs, who flocked there by the planeload.

The advent of the Playa Blanca village foreshadowed the development of a close relationship between Club Méditerranée and the Mexican government, a partnership that would eventually see the company involved in nine resorts in Mexico by 1986.

Another opening in 1974 was that of the company's second holiday village in the United States, the Hanelei Plantation resort on Kauai in the Hawaiian Islands. The village, a snazzy hotel-bungalow combination that was franchised to a company from Japan, was designed to serve the bizarre mixture of Japanese honeymooners and American singles. Club Méditerranée tried to market the Kauai resort like a United Nations conference. "The Hanelei Plantation has been chosen for an Oriental-Western dialogue, where members from Japan, Europe and North America will come together to exchange thoughts and learn about one another," explained the company's 1974 travel brochure.

Needless to say, this peculiar concept, which was also catalogued as "a cosmopolitan, multi-lingual vacation experience" and "a delightful tri-cultural holiday" was not popular with the GMs, and the village was quietly closed after a few unsuccessful seasons.

But none of this had much impact on Club Méditerranée's global operations as hundreds of thousands of enthusiastic GMs from around the world pushed total sales to about $170 million in 1975. Of this amount about 9 per cent, or slightly less than $20 million, was generated in North America, a remarkable statistic when one considers that the company was operating only five resorts in the western hemisphere at the time, two in Guadeloupe and one each in Martinique, Mexico, and Hawaii.

Acknowledging the widening popularity of Club Méditerranée, *Newsweek* published a feature story on the company in its January 5, 1976, edition, a tribute to the efforts of Gilbert Trigano and everyone else connected with the company. "The success of the Club Med is due to a brilliantly simple formula: it takes care of everything — and for one prepaid price," said *Newsweek*, summing up the company's prosperity.

Trigano, then 55, was also optimistic about the future. "By the year 2000, there will be 300 to 400 clubs worldwide," he predicted. "Just give us a world at peace and growing purchasing power and we'll take care of the rest."

Gérard Blitz was also back on the scene, working out of the

company's plush offices near the Paris Bourse. Although he was certainly not functioning in the same capacity as he had in the past, he helped Trigano out by giving interviews to the media, remembering the good old days in Alcudia and explaining the fabled Club Med concept.

Blitz, the spiritual father of the company, was still a valuable asset to Club Méditerranée, although he had earlier liquidated his holdings in the holiday enterprise. In recognition of his enormous contribution to the company, he was appointed *président d'honneur* (honorary president) of Club Méditerranée, a ceremonial title the 75-year-old Belgian retains to this day.

Basking in its unprecedented success, Club Méditerranée ventured farther afield in 1976 by opening the company's 74th holiday village, in Fidel Castro's Cuba. There the company operated its Bacuranao village, a dreary, 58-unit cement compound on Cuba's north shore, east of the capital city of Havana. The Bacuranao village was the result of five years of work by Gilbert Trigano and the combined efforts of the Cuban and French ambassadors, both of whom, reputedly, were fervent GMs.

Capitalistic Club Méditerranée in Communist Cuba was viewed with a certain amount of scepticism in some quarters in Paris. A reporter from *Le Point* asked Trigano about the odd arrangement. "The leaders think that their political ideas and the way we conduct our business are not morally incompatible," said Club Med's chief, surmising that the "sociologist" type of tourist might want to holiday at the Club Med village in Cuba.

The Cuban resort was another of Trigano's lead balloons, and it closed a short time after it opened. A key reason was that American tourists were forbidden by law to vacation in Cuba, so Club Méditerranée was unable to cash in on the nearby U.S. market.

Stefan Geissler, Club Méditerranée's director of international relations, also felt that the Cuban "economy was just not ready for us," citing an occasion when the GMs were forced to hang around the drab resort because delegates to a Third World political conference were monopolizing all the cabs and buses on the island.

Although the company was successfully operating vacation villages in three other Communist countries — Yugoslavia, Bulgaria, and Romania — Club Méditerranée also failed in its attempt to operate a resort in the Soviet Union. This time the Club Med village was located in Sochi, a Black Sea resort favoured by Soviet bureaucrats, unlike everyday Russian labourers, who enjoy their holidays in barbed-wire enclosed buildings known as sanatoriums. (Sanatoriums, in the Russian sense, are not always mental institutions or tuberculosis hospitals. Instead, they are used by Soviet workers for healthy and inexpensive vacations, one of the few bonuses available to the average citizen in the USSR).

Unfortunately, the Sochi Club Med village was another fiasco for the company and closed after only two years of operation. "It wasn't very attractive," admitted Stefan Geissler, summing up the reasons for the Black Sea blunder. "We found that most visitors to Russia wanted to tour and not spend two weeks in a club hotel."

Despite the problems in the Soviet Union and Cuba, the good news, financially speaking, far outweighed the bad. In 1975, Club Méditerranée launched a new subsidiary, Maeva, a chain of apartment resorts, mostly on the French Riviera, that are available for time-sharing purchase and holiday rental. A year later, in 1976, the company bought 45 per cent of Valtur Vacanze, a Club Med–like hotel operator in Italy. Then, in an unusual acquisition in December of the same year, Club Med purchased a 55-per-cent interest in Club Nature, a small chain of eight resorts that catered exclusively to nudists.

"We feel that nudism is legitimate," explained Club Med executive Stefan Geissler. "Those who wish to practise it should be allowed to do so in peace without being stared at and without paying three times over the norm."

However, the nudist customers seemed unimpressed by Club Med's ownership of the resorts. In 1977 only 3,246 of the sun-worshippers holidayed at Club Nature.

That same year, the company took over Clubhotel, a multi-property vacation business in France. It was also the year in which terrorism against Club Med properties hit the headlines.

It started on April 22, 1977, when two powerful bombs destroyed eight bungalows at Club Med's Cargese village on Corsica, the seventh attack against the vacation company since it had set up shop on the French island. The FLNC, the Front de Libération Nationale de la Corse, a shadowy and extremely violent local terrorist group that wanted independence for the island, claimed responsibility for the blast in protest against the "colonization" of Corsica by tourists.

A little over two weeks later, on May 9, another big bomb, an 11-pound package of TNT, was placed in the centre of Club Med's Sant'Ambrogio village, also on Corsica. However, this time there was no explosion because French experts managed to defuse the bomb at the last minute. Once again the FLNC was suspected.

Although no one was injured in the two incidents, the resulting damage at Cargese forced Club Méditerranée to close the resort for repairs.

Why had Club Méditerranée, a holiday company, suddenly become the target of a terrorist group? The answer is complex and the dispute long-standing, but to understand the situation one must first examine the relationship between the French government in Paris and Corsica, a full-fledged department of France.

Corsica, the birthplace of Napoleon and home to some of the world's most notorious heroin traffickers, is the third-largest island in the Mediterranean. A ruggedly beautiful place that is occasionally called "the Scented Isle," Corsica was an Italian colony for six centuries before finally succumbing to France more than 200 years ago.

Despite the all-pervasive influence of France, many of the native Corsicans, who number about half of the island's population of 300,000, have never forgotten their roots and remain very proud of their distinctive culture, history, and language. Old-fashioned and fiercely traditional, a large number of Corsican-born islanders still speak a form of Italian in everyday conversation rather than French. Corsica's weak and backward economy is dominated by French nationals who control the two main industries — agriculture and tourism — a circumstance that has left many Corsican natives feeling exploited, abused, and bitter about what they see as a one-way relationship with France.

The source of the current conflict in Corsica is partly attributable to France's capitulation in Algeria in 1962. Then, the retreating French were forced to cope with the enormous burden of one million *pieds-noirs* (black-foots), the French settlers in Algeria, who had become refugees as a result of the Algerian nationalists' successful fight for independence.

To make their plight easier, the French government relocated about 15,000 *pieds-noirs* in Corsica. To get the newcomers started, the government also granted low-interest loans and economic favours that were not normally available to the native Corsicans. Soon the hard-working *pieds-noirs* began to prosper and flex their financial muscle, grabbing up much of the best farmland and sticking closely together, especially in matters of business.

The situation was compounded by the simultaneous arrival of large numbers of prosperous mainland French who wanted to take advantage of Corsica's tourism opportunities, building villas and resorts and monopolizing most of the island's prime beachfront property. To make matters worse, many of the local Corsican businesses were bought up by French interests to service the invasion.

Among the native Corsicans, a feeling began to develop that everyone on the island was getting rich except for those who happened to be born on Corsica, a situation many of the locals blamed on French government policies that were viewed as discriminatory.

The issue boiled over in August 1975 when 50 armed and angry Corsican nationalists seized a vineyard belonging to a *pied-noir* farmer near Aleria on the island's east coast. Although intended as a symbolic act to bring attention to the problem, it turned into a much larger conflict when a stunned French government sent in tough anti-riot squads to deal with the militants, a decision that led to the killing of three French police officers in subsequent confrontations and the formation of the murderous FLNC in 1976 as the violence escalated.

Soon after, Club Méditerranée, probably because of the company's close association with the French government, was identified by the extremist FLNC as an instrument of French exploitation and control in Corsica, a notion that put the holiday company's villages in the front line of the terrorist group's campaign against French rule. The dirty and little-known war continues to this day.

Two months later, in July 1977, a different kind of tragedy struck Club Méditerranée. This time it was in Tunisia, a small Arab nation that had been a protectorate of France from 1881 until it achieved its independence in 1956, following many years of bloodshed.

The story started on July 9 at Club Med's Djerba village on an island off Tunisia's Mediterranean coast. At seven that morning, a ten-member group, five men and five women (five French and five Belgian), left the resort in four Citroën Meharis (not Land Rovers, as advertised in the company's brochure), for a multi-day excursion into the country's desert interior. It was extremely hot at this time of the year and the expedition was plagued by mechanical problems from the outset.

The first leg of the journey was a 130-mile jaunt from Djerba to Ksar Ghilan via the town of Chenini, a relatively short distance that took the Club Med group 17 hours to complete. The delays were caused, in part, by the condition of the Club Med vehicles. One car had to be replaced and another abandoned before the group departed for the second day of the excursion on July 10.

Besides mechanical problems, the health of some of the participants was far from perfect. Two of the women should not have been permitted to travel on the rugged excursion — one had a bad heart and another was recovering from throat surgery and could only drink with a straw. But it was too late and the group once more set out deeper into the desert. They were headed for Douz, an outpost at the edge of the Sahara.

After leaving Ksar Ghilan in three vehicles instead of four at a time when the temperatures were climbing rapidly, the Club

Med group once again ran into trouble. They repeatedly got bogged down in the sand. "Four tires were flat and the starters of two of the cars had broken down," said the official Tunisian report, compiled by Al Arbi Al-Baz, the National Guard commander in Douz. "The tourists were then obliged to push the cars to get them out of the sand as well as to make them start. These efforts were strenuous."

Finally, the group came to a complete stop only 19 miles from Douz. All the vehicles were immobilized in the sand. Worse yet, the woman with heart trouble began having severe problems. The excursion's youthful guide, a 24-year-old Club Med GO named Alain Richez, immediately realized the life-threatening nature of the situation. He knew the woman needed medical attention fast. Somehow, he and the others managed to free one of the vehicles and get it started. Then he and two young male members of the group headed for help in Douz.

Richez and his mates travelled only five miles farther before getting stuck in the sand once more. Then, in a desperate and foolhardy attempt to get assistance, Richez, leaving his two companions in the relative safety of the vehicle, set off alone on foot, a virtual act of suicide in the Tunisian desert.

"He had started to walk around 2:15 P.M., in other words at the hottest time of the day," detailed the Tunisian investigation. "He did not take anything with him to help him fight against thirst. The heat was terrible, especially that day where the wind known as 'chili' was blowing."

Richez never made it to Douz. Neither did the woman he was trying to save; she died at five that afternoon where the vehicles first got stuck. Three hours later, the remaining six members of the original group finally freed another vehicle from the sand and started the drive to Douz. After a short distance, they picked up the two men who had accompanied Richez. Further along, they discovered Richez's body lying face down in the middle of the road. He had died from heat exposure after walking for seven miles, an amazing distance considering that he had no water.

Shortly after finding Richez's corpse, the survivors met up

with a Tunisian who was collecting stones in his tractor. He offered them water and transported them to safety in Douz. The nightmare in the desert was over.

"It's incomprehensible," said a shocked Gilbert Trigano about the disaster that had claimed two lives in the Tunisian desert. "This tragedy should never have occurred. Believe me, I have gone through all the hypotheses in my head and I keep coming to a dead end on two questions that, unfortunately, will never be answered. Why did the convoy leave so late from Ksar Ghilan? Why did Alain continue on foot, which was suicidal?"

The first of Trigano's questions was addressed in the official Tunisian report on the incident prepared by Al Arbi Al-Baz. According to the report, the Club Med group departed Ksar Ghilan at seven-thirty on the morning of July 10, but it is possible that the condition of the vehicles, which was described as "poor" by the Tunisians, may have caused further delays.

The answer to Trigano's second question will always remain a mystery because of Richez's death, but the controversy over Club Méditerranée's professionalism in the tragedy will linger. Why didn't at least one of the Club Med vehicles carry a short-wave radio for emergency communications? Why did Club Méditerranée use Citroën Meharis instead of four-wheel-drive Land Rovers as advertised?

"The GMs prefer the Mehari," Trigano told the French newspaper *Journal Dimanche*, confirming that the Club Med brochure had indeed mentioned Land Rovers. "That's what they have always told us in the preceding excursions. They find them more comfortable."

An investigation by *Journal Dimanche* also determined that problems with the vehicles were not unusual on the Tunisian excursions. The paper reported that on the previous expedition, from June 25 to July 2, there were all kinds of mechanical malfunctions and several of the GMs complained vehemently about the situation when they got back to the Djerba village. "We would spend three to four hours a day on mechanical repairs," an angry GM told the paper.

On October 9, *Journal Dimanche* also published excerpts

from letters Alain Richez had written before his death. They graphically describe the difficulties he was encountering. "Three hours to travel three kilometres in insane heat, daily and perpetual mechanical breakdowns, a crazy and very tiring route," he wrote. "After 45 minutes, our four spare tires were flat. There was only one thing left to do, stop there and wait for sunrise . . ."

Trigano did not deny the obvious. "It's true that these vehicles were not perfect," he said candidly. "They broke down, but they left again. They were equipped with all the necessary materials such as spare tires, tool kit, first-aid kit, litres of water, wine, beer, etc.

"These vehicles are rented on location for the season," he continued. "Two Tunisian mechanics take care of them. It's one of our rules. We use the local services, with all that includes. It is obvious that in the south of Tunisia we cannot ask for such impeccable cars as we find in Germany.

"Every year we transport in the course of our different excursions more than 150,000 people. Without accident. This one, I repeat, is incomprehensible, but in all human activities, fatality and irrationality have a part to play."

CHAPTER ELEVEN

Murder in Corfu

"I don't find it troublesome to think about death. I happen to think about mine quite often."

Gilbert Trigano, 1973

Six days after Alain Richez's needless death in the Tunisian desert, another Club Med GO, Jean-Maurice Picimbono, was brutally murdered in a hold-up at Club Med's sprawling Ipsos village on Corfu, a normally idyllic Greek island in the Ionian Sea near Albania.

It was a typical Saturday afternoon at the Ipsos village. Many of the GMs were finishing up the standard Club Med lunch — mountains of excellent food, French and Greek, washed down by copious amounts of wine and ice-cold beer. Still others basked in the glorious Greek sunshine or splashed about in the warm water.

Saturday was also arrival day at the resort, a very busy time when hundreds of incoming GMs would have to be checked in and have their valuables put away for safekeeping. In the administrative wing, Dimitrios Carras, a Greek cashier at the resort, and his two assistants, one of them Picimbono, were doing just that, processing and sorting out the belongings of the 600 or so newcomers, a laborious task that takes several hours.

Suddenly the telephone wires went dead. Shortly thereafter, three masked gunmen, carrying bags and speaking French, invaded the Club Méditerranée village. They went directly to the office where Carras and his associates were working. At gunpoint, they ordered the Club Med employees to fill their bags with loot.

"We were all caught by surprise when the masked men burst into the office, carrying sacks and waving pistols," said a shaken Carras. "They ordered us in perfect French to keep still. Picimbono tried to resist and they fired, killing him instantly. Then the men fled through the open windows and we ran after them, trying to hit them with rocks," he continued. "They fired at us, wounding two persons, one seriously. They got into a car and drove off at high speed, and we lost sight of them."

The bandits, whose total take in the robbery was estimated at about $500,000 in cash and jewellery along with 600 passports, escaped from the holiday village in a Fiat 127. The Greek police quickly traced the Fiat to a rent-a-car company on Corfu, where the vehicle was registered to a Frenchman named Michel-André Legendre. Further investigation revealed that this was an alias and the Paris address given to the rental company was non-existent.

But it is known that after leaving the Club Med village, the gunmen drove directly to the nearby port of Kerkyra, about 12 miles from the resort. There they boarded the *Alexia*, a speedy 40-foot motor yacht owned by a 33-year-old Italian journalist, Alessio Monselles, who claimed that he was vacationing on Corfu with his 19-year-old girlfriend, Daniela Valle.

Monselles, who was later charged with complicity in the affair, told the Italian police that he and Valle, who was also charged, were alone on the boat on Saturday when the three blood-soaked gunmen hijacked his vessel for their getaway. He added that three Frenchmen had chartered his yacht prior to the Corfu robbery and that he had taken them on a tour of the Greek islands before docking at Kerkyra the day before the stick-up.

According to Monselles, the robbers had threatened to murder him if he didn't help them escape. Fearing for his life and his girlfriend's, he co-operated. First he took the *Alexia* to a tiny port in Yugoslavia, where he bought more fuel, then, at the gang's order, he navigated the boat to the Tremiti Islands off the coast of Italy. There, said Monselles, the bandits completed their escape by taking the yacht's dinghy and rowing ashore with their sacks of booty.

Free of the gunmen at last, Monselles did not immediately notify the police. Instead, he steered the *Alexia* back across the Adriatic Sea to the resort of Dubrovnik in Yugoslavia. Leaving the vessel in Dubrovnik, he and Valle returned to Italy aboard a ferry. On July 21, five days after the Corfu hold-up, the couple were arrested in Rome at the request of the Greek government.

Monselles and the *Alexia* had somehow been able to evade an air and sea dragnet mounted jointly by Greece, Yugoslavia, and Italy. There had been sensational reports in the press that the *Alexia* had sought refuge in Albania.

When Monselles was finally arrested, his version of the events was deemed highly suspect by the authorities. There were reports that the *Alexia*'s powerful motors were already running when the gunmen boarded the yacht in Kerkyra and that it had raced out of the harbour almost immediately after. In Monselles's favour, the Italian police had found the *Alexia*'s dinghy on San Nicola Island in the Tremiti group. It had been abandoned, but the police wondered if it had been left there deliberately to throw them off the track. There were simply too many pieces of the puzzle missing.

After his arrest, Monselles was held in Rome's Regina Coeli prison, but he was to remain behind bars for only a brief period. He was eventually released because the Italians decided that there was insufficient evidence to mount a prosecution.

Meanwhile in Paris, Gilbert Trigano was coping with the second major crisis to hit Club Méditerranée in less than a week. He had his own theory about the Corfu robbery. After the hold-up, he speculated that the robbery might have been the handiwork of someone staying at the Club Med village. To back up his theory, Trigano pointed out that during the course of the stick-up a member of the gang had referred to a fake robbery that had been staged by the resort's GOs to amuse the clientele.

Two weeks after the Corfu murder-robbery, on July 29, 1977, Club Méditerranée was once more the victim of a criminal outrage. This time it was arson at the company's alpine village in Tignes. There someone deliberately set two small fires that, fortunately, caused little damage and no injuries. "It's possible it's a pyromaniac or a little revenge," Gilbert Trigano said after the incident.

Three days later, on August 1, another Club Med village was robbed. The setting on this occasion was Club Med's Vittel village, in the French province of Vosges. The 1,000-acre complex, which is known as the "Green Island" village because of its verdant location, features an impressive 1920s-style hotel with nearby polo field and other amenities.

The robbery at the Vittel village was a solo effort. The lone gunman, crudely disguised in a mask and wig, walked into the cashier's office at ten-thirty in the evening. He pointed a pistol at an employee and demanded that she hand over the valuables. As she was alone at the time, she readily co-operated. After quickly stuffing cash and jewellery into a suitcase he had brought with him, the robber fled into the darkness.

The employees of the Vittel village were convinced that the hold-up was the work of someone who was very familiar with the resort. He seemed to know too much about the layout and operational practices. Some GOs even suspected that the culprit was a GM who was staying at the village.

On August 4, only three days after the Vittel heist, yet another robbery took place at a Club Med village, at the resort of Nicotera in Calabria, in southern Italy.

It was eleven-thirty on a Thursday morning. The robbers were much more creative and bold than their predecessors. It started when three men drove into the village. Two were wearing the uniforms of the Carabinieri, Italy's national police; the third member of the group said he was a plainclothes inspector and established his credentials by flashing false identification. They explained that they had come to the Nicotera resort to look at the identity papers and passports of the GMs and staff.

Everyone was convinced that the trio were legitimate law enforcement officers, and they were politely directed to the administrative section of the Club Med village. Once there, the inspector and one of the fake Carabinieri walked into the cashier's office, while the other counterfeit cop waited outside to supervise the growing crowd of GMs who wanted to find out what was going on.

However, the ruse quickly evaporated when the bogus Carabiniere pointed his machine-gun at the two Club Med employees in the office. The inspector tied them up and loaded the valuables, which were later estimated at about $60,000, into a large bag they had brought with them. Their mission accomplished, the gang made their getaway by car; the vehicle later turned out to be stolen.

Unbelievably, the string of crimes at Club Méditerranée still hadn't run out. Three days after the incident at Nicotera, on August 7, the mad arsonist was at it again in Tignes, starting fires and disrupting the resort. Like the blazes that were intentionally set ten days earlier, the new fires caused minimal damage and no casualties.

If that wasn't enough, the Club Med village in Playa Blanca, Mexico, was robbed on August 13, the fourth heist at the resorts in less than a month. This time, the bandits were interested only in cash, taking more than $25,000 in bills but carelessly discarding thousands of dollars in travellers' cheques and jewellery by the side of the road.

"The thatched huts of Club Méditerranée villages welcome half a million holidaymakers every year, eager for wine, sport, sea, and sociability," said the London *Times*, noting the rash of robberies at the French company's resorts. "This year, however, they have become quite fashionable for quite a different group — the gangsters."

The *Times* estimated that Club Méditerranée had been victimized to the tune of more than £500,000, or well over a million dollars, in the four robberies. The paper also detailed how 800 passports had been stolen, which the *Times* figured could provide another bonanza of cash for the gangsters; each passport was worth up to £140 ($300) on the international black market.

Gilbert Trigano was convinced that the four heists had not been orchestrated by an organized criminal gang. Rather, he believed that the success of the robbery in Corfu had spawned the other attacks on the relatively defenceless Club Med villages. But the heist at Nicotera was hardly an amateur operation.

"Violence is part of our society today," said Trigano, philosophizing about the outrageous series of events. "We have to live with it. Banks are too well guarded; you cannot have such strict security measures for people who are on vacation to enjoy themselves. So we have to tackle the evil at its root, which is money."

"All the losses will be reimbursed," Trigano told the French newsmagazine *Le Point*. "But as far as the hold-ups are concerned, we wont talk much about it, I guarantee you, because there won't be any cash left in the villages before long."

Was he concerned that the recent outbreak of crime might hurt Club Méditerranée's business? "We thought we might lose some of our members because of the hold-ups," admitted Trigano, who was pleasantly surprised by the GMs' strong show of support. "But on the contrary, we have phone calls every day for new applications. It has not affected our reservations."

Despite Trigano's upbeat and calming tone, he was in fact very worried about the potential loss of business for the company, a nasty consequence of the robberies. Behind the scenes, he had ordered his staff to notify the GMs about the dangers of using cash at a Club Med village.

"We have sent letters to all our members," Trigano later explained, outlining one of the precautionary measures the company was suggesting to the GMs. "We explain to them that from now on, they should not carry cash, but should use money chits issued by the organization."

Trigano was a little peeved about the sensational media coverage of the robberies, implying that Club Méditerranée was being singled out over its competitors. "Last weekend several other vacation villages in Italy were robbed. Nobody talked about that," he complained to *Le Point*. "We are well known and that excites commentary."

In an interview with the London *Times*, however, Trigano

was singing a slightly different song. "Nobody suffered any losses," he told the *Times*. "We are insured by Lloyds and, after all, it was good publicity."

One cannot help but wonder if the family and friends of Jean-Maurice Picimbono, the unfortunate Club Med GO who was murdered in the Corfu hold-up, would agree with Trigano's "good publicity" declaration.

CHAPTER TWELVE

Brickbats and Copycats

"If we do a good job, we don't have anything to fear."

Gilbert Trigano, 1982

Although Club Méditerranée had been bloodied and battered in 1977, it still managed to attract well over 500,000 GMs to its resorts, a record for the company, and generate total sales of FF1.35 billion, another all-time high.

The financial performance of Club Méditerranée in 1977 is remarkable when one considers the numerous calamities that wreaked havoc on the holiday enterprise during the summer season: four hold-ups, at Corfu, Vittel, Nicotera, and Playa Blanca; a murder in Corfu, two deaths in the Tunisian desert; two arson attacks in Tignes; and two terrorist bombings, one successful, in Corsica. With all that and the accompanying barrage of sensational publicity in Europe, it's amazing that the GMs weren't terrified by the prospect of a Club Med vacation. But everyone seemed to accept that this was only a temporary aberration, the deranged actions of a criminal or lunatic fringe or, in the case of Tunisia, just a very sad, albeit unnecessary, human tragedy.

However, the next year also got off to a bad start for Club Méditerranée. Early in the year, the Calvi village in Corsica was once again attacked by the FLNC, the terrorist group that claimed responsibility for the Cargese bombing the year before.

95

There was also another robbery at Club Med's swank St. Moritz village in Switzerland.

Then, at about ten past four in the morning on June 11, three powerful explosions rocked Paris's Bourse district. The target was the headquarters of Club Méditerranée, the most direct attack to date on the holiday company and the fourth incident involving explosive devices in 14 months.

The bombs, which started a fire in the company's executive offices, also shattered windows throughout the area and damaged a few of the neighbouring buildings. A night watchman, who was making his rounds when the blasts occurred, was wounded in the legs when he was hit by flying glass.

An hour later, Agence France-Presse, France's national news agency, received an anonymous telephone call from someone claiming to represent the French National Liberation Front, a previously unknown group that took credit for the bombing. The caller linked the Club Med headquarters bombing with other attacks against the company. "Our successive attacks against Club Méditerranée are an act of resistance against the Jewish occupation of the country," the caller raved.

Gilbert Trigano was confounded by the bombing, labelling the attack incomprehensible, "unless one established a connection between them and the Corfu hold-up, of which one of the authors is still on the run," he told the press in the chaotic aftermath, expressing doubt about the legitimacy of the phone call to Agence France-Presse.

While Trigano was at a loss to explain why Club Med was the target for the bombing, another Club Med executive, Stefan Geissler, speculated that the call may have been genuine, because of the volatile political tone. "They were aiming at the Club's liberal image," said Geissler. "This makes us think it could indeed have been this so-called front, which seems to be a pretty sick group against Jews, Arabs, and everybody who isn't 100-per-cent French."

Trigano's opinion that there might somehow be a connection between the perpetrators of the robbery-murder in Corfu and the bombing of Club Med's headquarters was a theory that would never be tested. Four months later, on October 9, the

French police killed two well-known hoodlums, Gaston Ruquois and Christian Tricoire, in a wild shoot-out at a check-
point on the Paris–Bordeaux highway. Both men were thought
to have had strong links to the events in Corfu more than a year
before. If there was in fact a connection, the answer died with
Ruquois, the alleged mastermind of the gang.

Fortunately, the news for Club Méditerranée wasn't all bad in
1978. In fact, there were some exciting developments that far
overshadowed the bombing of the company's headquarters.
First, the Club Med villages in Cancún, Mexico, and Paradise
Island, Bahamas (opened in 1976 and 1977 respectively), were a
big success. Both resorts were attracting huge numbers of GMs,
mostly from the United States and Canada.

In Europe, Club Med had also managed to resuscitate the
previously unprofitable Don Miguel hotel in the Spanish resort
of Marbella, on the Costa del Sol. The Don Miguel, which has
been described as "monstrously ugly," had been taken over by
Club Méditerranée during one of the periodic real estate
slumps in southern Spain a few years before.

"I didn't think we could make a go of it," said Stefan
Geissler, Club Med's director of international relations. "But
after two years the hotel is booked almost solid."

How did Club Méditerranée manage to turn it around when
others had failed? There were many reasons: the opening of a
day-care centre for the GMs' children; the construction of 12
first-rate tennis courts; the organization of Scrabble and bridge
tournaments; the building of a night club in the hotel's basement; and the important addition of a private beach.

Club Méditerranée was also making big strides elsewhere
around the world. In Eastern Europe, the Romanian government was so pleased with the success of its only village that it
asked the company to open another one. In Egypt, the 400-bed
Hurgada complex on the Red Sea, financed in part by the
tourist-hungry Egyptian government, was also added to the
roster of Club Med villages.

In the small African nation of Liberia, Club Méditerranée
was asked to manage a hotel that had been opened for a Third

World conference. But it just didn't work out. "We had to say no," explained Geissler. "They wanted us to run the hotel during the conference and then transform the centre into a tourist operation."

On a potentially more profitable scale, Club Méditerranée also disclosed that it was negotiating with the People's Republic of China. "We are interested. They seem interested," said Geissler, years before a deal was finally arranged.

In North America, Club Méditerranée also announced that it was going to take another shot at operating a vacation village in the United States. The project, wholly owned by Club Med, was a 470-bed skiing resort known as Copper Mountain in Colorado. The Copper Mountain village, which would open a couple of years later in 1980, was Club Med's third attempt in America. The first two Club Med villages, at Bear Mountain in California and on Kauai in the Hawaiian Islands, had both flopped years before.

To finance the Copper Mountain village, the French holiday company sold an industrial revenue bond to Aetna Insurance and the European-American Bank and Trust Company. (Club Méditerranée also had plans for a second resort in Breckenridge, Colorado, if a similar financing package could have been organized, but apparently it never materialized.)

One of the problems for Club Méditerranée in the United States was the tough American immigration laws, which prevented the company from importing its own labour force from around the world. However, the issue in Colorado was resolved when American immigration authorities relented and granted job-specific visas to Club Méditerranée. The visas, which were valid for only half of the resort's 60 employees, meant that a GO could work only in a clearly defined capacity. At the end of the six-month period, when most of the GOs were transferred to other Club Med villages, the job-specific visas would then be applied to other incoming GOs.

Why didn't Club Méditerranée simply hire only American-born GOs to work at the Copper Mountain village and avoid all the hassles of dealing with the U.S. immigration service? A primary reason was that the company wanted to preserve its international vitality, a feature that separates Club Méditerranée from most of its competition.

Another factor might have been the low wages Club Méditerranée pays some of its GOs. Although the company does provide room and board and gives its employees various perks including free wine and beer with meals, a number of GOs, including one who worked at the Copper Mountain village, were still earning only $400 a month in 1986. This was in exchange for a brutal schedule that often added up to 70 or 80 hours a week, especially when one counted in the virtually mandatory socializing that GOs have to take part in if they are to get favourable reports from their immediate superiors at the resort. "Paid overtime" being unknown in Club Méditerranée's vocabulary, $400 a month works out to less than $1.50 an hour, a parsimonious rate that does wonders for the company's bottom line. The advantage would be quickly wiped out if Club Med had to pay its employees on an hourly basis like most other hotel companies in the United States.

Gilbert Trigano angrily defends Club Med's payroll structure. In 1978 he told a French magazine that the salaries the company pays are "normal" and that the GOs work only 32 hours a week. However, it is clear that a significant part of Club Méditerranée's staggering success is attributable to the financial exploitation of some GOs.

The GOs, who do experience the joy of foreign travel as part of their employment package and who do not have a gun pointed at their heads to make them work, are essential to the success of Club Méditerranée, not only because they work for low pay. The GOs, who are famous for their endless enthusiasm and *joie de vivre*, also give the company a formidable edge over their competition in terms of ambience and style. "The Club does not really hold a monopoly, but nearly so, and part of the reason is that the imitators have been unable to reproduce the GO team," said Hubert Levin, a Paris stockbroker, interviewed by *Business Week* in 1981.

Club Méditerranée's enormous popularity caught the attention of other hoteliers in North America, who envied the French holiday company's ability to make money in the mid-1970s. Soon all kinds of imitators popped up, trying to cash in on the Club Med theme. The most blatant of the copycat resorts are on the Caribbean island of Jamaica.

By far the best-known of the Club Med–like hotels is the Negril Beach village on Jamaica's north shore. Looser and lustier than Club Méditerranée, Negril Beach was initially marketed on the unabashed "hedonism" theme, featuring a nude beach, lavish food, raunchy night life, and heavy hints of uninhibited sex to lure the clientele. It was also hardly a secret, although village management did not promote the fact, that strong Jamaican ganja (marijuana) could be easily and inexpensively purchased in the area, sometimes with less effort than it took to buy a drink.

"The idea was to provide a direct alternative to Club Méditerranée and to roll on their success," Franklin Rance, general manager of the Negril Beach village, explained to *Business Week*. "In 1977, Negril Beach became the most successful resort in the Caribbean and made a profit of $2 million."

The Negril Beach village was promoted in a campaign developed by a Canadian travel consulting firm, J. Allan Murphy Limited, the company responsible for the wildly successful hedonism concept. A key feature of the first hedonism campaign was an advertisement showing the upper body of a woman with a string of shark's teeth draped in her cleavage. It bore a remarkable resemblance to an earlier Club Med advertisement that pictured the top half of a woman in a bikini with a string of beads nestled between her breasts. The beads in the Club Med ad represented the currency at the French vacation villages, while the shark's teeth, perhaps in tribute to the Jamaican hotel industry, were the money of choice at the Negril Beach village.

J. Allan Murphy Limited later became involved in the campaign for the new Couples resort, which opened at Jamaica's Tower Isle Hotel in January 1978. The hotel went one step farther than the other all-inclusive resorts by offering the guests free liquor and cigarettes. It was designed for couples rather than the swinging singles crowd, hence the name.

To get the ball rolling for the reconditioned resort, J. Allan Murphy prepared a poster that showed two lions in the act of copulation, a definite attention-getter that helped raise occupancy rates at Couples to 92 per cent, compared with the 30 per cent that the much straighter Tower Isle Hotel had garnered the year before. But the copulating lions were too much for some members of the travel trade, who were too embarrassed to display the Couples poster.

Despite the phenomenal success of some of the newcomers, Club Méditerranée didn't feel that its vacation empire was in jeopardy. On the contrary, the company increased its sales by 53 per cent in North America in the same period when hedonism and the Negril Beach village were making such a splash. "The more advertising others do for the all-inclusive concept, the better it is for us," explained Jacques Ganin, president of Club Med in New York, in an interview with a reporter from *Business Week*.

Besides, Club Méditerranée had been through it all before. In Europe, the company had outgrown or devoured several competitors over the years. In the United States, it had to contend with outfits like the American Express Club Continental and Diners Club's Club International, both of which were primarily vacation savings clubs. Members would pay a small amount of money each month towards a future holiday, a vastly different concept from the "fly now, pay later" schemes that are so popular with consumers today.

Then there were the smaller organizations that also sprang up in Club Méditerranée's wake. These ranged from the Passport Club in New York to the Matterhorn Sports Club, a travel club with offices in Washington, Baltimore, and New York.

Club Méditerranée also got into merchandising in a big way in 1978. The year before, the company had realized merchandising was a natural spin-off and had licensed four companies to manufacture products bearing the Club Méditerranée name and the famous trident symbol. The first line of products included suntan lotions and related cosmetics from L'Oréal, luggage by Besançon, towels from Santens, and sunglasses by BK Optics. In the spirit of generosity, the company announced that all profits from the new venture would be handed over to a charitable foundation that would use the proceeds to finance humanitarian causes. Today Club Méditerranée does much more merchandising than it did in 1978, especially in France. There the GMs who can't get enough of Club Med can choose from a wide selection of products ranging from beachwear to bicycles to watches.

But without question, the highlight of 1978 for Club Méditerranée and Gilbert Trigano was when the French business magazine *Le Nouvel Économiste* named Trigano France's manager of the year, quite a tribute for someone primarily engaged in the leisure industry.

Friends and business acquaintances buried Club Méditerranée's president in accolades. "Gilbert Trigano is an exceptional man," declared Pierre Moussa, president of Paribas, the French investment bank that had been a shareholder in Club Med since 1970. Moussa, who categorized Trigano as "an effective visionary," also pointed out that his old friend was a kind man who had "a heart of gold." From Italy, Giovanni Agnelli, Fiat's chairman of the board, was impressed by the "imagination" and the "originality" of the man. But perhaps the best analysis of Trigano was offered by Gérard Blitz, the founder of Club Méditerranée.

"Gilbert Trigano is the prototype entrepreneur and manager who identifies 100 per cent in his enterprise," said Blitz, detailing the magnitude and scope of Trigano's responsibilities. Blitz praised "the way with which this man directs one hundred villages in so many different countries in the midst of such diverse cultures, the way he negotiates with governments, his high intelligence, his vivacity and his open mind, his exceptional adaptability."

By the end of 1979, Club Méditerranée had become one of the world's fastest-growing vacation and resort companies. Although some major American-based chains — like Sheraton, Ramada, Hilton, Hyatt, Holiday Inn, and a few others — were raking in hundreds of millions of dollars in leisure-time revenues annually, none was as clearly identified by the consumer as a holiday company as Club Méditerranée. This image was a tribute to the success of the company's unique advertising program and the management policies of Gilbert Trigano.

The company seemed to be years ahead of the American chains in style and sex appeal. And Club Med's all-inclusive package — one price for everything except drinks and knick-knacks — was very popular with the harried North Americans who didn't want to spend every day of their one- or two-week vacations worrying about what to do and where. Ironically, Gilbert Trigano, who had noted the American hotel industry's penchant for producing look-alike rooms from coast to coast, had, in his own way, created the spiritual equivalent of that approach. After all, there were certainly no surprises in a holiday at a Club Med village, perhaps explaining in part why more than one-third of GMs are repeat customers.

In 1979 total sales for Club Méditerranée were just slightly under the FF2-billion-a-year mark, a healthy increase of 22.4 per cent over the 1978 results.

Record revenues and profits notwithstanding, Baron Edmond de Rothschild, the financial saviour of the company in the early 1960s, had already started to diminish his holdings in Club Med. As he explained to the French business magazine *Le Nouvel Économiste* in 1978, it was necessary for the quick growth of the company. "It was quite obvious that the Club would not have had such a rapid development if I had stayed on as a principal," said Rothschild. "There was and still is enormous risk to take every day: guaranteeing the rents over 20 years, moving into certain countries that were politically or socially unstable ... therefore by reducing my participation I facilitated the entry of other partners of substantial influence."

A good example of a "politically and socially unstable" country is Haiti, where Club Méditerranée finally opened its 700-bed Magic Isle village in 1980. Miserable and impoverished, the fascinating Caribbean nation has a long legacy of murder, brutality, and corruption, especially under the dreadful Duvalier regime, which was in power when the company decided to open a resort there.

Club Méditerranée developed an innovative way of financing

Magic Isle village, north of Haiti's capital city of Port-au-Prince. The key element was a 16-year, $8-million (8,000 units at $1,000 each) indexed bond that paid off in escalating sums depending on the occupancy rates of the Club Med village. Developed and offered in conjunction with Crédit Lyonnais, a large French bank and a major shareholder of Club Méditerranée, the indexed bond worked as follows. In the first year of the bond, Club Méditerranée agreed to pay the investor a flat 10-per-cent return. This was to cover the period when the resort was being constructed. Once the Club Med village opened, however, the benefits and risks of the indexed bond became apparent.

In subsequent years, Club Méditerranée would guarantee investors only a minimal return of 8.5 per cent a year, or $85 for each $1,000 unit of the bond. But this figure would be enhanced by a series of bonus payments geared to the occupancy rate of the Haitian village. For example, the company would toss in an additional $6 for each holidayer when the occupancy rate reached 65 per cent. At 70 per cent, the supplement was raised to $7 per vacationer, and at 80 per cent and above the bonus was set at $8. With an occupancy rate of 80 per cent, not an unreasonable prospect in the Caribbean, the bonus system translated into an additional $255,500, or $31.94 per unit of the bond. This was in addition to the $85 already guaranteed by Club Med, thus effectively raising the return on investment to 11.69 per cent. At 85-per-cent occupancy, the bonus payments would reach $357,700, or $44.71 for each unit of the bond, a 12.97-per-cent return.

In addition to the bonus based on occupancy, Club Méditerranée further sweetened the offer by linking the cost of a vacation at the six other Club Med villages in the Caribbean to another supplemental payment. In this arrangement, the bondholder would receive an additional bonus of 28 cents for every 1-per-cent rise in the price of a holiday, a dividend to be paid on top of the existing incentive.

For Club Méditerranée, the financial benefits of the indexed bond were substantial. On the open market, the company was looking at borrowing money at 12.5 per cent to finance the

Haitian resort, the going rate at the time. With the indexed bond committing the company to a firm pay-out of only 8.5 per cent and the rest of the money tied to performance and the price of a Club Med holiday, the scheme meant a considerable saving for the company.

"The benefit for us is that we get cheap finance, and we only have to pay more than 8.5 per cent if the venture is successful," remarked Olivier Michel, Club Méditerranée's finance director, in an interview with *Business Week*.

The novel idea of using an indexed bond as a financing vehicle evolved out of management contracts employed by the French vacation company at villages and resorts owned by other companies. Crédit Lyonnais simply adapted the concept to the requirements of the financial markets.

The indexed bonds were a big hit from the outset and the issue was quickly oversubscribed, a testament to the faith that the investment community now placed in Club Méditerranée, in sharp contrast to the haphazard days of an earlier era.

In 1979 Club Méditerranée also opened its first resort in South America, the colourful Itaparica village near Salvador de Bahia in Brazil. Another milestone was the inauguration of the company's first resort in the Asian sector, the 550-bed Château-Royal village on the Pacific island of New Caledonia, a politically troubled territory belonging to France and located 930 miles east of Queensland, Australia.

In another intriguing breakthrough, the company also found time to set up shop in the remote Maldive Islands, a little-known, Robinson Crusoe–like backwater in the Indian Ocean that was a British protectorate until it achieved independence in 1965. There Club Méditerranée took over an intimate, 100-bed beachfront hotel owned by the Maldive government and converted it into Farukolhufushi village, arguably the least pronounceable and most exotic resort in the entire chain.

In addition to the Brazilian, New Caledonian, and Maldive Islands resorts, the company opened its second holiday village in the Bahamas, a 600-bed complex on the out island of Eleuthera. Then there were the Archeological Inns in Mexico, five small hotels with a combined total of only 400 beds situated near the well-known ruins of Chichen Itzá, Uxmal, Coba, Cholula, and Teotihuacan, the site of Mexico's two famous pyramids.

The Archeological Inns were a special deal for Club Méditerranée. First, the hotels are not marketed under the Club Med name and are known as "managed" villages, in the language of Club Med. Although they are promoted and sold by the French holiday company, the Archeological Inns are owned by the Mexican government through FONATUR, the Fondo Nacional de Fomento al Turismo, a state-controlled agency that was established to develop tourism in the country. As manager of the facilities, which do not require seven-day stays or Club Med membership, Club Méditerranée supervises the day-to-day operations of the hotels — staffing the resorts and collecting the sales revenues. For its trouble, Club Méditerranée is paid a management fee, while handing over the majority of the profits to FONATUR.

Surprisingly, Club Méditerranée is not the majority owner of any of the holiday resorts bearing its name in Mexico. In fact, all the Club Med villages (Playa Blanca, Cancún, Ixtapa, and Sonora Bay) are indirectly owned by the Mexican government, a circumstance brought about chiefly because of the country's tough laws on foreign ownership of beachfront property.

For example, the very popular 750-bed Cancún village on Mexico's Yucatán Peninsula is wholly owned by FONATUR. And at Ixtapa, a 750-bed village on Mexico's Pacific coast that opened in 1981, FONATUR, through its subsidiary PROFOTUR, owns 60 per cent of the resort, while Club Méditerranée, having paid $4.8 million to become a partner in PROFOTUR, controls the remaining 40 per cent.

At the robbery-plagued Playa Blanca village, which opened in 1974, Club Méditerranée has only an 8.33-per-cent interest, with 91.67 per cent controlled by Financiera Banamex, a subsidiary of Banco Nacional that was nationalized by the Mexican government in September 1982.

A similar financial arrangement exists with Banco Nacional concerning the ownership of the Sonora Bay village, one of the newer Club Med villages in Mexico (it opened in 1984 as the Guaymas village). At Sonora Bay, located on the Sea of Cortez across from the Baja Peninsula in north-western Mexico, Banco Nacional owns 61 per cent of the "corporation which owns the beneficial rights to the village," according to documents filed with the Securities and Exchange Commission prior to the listing of Club Med Inc. on the New York Stock Exchange. The French holiday company, however, owns the remaining 39 per cent of the company.

This arrangement, not at all unusual in nationalistic Mexico, safely ensures that the extremely important tourism industry will stay in the hands of locals and not be entirely swallowed up by foreign-owned businesses, a mistake too many other cash-hungry nations have made.

Club Méditerranée doesn't widely promote the details of its financial relationship with the Mexican government. In fact, many GMs, GOs, and travel agents, for that matter, are completely oblivious to the fact that the Mexican government is the principal owner of all the Club Med villages in Mexico. Nevertheless, the arrangement is working out so well that Club Med is prepared to invest millions of dollars more in future development. One project is the controversial Huatulco village, a large 1,000-GM facility at Mexico's newest super-resort in Oaxaca on the Pacific coast that is scheduled to open in late 1987.

At Huatulco, Club Med and other resort developers have come under strong attack for dislocating many of the local residents, many of them low-income Mexicans who were paid only $100 for their beachfront properties when they were evicted by the Mexican government to make room for the new resorts.

Some of the residents blamed FONATUR for the disruption. "It's clear that FONATUR wants to kick all the people out," Pedro Lara Vizareta, a local restaurant owner, told the *Toronto Star*. "And when we are out, no one will be allowed to enter here."

Vizareta also detailed an October 1986 incident in which the state government sent in the police to help tear down the local school. "The government sent a lot of police," he remembered. "They took all the furniture out and then the heavy machines came and knocked down the classrooms."

Mexican officials deny that they are forcing out the locals to make room for the sun-seeking foreigners. "We don't want people to leave here," explained Eugenio Gonzalez, human resources director for the Huatulco project. "We are creating work at all levels. Planners say this wilderness will be a city of 300,000 in 30 years."

In Egypt, there was a different kind of problem in 1979. There a vicious attack against Club Med was launched in the pages of *Al Akhbar*, a semi-official Egyptian government newspaper. "An enclave of French colonialism," snarled the paper, which also accused the company of "tax evasion" and of being "racist," a claim it undermined by anti-Semitic remarks of its own. "Mr. Trigano, the Club's proprietor, is a moneyed Jew from France. The Club will be a dispensary of information servicing Israel."

Al Akhbar's campaign against Club Méditerranée, which began in June 1978, was a surprise to French and Egyptians alike. Club Méditerranée, which had several facilities in the country, had always enjoyed cordial relations with the Egyptian government and was one of the country's biggest players in the tourist industry. When Alain Fouquet-Abrial, Club Méditerranée's man in Cairo, asked the Egyptian government for an explanation, he was given an evasive answer. "It's a political issue," said Mahmoud Amine Abdel Hafez, Egypt's minister of tourism at the time.

Publicly, the matter seemed to have originated with the allegedly discriminatory practices at Club Med's Manial Palace village in Cairo, the former residence of Egypt's elephantine King Farouk, who had been forced to abdicate in the coup of 1952. There were accusations that Club Méditerranée was somehow excluding the local residents from using the facility. However, *Le Monde*, France's leading newspaper, concluded that the Manial Palace was not a "closed" village, but a normal hotel where anyone with the ability to pay was permitted to use the restaurant, bar, cabaret, and other facilities.

The attack may have been spawned for a much more ominous reason — the perceived Jewish ownership and control of Club Méditerranée. What with Baron Edmond de Rothschild's close association with the state of Israel and the Bronfman family's generous support of leading Jewish causes in North America, it isn't difficult to imagine how some Egyptians might interpret the establishment of a Club Med village in Egypt as a Zionist conspiracy, especially in the tense atmosphere of early 1979, just before Egypt signed its historic peace accord with Israel. There were sensational stories floating about that Gilbert Trigano, Club Med's Jewish chief executive, had been placed on the infamous blacklist of the Arab Boycott Office, an intelligence-gathering organization based in Damascus that was established to prevent any company or individual doing business with Israel from making money from the oil-rich Middle Eastern nations. For Club Méditerranée, which operated vacation villages in four Muslim countries, Morocco, Tunisia, Turkey, and Egypt, the rumour was potentially very damaging.

If Gilbert Trigano was worried about *Al Akhbar*'s campaign against Club Méditerranée and himself, he didn't let on publicly. "I attach no importance to it," he calmly told the French publication *L'Aurore*. "We have always respected the laws of the countries that we operate in."

A year later, in December 1980, Club Méditerranée was embroiled in controversy once more, this time over an incident at the Cancún village involving four busloads of arriving GMs, many of them from Canada. Although intended as a harmless practical joke, it upset many of the guests.

It started when the plane carrying the GMs landed at Cancún's small but modern airport. After retrieving their luggage and passing through Mexican customs, the Club Med group were then ushered into the buses that would take them the short distance from the airport to the vacation village, a trip of about three miles. It was a ride many of the GMs would like to forget.

Shortly after departing from the airport, the convoy of buses came upon an obstruction in the road and were forced to stop. The buses were boarded by pistol-toting gunmen, their faces hidden by nylon stockings. To the GMs it was a hijacking. "Money, give me money!" the gunmen yelled at the terrified passengers, many of them women with small children.

The drama was played out all the way to the entrance of the Club Med village, a journey that lasted about 25 minutes, according to one of the eyewitnesses. Once there, the driver of one bus and one of the fierce-looking gunmen exploded into riotous laughter. It was a practical joke, just a "Welcome to Mexico" gag perpetrated by the GOs, who didn't think about the consequences of their farce.

Bill Glassco, a well-known theatre director in Canada, was one of the passengers. He wasn't amused by the prank. "It was really unpleasant," Glassco later told the Toronto *Globe and Mail*. "It was so fraught with danger. Any person on the buses could have had a heart attack. Some of the passengers were considering jumping the gunmen. Someone could have got badly hurt."

Glassco, who should know because of his years of working in live theatre, was stunned at how realistic the fake hijacking was. "These guys were really good actors and they were very scary," he said. "The first two days of our holiday were wiped out while we recovered from the shock."

Besides Glassco, who was in Cancún along with 31 others for a family reunion, two of the other GMs were John Evans and his wife, from Toronto. Evans, the former president of the University of Toronto, Canada's largest academic institution, didn't want to discuss the incident. But his wife, Gay, tried to put it into perspective. "It was unfortunate. They realized it was a mistake. It won't happen again," she said.

Later, the *chef de village* of the Cancún resort apologized to the GMs for the behaviour of his staff, telling them that there was nothing they could do about it after the fact. But for some of the GMs, the apology wasn't enough to soothe their spirits. Their vacation had already been ruined.

At the same time Club Méditerranée was being sued for

$2.8 million by two New Yorkers, who said that they had become ill either from food poisoning or by drinking contaminated water while on holiday at Club Med's new Eleuthera village in the Bahamas. In a suit filed in New York's state supreme court, Alan Reis and Charles More claimed that they and about 160 other GMs had become very sick, exhibiting symptoms such as "headaches, fever, cramps, profuse sweating, nausea, chills and vomiting." The pair also charged Club Med's staff with "intentional and callous disregard."

Amazingly, these events had virtually no impact on Club Med's sales. In 1980, the French company once again reported record revenues of FF2.46 billion, an increase of 24.4 per cent over 1979.

However, the strong financial performance wasn't enough to persuade Canada's Bronfman family to maintain its holdings in the company. In March 1981, it announced that CEMP Investments, the Bronfman family holding company, had sold its interests in Club Méditerranée for $13 millon to REDEC, the Saudi Research and Development Corporation, a Paris-based investment company controlled by Ghaith Pharaon, a 41-year-old, Harvard-educated Saudi Arabian tycoon.

CHAPTER THIRTEEN

The Man from Riyadh

"At the far end of the Champs-Elysées — past a mammoth winged horse flanking a grand boulevard; past the towering Egyptian obelisk commemorating the European conquests in the Middle East; past the Jeu de Paume, which houses the works of Cézanne, Degas, Monet, Renoir and van Gogh; past the École Militaire, where Napoleon Bonaparte first entered military training as a teen-age cadet; just through the far walkways of the Tuileries Gardens; at the exact center point of Paris — is the office of Ghaith Pharaon. The building — at 4 Place de la Concorde — is the most exclusive commercial address in all of France."

Hoag Levins, *Arab Reach*, 1983

Ghaith Pharaon, the son of Saudi Arabia's most illustrious physician and the prime tenant of 4 Place de la Concorde, was born in the desert city of Riyadh on September 7, 1940, just two and a half years after the March 4, 1938, oil strike at Dammam Number 7, a discovery that changed the economic future of the world. As a child, he witnessed the financial domination of his country by foreigners, mainly the Americans, through holdings in the Arabian American Oil Company, better known as ARAMCO. The consortium of four American oil companies — SOCAL (Standard Oil of California); Esso, now Exxon (Standard Oil of New Jersey); Mobil (Socony-Vacuum); and Texaco — held the gloriously profitable oil concession in Saudi Arabia, America's largest single overseas investment.

But all this changed dramatically in March 1980 when the Saudi Arabians purchased 100 per cent of ARAMCO and thereby gained complete control over their own resources, a monumental puddle of black gold that was earning $315 million a day, or over $114 billion a year in clear profit in 1981, the same year that Ghaith Pharaon acquired a stake in Club Méditerranée.

Pharaon's career is closely linked to the incredible growth of Saudi Arabia's oil industry. After attending the Lycée Janson de Sailly in Paris and the International College in Beirut, he studied in the United States, like many of his contemporaries, earning a bachelor of science degree from the Colorado School of Mines and Stanford University in 1962. Three years later, in 1965, he picked up his MBA from Harvard University.

The same year he graduated from Harvard, Pharaon founded the Jeddah-based Saudi Research and Development Corporation (REDEC), a financial, engineering, and management group that formed the basis of his empire in the early days.

By 1981, when he purchased the Bronfman family's interest in Club Méditerranée, he was already listed as chairman of the board of 17 companies; he was an investor in countless others and one of the richest wheeler-dealers ever to come out of Saudi Arabia. As with Baron Edmond de Rothschild and Giovanni Agnelli, two of Club Méditerranée's other major shareholders, Pharaon's net worth could be measured accurately only by a battalion of accountants.

Besides his holdings in REDEC and the French vacation company, he has, at one time or another, had a substantial interest in a variety of companies around the globe. In the United States, these include Hyatt Hotels, one of the world's biggest hotel chains; the Sam P. Wallace Company, a Dallas-based conglomerate with subsidiaries in everything from construction to nuclear technology; the CRS Group, a Houston firm specializing in multimillion-dollar architectural and engineering projects; and the Arabian Services Corporation, a Pharaon-controlled company that held a big interest in another company that owned a sizeable chunk (about 50 square miles) of Louisiana's multibillion-dollar Tuscaloosa Trend, one of the largest natural gas deposits in the United States.

Naturally, there was more. There was Saudi Arabian Parsons Limited, a joint venture with the California-based Ralph M. Parsons Corporation, an enterprise that secured a huge contract from the Saudi Arabian government after its formation. Another joint venture was arranged between the International Pharmaceutical Products Company and the Sterling Drug Company of New York, a deal that created one of the largest drug and medical equipment companies in Saudi Arabia. In addition to all of the above, Pharaon's American holdings have included the International Maritimes Carriers, a bulk shipping line, and the International Control Systems Corporation, a company that manufactures prefabricated hotel rooms and other concrete structures in Mobile, Alabama.

Then there are the Pharaon-owned U.S. banks that first brought his name to the attention of the American public. In the emotional aftermath of the Arab oil embargo in 1975, he acquired a controlling interest in the $1-billion Bank of the Commonwealth in Detroit, Michigan, a controversial take-over that the Saudi financier had been directed to by no less a personality than John Connally, the former governor of Texas who served as Richard Nixon's secretary of the treasury in 1971 and was himself a failed Republican candidate for the Presidency in 1980.

In a remarkably candid interview with the intrepid Linda Blandford, a Jewish writer who spent a considerable amount of time hobnobbing with the élite in Saudi Arabia for her book *Super-Wealth*, Pharaon frankly disclosed his reasons for buying the Michigan bank.

"I wanted an American bank in the center of an industrial city, not a small town," he explained to Blandford. "Saudi Arabia's buying into technology and industry, not tennis clubs.

A small-town bank without enough capital assets wouldn't have been the right vehicle for me. It had to be a bank with one major shareholding and not too high a percentage of Jewish money on deposit in case of a run after the takeover. My lawyers went through every bank in the States that could be up for sale. I went through their list, found four that met my particular specifications and settled on the Commonwealth."

Contrary to popular perception, Pharaon's take-over of the Michigan bank didn't mean instant dismissal for the institution's Jewish employees. "Fire Jewish employees from the bank in Detroit?" the Saudi billionaire laughed, admitting that some Jews had withdrawn their funds after the purchase. "I'd lose some of my best staff."

It came as a surprise to Pharaon that the Commonwealth Bank's board of directors were more concerned with issues of race than with the Jewish question. There was a reluctance to open branches in the poorer sections of Detroit, but Pharaon insisted that everyone, regardless of race or colour, should be served.

"First, it's a public service. You can't refuse black people banking facilities," said Pharaon, explaining that his thinking was not entirely motivated by his compassion for civil rights. "The board argued against it on a question of security. I said, 'Buy security but open those branches.' It's not altruism. Blacks work; those branches will make money."

However, Pharaon's ownership of the Bank of the Commonwealth was short-lived. A few years later he sold the Detroit bank to Roger Tamraz, the head of another Arab consortium of investors. But he made up for it, at least in publicity terms, by acquiring the National Bank of Georgia, a financial institution owned by Jimmy Carter's long-time friend and budget director, the beleaguered Bert Lance, who was reportedly millions of dollars in debt and under investigation by numerous government agencies.

Pharaon's purchase of the Georgia bank raised eyebrows because it occurred at a time when Lance was in deep trouble — the ongoing controversy swirling around Lance had devalued his bank's stock and lowered public confidence in the institution. Pouring gasoline on the critics' fire, Pharaon was also offering $4 to $5 a share above the market value for the bank's stock, an act of generosity that drove more than a few of the conspiracy-mongers into a frenzy.

Ghaith Pharaon's holdings in his homeland are appropriately staggering and cover the full spectrum of industrial activity. A short list of his investments includes the Arabian Pipeline Construction Company, the Saudi Inland Transport Company, Saudi Mowlem Ltd. (construction), the Jizan Cement Company, the Najd Maritime Company (shipping), and the United Commercial Agencies, one of the largest insurance companies in the Middle East. In addition to all these ventures, Pharaon has reportedly been involved in fertilizer plants, steel mills, reinsurance companies, and innumerable other enterprises in Saudi Arabia.

If this isn't enough to fill his daily calendar, then there are also his considerable holdings in Europe, Asia, and Latin America. Over the years, Pharaon's name has been linked to a variety of companies around the world. These have included France's BSN-Gervais Danone, a large food consortium, Great Britain's International Foley and Company, and the Mowlem International Company, a big British construction company. In Hong Kong, he is a major backer of the Saudi Hong Kong Real Estate Company, a joint venture with Lebanese businessperson Nagy El-Azar that is involved in multimillion-dollar residential development projects. In South America, he was involved in the purchase of 90,000 metric tons of frozen chickens from Brazil's UNEF export group, a $90-million deal that called for 5,000 metric tons of poultry to be shipped to Saudi Arabia each month. Added to this are a hotel in the Portuguese enclave of Macau, a timber concern in Sabah, and dozens of other businesses. The list goes on and on and on.

How wealthy is Ghaith Pharaon? It would be difficult to come up with a precise figure, but in 1979 he estimated his annual turnover at $2.5 billion, a tidy amount of money in anyone's terms. At the time, he also revealed that he had a $1-billion investment program to ensure that the juggernaut kept rolling.

In September 1980, a couple of months before the American presidential elections, one of Pharaon's investments, the National Bank of Georgia, caused a bit of a stir when it was learned that the bank had loaned more than $1 million to President Jimmy Carter's peanut business. Carter had negotiated the loans in 1975/76 (before he came out of nowhere to capture the presidency and before Pharaon invested in the bank) in order to build a new warehouse and peanut sheller. At a news conference in 1980, he was asked if the loans represented an "actual or potential" conflict of interest because he was considering the sale of 60 F-15 fighter planes to Saudi Arabia; some of the loans were still outstanding at the time and Pharaon was the principal owner of the bank.

"I've never accepted any loans from an organization that's owned or controlled by any foreign government or foreign nationals," said President Carter, dismissing the reporter's assertion. "The only loans that I have gotten were long before I became president, from American-controlled banks in Atlanta, and I have so far paid those loans off as required by the bank itself."

Pharaon, who owned 98.3 per cent of the bank's 1.5 million shares in March 1980, was described by a National Bank of Georgia official as "an absentee owner" who only inherited the Carter loans when he bought the financial institution.

Ghaith Pharaon started to encounter much more serious economic turbulence in February 1986. The problem centred on debts incurred by Pharaon's Saudi Research and Development Corporation (REDEC) to more than 60 creditor banks, debts that reportedly amounted to $274 million and several hundred million more in contingency payments.

The creditor banks, who in the past had had a hard time saying no to the ambitious Saudi financier, included numerous U.S. banks, Saudi American banks, and the National Commercial Bank of Saudi Arabia.

In December 1985, Pharaon was paying only the interest on REDEC loans and not the principal, and he decided to tough it out. At a meeting of REDEC's creditors in London three months later, a gathering Pharaon chose not to attend, the banks were informed that he would not bail out REDEC by using assets from Pharaon Holdings, a holding company for his extensive non–Saudi Arabian business interests. However, the creditor banks were assured that REDEC intended to pay off the remaining debts fully.

While obviously concerned, the creditors didn't panic. "If the banks work with the company then there's a good chance they'll get 100 cents on the dollar," one banker at the meeting told Reuter. "Its [REDEC's] assets are far in excess of its liabilities."

Pharaon's financial problems with REDEC were brought about primarily by the declining price of oil; with their revenues down, many of the Saudi Arabian companies for whom REDEC had imported goods, mainly cement, were unable to pay their bills. At the London meeting, the bankers estimated that REDEC was owed approximately $411 million, of which only half was collectible, according to company officials.

With all REDEC's financial problems, one cannot help but wonder if Ghaith Pharaon availed himself of a Club Med vacation to ease the stress of civilization.

CHAPTER FOURTEEN

Club Med Enters the 1980s

"Me, I am not a man of political declarations, but a practical man."

Gilbert Trigano, 1984

As chief executive officer of Club Méditerranée, Gilbert Trigano was working with quite a group of major shareholders following Ghaith Pharaon's purchase of the Bronfman family interests in 1981. Politically diverse and worth billions of dollars, the high-powered assemblage was proof enough that truth was stranger than fiction — at least at Club Med.

Other than Pharaon, the Saudi tycoon who had close links to the desert kingdom's anti-Israeli royal family, there was Baron Edmond de Rothschild, who just happened to be one of Israel's most important financial backers. Then there was Giovanni Agnelli, who as Fiat's chairman listed Muammar Gaddafi's Libyan government among his business partners. Finally there was the French government, through its nationalized holdings in Crédit Lyonnais and other financial institutions that held large numbers of shares in the holiday enterprise.

The French business magazine *L'Expansion* catalogued the holdings of the various participants in a September 1982 edition. Leading this impressive group of investors, though not nearly as powerful an economic force as in the past, was Baron Edmond de Rothschild, whose shareholdings were reported at

7.6 per cent. Also at 7.6 per cent was the Union des Assurances de Paris (UAP), a big insurance group owned by the French government. Next, at 7.2 per cent, was Crédit Lyonnais, a French government–owned commercial bank. Ghaith Pharaon was down for 4.9 per cent, and Giovanni Agnelli's group was listed at 3 per cent. Club Méditerranée's employee investment fund controlled 3.6 per cent, and another 6 per cent was attributed to Paribas, a huge investment consortium owned by the French government.

The year before, in November, a European management forum had recognized the accomplishments of Trigano and his staff by listing Club Méditerranée as one of the 100 most dynamic companies in Europe, a tribute that firmly established the vacation company as one of the élite corporations in the European financial community. Only eight other French companies had made the prestigious list; they included such economic heavyweights as Airbus Industries (a multibillion-dollar conglomerate that was effectively challenging the long-standing domination of the American aviation manufacturers) and Novotel, one of Europe's biggest hotel companies.

It wasn't difficult to understand why. After all, the financial performance of Club Méditerranée had been outstanding. In the eight years from 1974 to 1981, profits had increased by slightly more than 500 per cent. In the same period, the number of GMs had similarly leaped, from 330,000 a year to over 770,000, more than doubling business. In addition, the French GMs were no longer a majority of the clientele, as they had been in the past.

Overall, Club Méditerranée racked up gross revenues of FF3.18 billion (approximately $553 million) in 1981, a record total that translated into an increase of 29.2 per cent over the preceding year. Sales generated an impressive $8.10 per share in earnings, while the price of the stock on the Paris Bourse fluctuated from a high of $94 to a low of $64.

In the all-important North American sector, where Trigano had big plans for Club Méditerranée in the years ahead, the company registered about a third of the company's total. This

120

resulted in a gross operating profit of $46.7 million and a net income of almost $8 million.

The company also continued its ambitious expansion program. There were several new villages, including a 600-bed resort at Punta Cana in the Dominican Republic and a flashy 750-bed hotel at Ixtapa, Mexico's latest jet-set resort on the Pacific coast. The 75-acre Punta Cana village was wholly owned by the company; the Ixtapa resort was a joint venture with the Mexican government, with Club Med a minority partner.

In 1981 Club Méditerranée contributed to the city of Atlanta's "Safe Summer" program, which had been established in the aftermath of the Atlanta child murders, a homicidal spree in which 28 black children were killed. The holiday company donated 160 vacations at its Fort-Royal village on the Caribbean island of Guadeloupe, a thoughtful gesture that gave many of the low-income black children the thrill of a lifetime.

"I want to go swimming, sailing, just have fun," said an excited David Baker, a 10-year-old who lived in one of the city's public housing projects with his mother and was one of the lucky kids to get selected for the Club Med holiday. Beverley Baker, David's mother, was just as thrilled as her son because a Caribbean vacation for inner-city children "doesn't come every day." However, she did admit to being somewhat confused about exactly where her son was going. "We thought it was some kind of camping trip in Georgia," she explained, "and then we found out that the West Indies is not in Georgia."

Unfortunately, not all the news coming out of Atlanta was as heartwarming. At about the same time that the first group of children were returning from their Club Med holiday in Guadeloupe, Atlanta's highly respected Centers for Disease Control (CDC) was warning of the dangers of cutaneous larva migrans, a hookworm-type infection that had been contracted by seven American GMs, five men and two women, after vacationing at Club Med villages in Mexico and Martinique, the sister island of Guadeloupe in the French West Indies.

According to the CDC's *Morbidity and Mortality Weekly Report*, the seven holidayers, who had stayed at Club Med at various times since October 1980, had come down with painful, purple-reddish sores on the soles of their feet after spending time on beaches contaminated with larva-bearing dog and cat excrement. The hookworm larva, which thrives in the hot, wet sand found in the tropics, had apparently burrowed its way into the victims' bodies after coming in contact with exposed skin. The CDC duly notified the resorts in question and recommended that stray dogs and cats, which can be a problem in Mexico, not be permitted on the beaches.

Early in 1982, on February 9, labour problems threatened Club Méditerranée, this time in the form of a strike by 453 disgruntled immigrant workers, mostly poor North Africans escaping the poverty in their homelands in Morocco and Tunisia. The strike, which partly paralyzed several of Club Med's Alpine resorts in France, occurred at the height of the lucrative winter season.

Typically the foreigners performed all the menial jobs such as cleaning the toilets and showers, dishwashing, and garbage disposal. They often toiled for 10 hours a day, six days a week. For their efforts, they were fed and paid a small salary of about FF15 an hour. In addition, they were housed in what some claimed were cramped and dehumanizing conditions.

The striking workers forged a relationship with the Confédération Française Démocratique du Travail (CFDT), one of France's most powerful left-wing trade unions. The CFDT, which was surely aware of the French government's indirect and partial ownership of the vacation company, wasted no time making political capital out of the dispute.

But whatever the political motivations, some tough allegations were levelled at Club Méditerranée. A kitchen worker at one of the villages complained of harassment by management. "He told us the first one who creates problems will be sent back home without pay," recalled the North African. "It broke our hearts. We would have preferred to have been welcomed."

As for the accommodation provided by Club Méditerranée, some workers pointed out that they were forced to sleep three abreast in tiny rooms with virtually no space to move about.

Another said that his room was so small that it was physically impossible to stand up straight in it. Still others complained of having to share one toilet and one shower among 40 persons.

Surprisingly, what had the makings of an extended stand-off fizzled out quickly. The Moroccans and the Tunisians went back to work when the company agreed not to dismiss any of the strikers and promised that everyone involved would be re-hired for the coming summer season. Other key issues, like salary and adequate housing, were put off to a later date. It was over — for the time being.

In October Club Méditerranée let the word out that it was going to open another vacation village in the Far East, a 600-bed resort on Phuket Island in southern Thailand. The village, which was not scheduled to open until three years later, in 1985, was only the second Club Med resort to be opened in continental Asia. The other village, the 600-bed Cherating resort in Malaysia, opened in 1980.

As usual, at least for Gilbert Trigano, Club Méditerranée was involved with the now-standard crowd of blue-chip investors in the project. The group included the powerful Italian-Thai Development Corporation, a diversified industrial conglomerate that has thousands of employees and is involved in all kinds of enterprises ranging from construction to machinery to hotels. Started in 1985 as a joint Italian-Thai venture, the company is currently controlled by the family of Chaijudh Karnasuta, a co-founder and one of the richest men in Thailand.

Typically, the financial arrangements for the Phuket Island village were convoluted. In documents submitted to the Securities and Exchange Commission in Washington prior to the listing of Club Med on the New York Stock Exchange, the resort was described as having been built by Holiday Villages of Thailand, a local company that is 49-per-cent owned by Club Med Inc., the Cayman Islands subsidiary of Club Méditerranée. The other 51 per cent of Holiday Villages of Thailand is held by the GMR Company, a consortium of local investors headed by the Italian-Thai Development Corporation. However, this arrangement did not necessarily mean that Club Med was a minority participant. For the purposes of this deal, Club

Med used the ever-popular "classified" method to exercise control. As the documents state, concerning the ownership of Holiday Villages of Thailand, "The Company [Club Med Inc.], through ownership of classified stock, will have the right to elect a majority of a classified Board of Directors and receive preferential distributions."

In other words, Club Med had effective control of Holiday Villages of Thailand. After all, there is little point in being a majority owner, like GMR, if you don't have the right to elect most members of the classified board. As for the "preferential distributions" that Club Med will receive, they are nowhere clearly spelled out.

Altogether, 1982 was another very good year for Club Méditerranée. Total sales were approaching the FF4-billion-a-year mark, and the return on shareholders' equity was still a robust 15.93 per cent. With the addition of three new villages — Santa Teresa in Sardinia, Kos in Greece, and Luxor in Egypt — the total capacity was now up to 70,243 beds, 22,767 for the winter villages and 47,476 for the summer resorts.

Although the occupancy rates fell slightly, to 71.27 per cent from 71.51 per cent the year before, this was certainly no indication that the company was losing popularity. The decline was attributed to several factors. First, the Santo Stefano village in Sardinia was transferred to the company's Valtur Vacanze subsidiary. Then there was a fire at the Pontresina village in Switzerland, which temporarily disrupted operations. Finally, the Palinuro village in Italy was closed.

Although no one, understandably, liked to trumpet it, 1982 was also the year that AIDS began to have an impact on the company. At Club Med's Magic Isle village in Haiti, the GMs, mostly North Americans who believed the fatal syndrome was rampant in the impoverished nation, stayed away in droves, severely affecting occupancy rates at the resort.

Club Med did its best to downplay the spectre of AIDS. The chances of being stricken were minimal unless, of course, one took a private excursion to the disease-infested whorehouses of Port-au-Prince, the capital city. Club Med attributed the decline in business in Haiti to "rumours of health hazards in that country." The company optimistically believed in 1984 that "the operations of that village should return to normal in the future," a statement that didn't anticipate the 1986 overthrow of Baby Doc Duvalier, the country's corrupt dictator, a tumultous event that would force the closing of the Magic Isle village.

The new year, 1983, got off to an uncertain start when the Moroccan and Tunisian workers at Club Med's ski resorts in France went on strike once more at the busiest time of the winter season. However, this time the testy North Africans, who numbered about 400, were much more militant; they occupied five of the six Alpine villages the holiday company operates, an ugly tactic that forced Club Méditerranée to close the affected resorts and reportedly lose $600,000 a week because of the disruption.

The Club Med villages that were forced to close were the resorts at Tignes, Val d'Isère, Les Arcs, Avoriaz, and Monnetier-les-Bains. Spared in the labour dispute was the resort complex at Chamonix, which remained open. The strike, which lasted about three weeks, was eventually settled when the workers were guaranteed jobs on a year-round basis, spending the summers at Club Med villages in their homelands before returning to France for the winter season.

In early March, just a couple of weeks after the costly strike ended, Gilbert Trigano, who had had his hands full lately, was assigned the herculean task of heading up the 1989 Paris Universal Exposition, a mammoth international event to commemorate the 200th anniversary of the French Revolution. Trigano's appointment was made by his old friend François Mitterrand, France's Socialist president.

However, Trigano's assignment was short-lived and, in fact, he seemed to be the architect of his own demission. Four months later, in July, President Mitterrand pulled the plug on the Paris Expo after receiving a report prepared by Club Méditerranée's chairman; the report indicated that the project was going to cost French taxpayers billions of francs, a needless expenditure in light of the Mitterrand-inspired austerity programs that had been implemented. Just weeks after Trigano was appointed to the Expo project, Mitterrand had dropped a bombshell on his astonished countrymen by introducing tough financial measures aimed at remedying France's sick economy, which, according to some estimates, was running a deficit of $1 billion a month.

The new measures, which included "forced" loans to the government, tax increases, and higher rates for telephones, electricity, and gasoline, were not, to put it mildly, universally popular. But without question, the most controversial feature of the financial package was currency controls, whereby each citizen could take only FF2,000 (about $275) out of the country. Naturally, the currency restrictions put a serious crimp in many Frenchmen's travel plans, unless they booked pre-paid packaged holidays. These were quickly exempted from the controls.

French travel agents were outraged, believing that their livelihoods were in jeopardy. A few days after the controls were announced, thousands of angry agents led a demonstration at the finance ministry, protesting that the restrictions represented a serious loss of individual freedom and a real threat to their businesses.

"It not only hits those who travel," Jean-François Ricordeau, a French travel agent, told the *New York Times*, "but also those who dream of travelling."

Another agent, François Berthier, felt that the issue was more cerebral. "It's psychological," he said. "Taxes are one thing. But when you in effect close down the border by telling people they can only spend so much outside, it touches them personally."

Gilbert Trigano, who had referred to French travel agents in the past as "useless" and "failures" and a profession having "no appetite for risks," didn't have much to say on the matter.

In June President Mitterrand jetted off to Corsica, the seething French-ruled island where the Socialist leader was so unpopular in some quarters that it took a combined security force of 4,500 to protect him. To mark the occasion of his two-day visit, which was to discuss his government's progress on limited home rule, the Front de Libération Nationale de la Corse

(FLNC) had gone on a bombing rampage prior to his arrival. In May alone, the violent terrorist group had claimed responsibility for placing more than 50 bombs around the island, 43 of which exploded. Members of the bomb squad managed to defuse 11 of the explosive devices prior to detonation and, miraculously, only one person, a civilian, was injured.

Of course, Club Méditerranée was not to escape the FLNC's attention. The day before President Mitterrand arrived, police experts managed to defuse a small bomb that had been planted at Club Med's Santa Giulia village, at the southern end of the island. Although the bomb failed to go off, it was a clear message to Club Méditerranée that the vacation company remained on the front line of the conflict.

Club Med was also the target of bombs in the Caribbean. In the pre-dawn hours of April 26, 1984, Club Med's Fort-Royal village in Guadeloupe was bombed by what local authorities thought to be the Alliance Revolutionnaire Caraïbe, a fanatical left-wing terrorist group that wanted independence for Guadeloupe, Martinique, and French Guiana, a French-ruled territory on the north coast of South America.

The blast, which blew out windows and wrecked furniture and a wall in the resort's main restaurant, occurred while most of the GMs were still sleeping. Although a number of the GMs were roused by the noise of the explosion, there were no injuries.

The bomb at the Fort-Royal village was just one of 14 that exploded on that violent Thursday morning. The other blasts took place at 11 different towns and locales around the island, and damaged facilities included three police stations, two banks, four tax offices, and other government buildings. Luckily, no one was hurt. Earlier in the year, on February 4, a time bomb planted in another French government–owned hotel had exploded, injuring five guests.

Less than two months after the Fort-Royal village bombing, disaster once more struck Club Méditerranée. A scuba diving expedition at the company's Ipsos village on the Greek island of Corfu went wrong — terrifyingly wrong.

The incident started harmlessly enough on June 18, when a

trio of Club Med GOs, Frenchmen Jean-Marie Masselin and Petrian Lambas and a Tahitian, Watun Pasari, decided to go diving in the narrow strait separating the northern Greek island and Albania, a small Communist country that shoots first and asks questions later. The problems began when an Albanian patrol boat spotted the GOs' rubber dinghy drifting just a few yards off Albania's coast. Instead of simply arresting the intruders for violating their territorial waters, the Albanians opened fire on the helpless GOs, who were reportedly just surfacing from a dive.

Watun Pasari, the 26-year-old Polynesian, was slightly wounded by the gunfire, but he and Lambas were still able to swim to the safety of a fishing vessel that was in nearby Greek waters. Unfortunately, the 33-year-old Masselin wasn't able to escape. As Greek fishermen and other eyewitnesses later reported, he was last seen on the beach with his hands in the air being taken into custody by Albanian soldiers.

In Paris, worried Club Méditerranée executives did everything within their power to get Masselin released. In addition, the French government, which was one of only about a dozen countries that maintained diplomatic relations with Albania, did its part by calling in Albania's ambassador to discuss the matter.

Optimism began to fade on Wedneseday, June 20, when ATA, Albania's official news agency, reported a completely different account of the incident. According to ATA's version, the Albanians had twice fired warning shots in an attempt to drive the three foreigners away from their coastline. The Albanian news agency also denied that anyone had been shot in the episode, despite the fact that Pasari had been treated in a Corfu hospital for a bullet wound.

Two days later, a spokesperson for the Albanian embassy in Paris denied that his country was holding Jean-Marie Masselin prisoner. "He is not being held on Albanian territory," said the spokesperson.

The following Sunday, Masselin's decomposed body was found by fishermen, floating in the sea approximately half-way between the Greek mainland and Corfu. According to medical reports in Greece, Masselin had been shot in the head.

Outraged at this ugly turn of events, an angry French government quickly recalled Ambassador Marcel Martin from his posting in Tirana, Albania's capital city. A French foreign ministry spokesperson later categorized the dramatic recall as "a decision with political significance," about as tough as the talk ever gets in diplomatic circles.

For its part, the Albanian government, through the ATA news agency, decided to blame the French media for creating the situation, despite the eyewitness accounts that clearly placed a living and breathing Jean-Marie Masselin in the custody of Albanian soldiers.

"Much was written in the French press and, in spite of our clear explanations of the event, there were great distortions of the facts and unjust attacks against Albania," said an ATA news release, once more denying that Albanian soldiers had murdered the Club Med GO and suggesting that all the fuss was a sinister plot to disrupt French-Albanian relations. "Reporters who accuse us of being savage, murderers, etc., blow up the issue in the interest of those who want to drive a wedge in the good French-Albanian relations."

CHAPTER FIFTEEN

Club Med U.S.A.

"Even though we live in an unpredictable world, we are confident of this: as life each year grows more pressured and complex, the true vacation will become an ever more precious commodity."

Gilbert Trigano, 1986

Apparently satisfied that some of his stringent financial measures had revitalized the country's sagging economy, France's Socialist president, François Mitterrand, decided to lift the controversial currency controls on December 20, 1983, just a few days before Christmas and less than nine months after the unpopular legislation was enacted. Mitterrand's Christmas goody meant that French people could haul out the travel brochures and plan holidays in Spain, Italy, Greece, and other foreign destinations that had been financially taboo, unless one travelled on a Club Med–like vacation.

But it hadn't been such a great year for Club Méditerranée either. The holiday company had been affected by the nasty economic climate, although it had not been as badly hurt as some other vacation organizations. A slowing of the company's previous rate of growth seemed to be the primary result. Gross revenues, which had jumped 24.4 per cent in 1980, 29.2 per cent in 1981, and 24.3 per cent in 1982, slumped to only 13.9 per cent in 1983, a figure that translated into about FF4.5 billion.

Along with the relatively sluggish increase in sales, the company had shown little improvement in the total number of GMs, which had risen by only 3,000 (from 804,700 in 1982 to 807,400 in 1983). But then again, Club Med had been racked by numerous problems throughout the year, ranging from labour strife to terrorism to the murder of Jean-Marie Masselin at the hands of the Albanians.

While the overall totals for sales and GMs were not escalating as quickly as in past years, the all-important profit picture for the holiday company remained strong. Despite the difficulties, Club Méditerranée had still managed to ring up a profit increase of 22 per cent over 1982, well in line with past performance.

In April 1984, Gilbert Trigano dropped a tantalizing hint of bigger things to come when he told the press that the company's policy was to implant itself firmly in North America. To this end, a new company, Club Med Inc., would be created; it would encompass all of the vacation enterprise's markets in North America, Asia, the Pacific, and the Caribbean, a vast territory that represented approximately one-third of the company's total business at the time.

A month later, on May 17, Club Med Inc. was formally incorporated in the Cayman Islands (a British-ruled tax haven in the West Indies) as a wholly owned subsidiary of the French Club Méditerranée.

The formation agreement, effective November 1, 1983, carved up the holiday company on mainly geographic lines. The parent, Club Méditerranée, which maintained a 100-per-cent interest in the new company, transferred virtually all of its subsidiaries, properties, and operations in the American and Asian zones to the new subsidiary. For reasons that weren't made clear, Club Méditerranée in France decided to hang on to the leases and assets pertaining to the four villages in Tahiti, New Caledonia, and Réunion and to the very successful Buccaneer's Creek village in Martinique.

As part of the formation agreement, Club Med Inc. was also permitted the "exclusive and royalty-free right" to use the trident, the symbol of the company. But once again, this "exclusive" right really wasn't so exclusive. The parent company maintained the same marketing rights in Tahiti, New Caledonia, Réunion, Guadeloupe, and Martinique.

A services agreement, effective on the same date, was also instituted between Club Méditerranée and its offspring. The agreement (which has a life span of 50 years, ending on October 31, 2033) calls for the parent company to supply, among other things, an endless number of GOs. In addition, if Club Med Inc. requests it, Club Méditerranée will send in advisers and consultants to evaluate the performance and quality of the operation. The French parent will also provide experts in resort development who would look after planning, site selection, construction, and expansion and renovation of old and new villages.

To keep track of everything, Club Méditerranée also gave Club Med Inc. access to the French company's highly touted computer system, an IBM 3033 system in Paris that handles all pertinent business data, ranging from reservations and sales to a management information system.

In return for all these business aids, Club Med Inc. agreed to "pay at cost" for salaries and fringe benefits for the GOs, an amount that added up to $6.75 million in 1983. The new company was also on the line for a "proportionate" share of the French parent's day-to-day overhead ($2.6 million in 1983), defined as any expenses incurred by Club Méditerranée's Paris office for business relating to Club Med Inc. The services agreement also included proportionate payments for computer services ($891,000), a profit-sharing plan ($2 million), insurance ($793,000), and various other items. Club Med Inc. even pays for its share of the entertainment props and costumes used by the GOs for shows and performances to amuse the GMs.

In the unlikely event of a dispute between the parent company and its subsidiary, both the formation agreement and the services agreement call for the matter to be resolved by binding arbitration in the International Chamber of Commerce in Geneva, Switzerland.

With most of the essential paperwork signed and sealed, Club Med Inc. filed an initial offering of 2,160,000 common shares with the Securities and Exchange Commission in Washington in mid-July, a preliminary step to getting the company listed on the New York Stock Exchange. The company, which was to be quoted as CMI on the NYSE, later raised the offering to 3 million shares and hoped to net about $48 million.

What did Club Med Inc. plan to do with the proceeds? Slightly over half of the money, approximately $26.2 million, was scheduled for debt repayment on loans due between 1985 and 1992. A large portion of the remaining funds, about $19.3 million, was to be used for construction, expansion, and acquisition and renovation of resorts. In addition, an unspecified amount of cash was to be used for "general corporate purposes."

At the time, Club Med Inc. had just embarked on a four-year expansion program estimated to cost $208 million, of which the new company calculated that its share was $136 million. The remaining money, around $72 million, would be financed by outside investors.

The tireless Gilbert Trigano was named chairman of the board of Club Med Inc., which, at the time of its formation, operated 16 resort villages and managed four others bearing the Club Med name. The company also managed the five Archeological Inns in Mexico for the Mexican government.

Besides Gilbert Trigano, who would now wear two hats as chairman of the French parent and chairman of its North American subsidiary, other veteran Club Med employees, like Olivier Michel, Jacques Giraud, and Jean-Robert Reznik, were brought in to launch the new company. Gilbert's 38-year-old son, Serge, who had already been running the vacation company's bustling operation in North America, was appointed the firm's first president.

Salaries, which had been a major point of contention for some Club Méditerranée employees in the past, didn't seem to pose much of a problem at Club Med Inc. for those fortunate enough to be in upper management. In total, nine of the senior employees listed as officers and directors of the company, including Gilbert and Serge Trigano, were collectively paid $1,191,000 in 1983, an average of more than $132,000 per employee, or considerably more than the $400 a month that some of the GOs were being paid.

Gilbert Trigano, the same man who had once vehemently argued that "a cent is a cent" to impress upon his employees the value of money, is also eligible for a bonus "equal to 1% of the consolidated income before profit-sharing plan provision and income taxes." The bonus payment, which can be terminated only by the company's board of directors (of which Trigano is chairman), carried a maximum of $250,000 for the years 1984 to 1986. After the initial three-year period, the quarter-million-dollar limit was lifted. In addition, Club Med Inc.'s board "has authorized the payment of bonuses to officers and employees of the Company and its subsidiaries" who provide "valuable services to the Company in connection with the Services Agreement or otherwise in an aggregate amount of up to an additional 3% of the consolidated income before profit-sharing plan provision and income taxes."

According to Club Med Inc.'s consolidated statement of income, examined by Arthur Young & Company, the vacation company's income before taxes in 1983 was $10,924,000. Of that, the 3 per cent eligible for bonus payments comes to $327,720. Who would be burdened with the task of deciding which Club Med execs deserved a share of the bonus money? "Determination of the recipients and amounts of the bonuses will be made by the Chairman of the Board," states Club Med Inc.'s prospectus; in other words, it is another of Gilbert Trigano's corporate duties.

Club Med Inc. also made 300,000 common shares of the company available to a number of officers, directors, and key employees before the stock was listed on the NYSE. While the everyday investor on the streets was asked to shell out $17.00 a share for a piece of the action, insiders at Club Med were offered the same shares for only $5.62 per share, a price that reflected the book value as of October 31, 1983; and the insiders' shares could be converted to cash, under certain conditions, just two years after the date of the public offering in September 1984.

Obviously, the key employees and directors knew a good deal

when they saw it, and they snapped up 192,000 of the 300,000 shares that were made available. The lucky buyers were 12 men (Club Med didn't have any women in this group) listed as officers and directors of Club Med Inc. Although it is impossible to tell precisely who bought how many shares, it is known that only 120,000 of the shares were paid for in full by the purchasers. The remaining 72,000 shares went for only a 20-per-cent payment, about $1.12 per share, with the left-over sums to be paid over the next three years, interest-free.

The Club Med executives eligible for this special deal were Gilbert Trigano, chairman of the board; Serge Trigano, president and chief executive officer; Olivier Michel, vice-chairman and chief financial officer; Jean-Robert Reznik, senior vice-president; Jacques Giraud, then a director; Jacques Ganin, secretary; Joseph Townsend, treasurer; Jean-Luc Oizan-Chapon, general manager of operations for the American zone; Mario Salsano, director of development and legal adviser for the Asian zone; Alexander Chemla, vice-president of transportation, and Harvey Krueger and Stanley Komaroff, both directors.

The same group of Club Med Inc. insiders were also eligible to participate in the company's incentive stock option plan, formally adopted by the board of directors in August 1984. "The purpose of the plan," explains the company's prospectus, "is to make options available to certain officers and key employees of the Company [Club Med Inc.] and Club Méditerranée in order to attract and retain officers and key employees of outstanding competence and to encourage their best efforts on behalf of the Company and Club Méditerranée."

According to Club Med Inc.'s own figures, the company's stock option plan is a smash hit with upper management. Options for 350,000 common shares were granted to certain officers, directors, and key employees of Club Med Inc. or Club Méditerranée, and 167,000 common-share options were granted to the same group of senior executives who had also availed themselves of the other $5.62 stock deal.

Serge Trigano, the chairman's son, also appears to have benefited financially from his association with the company. In 1981, as part of his agreement to move to New York to head up the North American operation, Serge borrowed $1.4 million in interest-free loans from the company, loans that were still outstanding three years later. Apparently, the younger Trigano required this sum for the purchase of residential property in New York. Serge had to pay back the loans "within 180 days and after written demand" by the company, very favourable financial terms in anyone's language. It was also Club Med Inc.'s responsibility to find a buyer for the property — after, of course, Serge had notified the company of his intention to move. Moreover, of the profits from any resale of Serge's residence, only "a substantial portion of any gain is payable to the Company." This is an amazing deal for Serge when one considers that he borrowed the money interest-free in the first place.

When Serge finally decided to return to Paris in 1985 to take over Club Méditerranée's European zone, the most important financial sector of the company, Club Med Inc. was repaid the $1.4 million he had initially borrowed as well as $360,000 in profits from the resale. But as Club Med Inc's annual report clearly states, this represents only "a percentage of the resulting gain from the sale." What profit, if any, Serge made on the deal was not divulged in the company's 1985 annual report.

It is interesting to note the difference between the treatment that Serge Trigano received and that accorded to another employee. Joseph Townsend, the Treasurer of Club Med Inc., also borrowed money, up to $269,000, over the years 1981 to 1984. Like Serge's loan, this money was used chiefly for the purchase of residential property. However, unlike the boss's son, Townsend didn't get his loans interest-free. In fact, he had to pay out an additional 3 to 12 per cent a year. By 1984, Townsend had reduced the debt to $42,000.

On September 25, 1984, Club Med Inc. began its initial public offering on the NYSE. In total, more than 3 million shares were subscribed, netting the company $47.5 million in cash. In addition, the parent company, Club Méditerranée in France, continued to own 10 million shares that were not offered to the public, a block of shares that was worth $170 million. Following the offering, the parent company maintained a 72.99-percent interest in Club Med Inc.

The successful quotation was orchestrated by a quartet of underwriters, firms that guarantee the sale of shares and securities to the public. Shearson Lehman/American Express, E.F. Hutton, Merrill Lynch, and Lazard Frères were the lead companies, each agreeing to purchase 274,200 shares of Club Med Inc.

Besides the big four, other underwriters to get involved in the offering were such well-known firms as Salomon Brothers, Dean Witter Reynolds, Paine Webber, and Drexel Burnham Lambert, each with 45,400 shares. Baron Edmond de Rothschild's Compagnie Financière was similarly down for 45,400 shares, while his Geneva-based Banque Privée picked up 23,200. In total, 104 underwriting firms around the world were involved in the offering.

For their efforts in raising all this cash, Club Med Inc. "agreed to reimburse the Underwriters for $300,000 of their costs and expenses in connection" with the offering. In addition, the underwriters were permitted a surcharge on each share sold to the public, an amount "not to exceed $0.60 a share." The final cost for launching the new issue was well over $3 million, not an exorbitant sum when one considers the flow of cash that suddenly became available.

New shareholders of Club Med Inc. had almost no say in how the company was run. Although each was allowed one vote per share on matters submitted to a vote, it was important to remember that Club Méditerranée was still the majority owner and it was highly unlikely that the minority would prevail. The French parent had the right to "elect all of the directors of the Company." Acording to the prospectus, other shareholders "will not be able to elect any directors."

Not only had they no control over who served on the board of directors, but the minority shareholders had no access to the vitally important books and records of Club Med Inc. "Shareholders of the Company will have no general right to inspect or obtain copies of the list of shareholders or corporate records of the Company," the prospectus stated, ensuring that shareholders will never know precisely who owns the company.

In the event that an outraged investor wanted to launch a

lawsuit against Club Med Inc., he would encounter a plethora of problems. First, he would run into difficulties trying to serve papers on the key personnel and companies connected to Club Med Inc., because many of these people and companies do not live or operate in the United States. As the company clearly pointed out, "It may not be possible for investors to effect service of process on such persons within the United States." Even if the investor managed to get a judgement against Club Med Inc. in an American court, the holiday company had been advised by its lawyers (Maples and Calder in the Cayman Islands and Klein & Associés in France) that it was doubtful that a court in either of those countries would "enforce judgements entered by United States courts."

A great deal of information about Club Med came to light as a result of the public offering. For example, potential investors were able to learn the fascinating details of what is involved in opening a Club Med village.

Club Med estimates that it takes "four to five years" to open a resort village from scratch, from the initial study phase through to the actual construction. A renovated village, like the Club Med resort in Bermuda, takes much less time to launch and can generally be opened within two years.

Profitability varies from village to village. Some Club Med villages are instantly a big hit with the GMs and are making money within one year of opening. Others may take as long as three years before they begin to make a profit.

To increase profitability, Club Med often negotiates financially beneficial packages in the countries in which it operates. Items on the table can include low lease rentals for its facilities, direct construction and operating subsidies, favourable local tax treatment, and special immigration arrangements. In 1984 the company estimated that it cost about $25 million to build a 600-bed village from scratch, depending, of course, on the price of the land, availability and cost of construction materials, workers' salaries, and other expenditures.

Once opened, a new Club Med village is subject to depreciation of property and equipment. A resort's buildings, for exam-

138

ple, were estimated to have a "useful" life span of 20 to 35 years, while furniture and other equipment was calculated to last between five and 16 years. (Regrettably, the vacation company provided no data on the useful life of the apparently well-used mattresses at Buccaneer's Creek village in Martinique.)

The company's "current marketing strategy is to continue to concentrate on advertising the concept of Club Med rather than a particular village and to increase repeat visits by GMs." To this end, in North America, Club Med Sales, the marketing arm of Club Med Inc., maintains a staff of more than 235 people, operating out of several offices throughout the continent. A key component is the sales reps who promote Club Med holidays to travel agents in the United States and Canada. The company also has local representatives or subsidiaries in Mexico, Australia, Japan, and Hong Kong.

Travel agents, who accounted for 85 per cent of Club Med's sales in the United States and 97 per cent of the sales in Canada in 1983, are generally paid a flat 10-per-cent commission based on the retail price of the holiday package. This means that on a typical all-inclusive package sold in New York in 1986, a travel agent earned between $74.90 and $124.90 for every holiday sold.

The remainder of Club Med's sales in North America are made directly to the public, either through snazzy-looking stores in a few North American cities that the holiday company refers to as Club Med boutiques or through a toll-free telephone number in Scottsdale, Arizona, a suburb of Phoenix.

To assist in the strategically important advertising and promotion of its vacation villages, Club Med gives away hundreds of free holidays every year "in exchange for various advertising and promotion services provided to the Company." In 1983 alone, the company dished out a whopping $2.5 million in free vacations, which might help to explain why Club Med is written about so frequently, usually in a gushing manner, in the underfinanced travel sections of certain magazines and newspapers.

In general, Club Med's marketing strategies pay off. In 1983, for example, the occupancy rate for the American-zone villages, those in the Caribbean, Mexico, and the United States, was 70.8 per cent in the winter season and 53.7 per cent in the summer season. For the much smaller Asian zone, the rate was 71.7 per cent in the winter and 62.6 per cent in the summer.

Club Med is doing its best to make summertime vacations in the tropics more attractive. "Through emphasis on year-round villages, special promotional efforts and lower pricing during off-peak periods, the Company is acting to moderate the seasonality of its business," says Club Med.

It is important to note that Club Med's occupancy rates, a vital yardstick in the hotel business, are not misleading and are, in fact, a very accurate way of gauging the company's performance. Unlike some other well-known American chains, which base their occupancy rates on the number of rooms with somebody actually in them, Club Med bases its figures on the number of GMs or guests, a more sensible and precise method of accounting. For example, if Club Med has 300 GMs staying at its 300-room, 600-bed Punta Cana village in the Dominican Republic, the occupancy would be recorded as 50 per cent. If there were 450 GMs at the resort, the occupancy rate would be 75 per cent, and so on. At another hotel chain, the occupancy rate for a total of 300 guests could be reported as anywhere between 50 per cent and 100 percent, depending on how many rooms were actually used by the guests. If there were 100 couples and 100 singles staying in the hotel, 300 guests in all, the occupancy rate would generally be recorded as 66.6 per cent; but if there were 50 couples and 200 singles (still a total of 300 guests), the occupancy rate would be listed as 83 per cent, a figure far greater than Club Med's but based on exactly the same number of guests. In a volatile industry where numbers can be deceiving and outright confusing, especially for bewildered investors, Club Med's way of counting seems sensible.

"The sale of packaged vacations (including transportation) and the operation of its villages has been and, for the foreseeable future, is expected to continue to be, the principal source of the Company's revenues and net income," Club Med told potential investors prior to the public offering in 1983, summing up how the company makes most of its money.

In 1983 Club Med Inc.'s gross operating profit (which is calculated before expenses for sales, administration, depreciation, and the like have been deducted) was $68,363,000, based on total revenues of $211,485,000. Of the gross operating profit, almost $60 million (about 87 per cent) was generated in two areas — the sale of land packages ($47.9 million) and transportation ($12 million).

The $12 million profit from transportation is interesting. Few people realize what a big operator Club Med is in the field of air travel. In 1983 Club Med, by purchasing weekly blocks of seats on scheduled services and, to a lesser degree, by booking airline charters, racked up total sales of $56.5 million, not bad for a company that most GMs believe to be primarily a hotel and resort business. It rarely occurs to anyone that Club Med is making a sizeable profit on ferrying people back and forth to its villages, a factor that tends to be obscured by the all-inclusive nature of the holiday package.

Club Med is very tight with some airlines; in fact, it is in full partnership with UTA, a French airline, at its villages in Tahiti and New Caledonia, where each has a 50-per-cent interest. There is also a joint relationship with UTA involving the Le Lagon village in Réunion, although the specifics, for some reason, aren't clearly spelled out.

The deal with UTA (actually with UTA's parent company, Chargeur Réunis) calls for either company to "notify the other of any vacation resorts planned for jurisdictions where UTA provides scheduled service," explains Club Med, pointing out that both parties have the option to establish a 50-per-cent joint venture by putting up 50 per cent of the necessary financing. UTA also acts as a sales agent for Club Med in Singapore, New Zealand, and South Africa.

The villages that are jointly owned by Club Med and UTA have been the sites of a number of violent incidents, particularly the troubled Château Royal village in New Caledonia, which opened in 1978. There, on the French-ruled Pacific island located 1,115 miles east of Australia, the Club Med village has been caught in a violent struggle for independence by the Kanak radicals, the indigenous natives of the island who are trying to overthrow French rule.

"Our ancestors sold our lands to the French for a handful of tobacco and we want it back," a Kanak villager told the London *Times* in 1985, explaining one of the main reasons for the conflict, a little-publicized dispute that has escalated at times into a state of near civil war, including murders, bombings, and sabotage.

Because of the ongoing violence, much of it carried out by the Kanak Socialist National Liberation Front (FLNKS), the local terrorist group, and the Caldoches, the diehard racist white settlers, many GMs from Australia and New Zealand have been too frightened to holiday in New Caledonia, a circumstance that has hurt Club Med's business. "The decrease in Australian and New Zealand GMs was due to the current political environment in New Caledonia," Club Med said succinctly on the matter in 1986.

Besides the problems in New Caledonia, the Club Med–UTA arrangement has suffered because of a labour dispute at the Le Lagon village in Réunion, another French-ruled island near Mauritius in the Indian Ocean. In that far-off part of the world, the argument became so bitter that the village was closed in 1984.

Whether or not Club Med likes to admit it, the company seems to have a problem at some of its villages located in French-ruled territories. What with bombings in Corsica and Guadeloupe, mayhem in New Caledonia, and labour strife in Réunion, it appears that the extremist elements closely identify the vacation company as an instrument of French foreign policy, a policy that is viewed as exploitive and exclusionary by the radicals.

Is Club Med really an agent of French economic imperialism? There is no question that the French government indirectly owns a significant portion of the holiday company, through its nationalization of several financial institutions holding shares in the vacation enterprise. Club Méditerranée, the parent company, had to get formal approval from the French ministry of finance before it could go ahead with its plans for Club Med Inc. in the United States. And if at a later date Club Méditerranée in France wishes to sell off more shares and reduce its financial stake in the subsidiary even more, the company will have to seek, according to Club Med documents filed with the SEC, "further approval from the French Ministry of Finance." (Club Med doesn't think there will be any problems getting approval as long as the parent company continues to own at least 51 per cent of the shares of Club Med Inc.'s outstanding shares.) Finally, Club Méditerranée has to make periodic filings with the French ministry of finance to keep the bureaucrats up to date on Club Med Inc.'s investment programs and other developments. That, according to Club Med, is all the French government currently requires of the company. Of course, this may change because of France's recently instituted policy of privatizing many French companies, including a number with holdings in Club Méditerranée.

Club Med does acknowledge the dangers of operating in some of the world's hotter spots, albeit rather cautiously. "Most of the Company's operations are conducted in various jurisdictions outside of the United States," Club Med lectured potential investors in its 1984 prospectus. "Accordingly, the Company is subject to the political and economic risks of operating in such jurisdictions, including expropriation and possible unilateral changes in tax and other contracts and agreements which could arise with changes in political administrations."

Translated from corporate gobbledygook, this basically means that Club Med is running the risk that some new crackpot dictator could come along and, with the flick of a finger, cancel all the deals — or, worse still, throw the holiday company out of the country. It sounds far-fetched, but it is important to remember that Club Med has villages in Haiti, the Dominican Republic, Spain, Portugal, and several other places that have a long legacy of tyrannical rule.

Bearing in mind that Serge Trigano, just three years before, had declared, "A week at Club Med is not a vacation — it's a house party," the company also had the amusing task of conveying the seriousness of its version of the holiday business to crusty Wall Street investors prior to the public offering. "The village atmosphere is informal and removed from the pressures of everyday life," said the company. "There is no need to carry money at the villages, since bar expenses are paid for with multicolored beads." The company even made the experience sound almost therapeutic. "At mealtimes," explained Club Med, "GMs generally are seated at tables of eight, a feature which is designed to enhance social interaction."

Club Med also attracted investors with a dazzling array of corporate accomplishments. By far the most glamorous was the apparent 1984 breakthrough in the People's Republic of China, which was finally opening its door to the west for big-time tourism. Serge Trigano hailed the deal in a press release. "It has been our dream to have a village in this exciting country," he gushed at the time. "The Chinese have a strong desire to be ready for tomorrow's tourism. We are very proud to be part of this challenge."

The proposed resort, a golfing and tennis complex located in the Shenzhen economic zone near Hong Kong, was expected to cost $7.5 million and was announced as a joint venture involving Club Med, the Shenzhen Development Corporation, the Bank of China, and Trilease International. Although construction of the 280-bed resort was initiated in the spring of 1984 and was expected to be completed by Christmas 1985, there was still no word on the resort's opening as of late 1987.

However, Club Med later managed to negotiate the opening of two small "villa" resorts on the grounds of Beijing's fabled Imperial Summer Palace, the one-time residence of the Empress Dowager Tz'u-hsi.

As one Chinese official explained to the Associated Press, Club Med was going to use two different locations at the immense 692-acre palace, which had been built in 1888 with funds originally designated for China's imperial navy. One villa, the Ji-Qing Xing, was at the serene-sounding Clear and Cloudless Veranda at the Garden of Harmonious Interest, while the other, the Nanhu, is at the comparatively drab-sounding South Lake Island in Kunming Lake, the summer palace's recreational area.

Besides the coup in the People's Republic of China, Club Med was also active elsewhere in the Far East. In the Philippines, which was then the private playpen of the corrupt Ferdinand Marcos and his wife, Imelda, the company pledged $1.5 million, under certain conditions that had not been met at the time of the offering, for a 30-per-cent share of a company that was going to build a 700-bed village in Batangas province, on the island of Luzon.

In addition, the company planned to spend many millions more on a two-year program to expand and develop other resorts in the Asian Pacific region. The program, which would add 1,600 beds to Club Med's inventory, included changes to the existing villages in Tahiti (Moorea) and Mauritius and the construction of two new villages, the Phuket complex in Thailand and an exotic 700-bed resort on the island of Bali in Indonesia.

But from a financial standpoint, probably the biggest development in Asia in 1984 was Club Med's corporate marriage to one of Japan's leading companies, the powerful Seibu Group, a multibillion-dollar conglomerate with nine divisions involved in everything from real estate, transportation, and insurance to large chains of restaurants and department stores.

To get the venture off the ground, both parties became 50-per-cent partners in a new company, the SCM Leisure Kaihatsu KK, an enterprise created to study the feasibility of operating vacation villages for Japanese GMs in and around Japan. It was reported that the two companies planned to open four villages in total, with the first expected to be a 400-bed complex at the foot of Mount Yatsugatake in the prefecture of Nagano, near Tokyo. However, the project was later changed to another site on the northern Japanese island of Hokkaido, where Club Med plans to open its Sahoro village in late 1987.

Gilbert Trigano wasn't appointed chairman of the new company. That lofty position fell to Seiji Tsutsumi, the head of the Seibu Group, while Trigano settled for vice-chairman. In addition, a veteran Club Med executive, Jean-Robert Reznik, was appointed president.

Seibu used its vast network of department stores to promote

the idea of a Club Med holiday to the Japanese. The company let Club Med open a number of information and sales booths within the stores; the first was opened on October 6, 1984, at Seibu's new Yurakucho store, which is located in Tokyo's bustling Ginza district.

Late the following year, on December 16, 1985, Gilbert Trigano was named to the board of directors of the Seiyo Corporation, one of Seibu's new subsidiaries, established to streamline the conglomerate's real estate operation.

Being named to Seiyo's board was an extremely rare honour for Trigano. After all, it isn't very often that a foreigner is asked to join the inner circle of a major Japanese corporation. But to those who have watched Trigano for many years, it really shouldn't have come as much of a surprise. By the time he became associated with Seiyo, he was already on the board of directors of the French auto giant Renault and of Bull, Europe's biggest computer company. As if that wasn't enough on top of his hectic schedule at Club Méditerranée, he also found time to serve his old friend, France's Socialist president, François Mitterrand, by being a member of the influential Economic and Social Committee and the National Council for Tourism.

In contrast with these honours, however, Gilbert Trigano's and Club Med's efforts in a forgotten part of the Caribbean were fraught with difficulties.

CHAPTER SIXTEEN

Trials and Tribulations in Lilliput

"Coats and ties have never existed in the Turks & Caicos. In fact, this corner of the Caribbean, with more than 140 miles of gold and white beaches, could have been the inspiration for Club Med's slogan — 'The Antidote for Civilization.'"

Club Méditerranée, 1984

Some time in July 1979, Gilbert Trigano paid a quiet visit to the Turks and Caicos, a small cluster of British-ruled islands in the Caribbean Sea south of the Bahamas. The purpose of his journey to this obscure part of the world was to discuss the prospects of opening a Club Med village on the island of Providenciales — Provo for short — with local government officials, who were enthusiastic about the idea of having one of the French holiday company's famous resorts in their own back yard but simply didn't have the financial wherewithal to pay for the infrastructure (airport, roads, electricity, etc.), a necessary prerequisite to attract Club Med or any other major hotel chain to the underdeveloped islands.

On December 22, 1984, more than five years after Trigano's trip to the Turks and Caicos, Club Med's Turkoise village opened its doors to the sun-seeking GMs. The 490-bed, $26-million jewel was extravagantly promoted "as the most upscale of all the Club villages in the Western Hemisphere."

147

However, in the period between Trigano's visit and the opening of the Turkoise resort, Club Med had been harshly criticized by the British parliament's Foreign Affairs Committee, which wondered about the company's indifference "to the performance of its obligations under the terms of the agreement" respecting the development of the Provo village.

The story begins in early 1979, when Club Méditerranée retained Marset International, a London-based consulting firm, to investigate the possibility of expanding its activities in the British Caribbean. As a result of Marset's work, Club Méditerranée acquired an option on a prime 70-acre site at Grace Bay on Provo from the American land development company Provident Limited. This set the stage for Trigano's meeting with the Turks and Caicos government in the summer of 1979.

Trigano drove a hard bargain. Club Méditerranée would come to Provo only if certain financially beneficial conditions were met, relating to taxes, roads, electricity, immigration visas, and countless other items. But by far the most controversial of Club Med's demands concerned the improvement of Provo's airport, which, at the time, wasn't much more than a landing strip for light aircraft. It was entirely unsuited to large passenger jets, the transport of choice for most big holiday operators.

The Turks and Caicos government was headed at the time by the popular chief minister James "Jags" McCartney and the People's Democratic Movement Party (PDM). However, McCartney, a strong leader in his early 30s, wasn't universally loved in the Caribbean dependency. His critics attacked him as everything from a Black Power fanatic to a stooge of his good buddy Fidel Castro. McCartney was also no favourite of the "pink gin" crowd, a pompous collection of administrators and civil servants sent to the Turks and Caicos by the British government. This group was remarkably insensitive to the local residents.

(Liam Maguire, a white Anglo-Irish expatriate who was McCartney's entrepreneurial minister of tourism and his most important cabinet officer, summed up the realities of British rule in an interview with the London *Times*. "I remember the British Administrator in the Sixties who said the Turks and Caicos were incapable of ever producing a doctor. He's the same man who said: 'They don't need electricity,'" said Maguire. Maguire also quoted an RAF wing commander who used the phrase "Big white bird, he come." "That was in the late Sixties and the man he was talking to was a skilled aircraft mechanic.")

McCartney's government "warmly welcomed the Club Med proposal," according to a memorandum of Britain's Overseas Development Administration. The ODA further noted that it "was recognized that private investment in tourism offered the best hope of generating new productive jobs and of improving the financial position of the Turks and Caicos Government."

But there was still one big stumbling block. Unfortunately, the Turks and Caicos had no money in its coffers to pay for the infrastructure Club Med had demanded. However, as a territorial dependent of Great Britain, the Turks and Caicos government could ask the British government to squeeze a few more pounds out of the British taxpayer to foot the bill. The cost was originally estimated at $7.68 million for all the components Club Med had requested, a lot of money for the little island of Provo; it had a population of less than 1,000, most of them already employed, in 1979.

Club Méditerranée prepared a document known as a "heads of agreement," which spelled out the details. It was formally presented to the British government by chief minister McCartney. According to the terms of the initial heads of agreement, Club Med proposed that it would build a 650-bed village, employing 100 foreign GOs and 200 local residents, at a cost of approximately $12 million, in exchange for the Turks and Caicos providing the necessary infrastructure and granting favourable tax concessions to Club Med over the 45-year life of the agreement.

Shortly after receiving an "outline" of Club Med's proposal, the ODA commissioned the civil engineering firm of Wallace Evans and Partners, in association with Maxwell Stamp and Associates, to conduct a feasibility study on the project so that the British government could decide whether or not to spend the taxpayers' money.

When the consultants' report was delivered in the fall of 1979, a preliminary meeting was held at the Foreign and Commonwealth Office in London. Participating were most of the key players: the British government officials, the consultants, Marset International, and a Club Med representative, who had been assigned responsibility for the Turks and Caicos project. Strangely absent from this crucial meeting was any high-ranking representative of the Turks and Caicos government, supposedly the primary beneficiary.

At the meeting, the details of Club Med's proposal were discussed and a number of significant changes were made to the initial agreement. Among the amendments, Club Med agreed to pay the full commercial cost of electricity as long as the Turks and Caicos government could guarantee a reliable and adequate supply. The vacation company also agreed to pay for its own supply of fresh water (an enormous problem in the Turks and Caicos) if it could somehow negotiate a "soft" loan for approximately £500,000, or $1,065,000, the estimated cost of the desalination equipment. Lastly, Club Med agreed to look after all the sewage and solid waste disposal at the resort. "This is a welcome advance on Club Med's original position," remarked an obviously pleased ODA.

Surprisingly, the loan for Club Med's desalination plant became a divisive issue. According to the ODA, the entire project was in danger of collapsing on this point. "Club Med are arguing that the need to manufacture water has increased the capital cost of the village and that they cannot raise additional finance for this given their other borrowing requirements," said the ODA. "This would seem an untenable argument and the Turks and Caicos Government should clearly seek to avoid any such involvement. However, we are then left with the danger that the project could fail on this point because U.K. aid funds would under no circumstances be available."

There was one other much bigger issue, namely the matter of independence for the Turks and Caicos Islands. In November 1979, when a delegation of ministers from the Turks and Caicos arrived in London to discuss the Club Med project, they learned that there was a much more serious subject on the agenda.

At what has been reported as a "stormy" meeting, Margaret Thatcher's minister of state at the Foreign Office, Nicholas Ridley, dropped a sledge-hammer on the Turks and Caicos officials. He offered them a special one-time foreign aid package of £11.8 million, which would include the money for the Club Med infrastructure, if they would formally declare independence in 18 months; or they could leave things as they were and survive on the meagre annual hand-outs of the British government.

Not wishing to see the Club Med deal evaporate, chief minister McCartney's PDM government "agreed to campaign at the general election which was due towards the end of 1980 on a platform advocating independence in mid-1982," according to the Foreign and Commonwealth Office.

Ridley later met with representatives of the official opposition in the Turks and Caicos, the sleazy Progressive National Party headed by Norman Saunders, a flashy local businessman who owned the vitally important refuelling station and control tower at the notorious South Caicos airport. This facility had been identified as a primary landing pad for big-time cocaine and marijuana traffickers, according to U.S. drug officials, who also estimated that 90 per cent of the marijuana making its way along the treacherous route from Colombia to the southern United States was passing through the islands.

Saunders and the PNP rejected Ridley's call for independence. "While they accepted independence as the islands' ultimate destiny," said Ridley, outlining the PNP's opposition, "it was their view that this could not be realistically considered for the time being. Since the Turks and Caicos government and opposition hold conflicting views about their future, any constitutional advance must await the outcome of the general election due to be held in the islands later this year."

With the big question of independence awaiting the outcome of the November 14 election, the final agreement between the British-backed Turks and Caicos government and Club Med was formally signed on February 5, 1980, less than nine months after Gilbert Trigano had first visited the islands to discuss the project. Despite the unresolved question of independence, almost everyone in the tiny Caribbean outpost was excited about the official go-ahead for the Club Med village, which, according to the French vacation company, would be fully operational by the end of 1982.

Two months later, in April, a United Nations mission, the Special Committee on the Situation with Regard to the Implementation of the Declaration on the Granting of Indepenence for Colonial Countries and Peoples, toured the Turks and Caicos and listened to a lot of complaints from the locals that they were not yet ready to cope with the responsibility of independence. A month later, chief minister McCartney died in a mysterious plane crash in the United States, an accident that might have been caused by sabotage, according to the American report, a document that was never publicized in the Turks and Caicos.

The UN mission and McCartney's death more or less ended Britain's plans for an independent Turks and Caicos. Summarizing the political impact of these events, the Foreign and Commonwealth Office declared: "These two facts are thought to have been the cause of a decision by the PDM to abandon its undertaking to campaign for independence in 1982." The British government was now financially obligated to live up to its end of the deal respecting the Club Med village on Provo, paying for the airport, roads, and other facilities. And there was no longer any local political support for independence, the goal that may have been the primary reason why the British government decided to back the scheme in the first place.

Also in 1980, perhaps to answer any questions that might be raised by development experts, the British government dispatched John Harrison, the social development adviser of the British Development Division in the Caribbean, to the Turks and Caicos to investigate the social ramifications of the Club Med village in Provo. His report examined the impact of the Club Med venture with regard to housing, employment, educa-

152

tion, medical services, the environment, and numerous other concerns.

Among his findings, Harrison pointed out that other hoteliers on Provo were afraid that Club Med was going to shanghai their staff. "Employers are concerned that Club Med will increase their difficulties and that they may lose experienced staff," the social adviser noted, explaining that most of the hotels are small (10 to 15 rooms) and that they recruit most of their labour locally.

Another area Harrison focused on was the escalation of real estate prices on Provo, an economic impediment that could muffle the prospect of future migration from other islands. "I heard of one old lady who owns 70 acres of scrub land behind one of the settlements who now values it at $350,000," he commented.

Harrison, who stayed three days on the island meeting with local businesspeople, residents, and officials, also offered some overall impressions about the social climate on Provo. He observed that the "dominant ambience is of seclusion, solitude and timelessness." He also offered an amusing description of the kinds of outsiders who were already flocking there. "Observing the visitors to Provo, predominant impressions are of sophisticates seeking the not too uncomfortable 'good life' and 'macho' water sportsmen."

The social adviser's report, which was dated September 26, 1980, surmised that the very things that made Provo appealing to visitors — the wonderful clean environment, the birds and animals, and the beautiful beaches — would be severely affected by the onslaught of large-scale tourism. "Paradoxically," he explained, "the attractions of tourism for Provo all, from the environmental perspective, militate against its commercial development. In short, the very features which make Provo attractive are those most likely to be impaired by the 'golden horde.'"

Norman Saunders and the PNP swept into power in the crucial November 1980 election in what was reported in the local press as a "landslide victory," winning by an 8-to-3 margin over the

McCartney-less PDM. The election, which was validated by a team of UN observers, was riddled with political hatchet jobs and allegations of vote-buying. There was even some violence.

Liam Maguire, a former cabinet minister in McCartney's government, withdrew as a candidate when his political opponents chopped off the head of his wife's pet dog and deposited it at the front gate of their house.

Regarding the Club Med project, new chief minister Saunders was just as gung-ho as his predecessor. "Club Med will be a magnet that draws other investors," he told the *Times*. "The British government made a wise decision." Despite Saunders's optimism, problems had arisen in Great Britain.

It started when the Labour-dominated Foreign Affairs Committee reported to the House of Commons on July 1, 1981, about the Thatcher government's expenditure of nearly £5 million in aid money to finance the infrastructure of the Club Med project — all courtesy, of course, of the long-suffering British taxpayer. The British public didn't learn about its generous financial assistance to Club Med until early August 1981, when the Foreign Affairs Committee published its report, almost 18 months after the deal had been approved.

Voters were not pleased that such a large sum of money (£4.69 million, far greater than the original estimate of £3.94 million) was being spent, supposedly to benefit the 1,000 or so residents of Provo. The British government, especially the Overseas Development Administration, also came in for a heavy barrage of criticism for not paying enough attention to the social consequences of the Club Med project.

Development experts, especially those who hadn't been asked to participate in the project, were furious at the waste of money. The British government, they charged, could have sponsored 20,000 village pharmacies, 10,000 classrooms, and schooling for 300,000 children in the Third World with just the money from the original estimate. They also pointed out that every resident on Provo was benefiting to the tune of over £4,000 a head in aid money, whereas the destitute of Bangladesh were getting only a miserly 55 pence per head.

The Foreign Affairs Committee could not comprehend why

the Foreign and Commonwealth Office had negotiated the Club Med deal on behalf of the Turks and Caicos government and then, in the final agreement signed on February 5, 1980, exempted the French holiday company from all taxes on profits and property for 20 years. This generous concession appeared to contradict the need for "improving the financial position of the Turks and Caicos government," purportedly one of the main objectives of the project. Instead, a minuscule, 50-cent-a-night bed tax (about 10 per cent of the rate charged in some other Caribbean islands) seemed to be the biggest fiscal benefit directly accruing to the local government.

Thatcher's government was further embarrassed by the revelation that there was almost no unemployment on the island of Provo and that the ODA had fudged the true picture. The ODA had originally calculated that there were a total of 510 unemployed people in the Turks and Caicos, but had neglected to mention that out of an adult labour force of 357 on Provo, only ten women and not a single man were out of work.

The London *Times* also got into the act with a sharply worded editorial on August 5, 1981, the day after publication of the controversial report. "The picture presented is of Foreign Office greenhorns who did not do their homework and did not impose financial control, taken for a ride by Caribbean tourism developers, with the local inhabitants nowhere," said the *Times*.

However, the *Times* also acknowledged the partisan nature of the Foreign Affairs Committee report. "The recent tendency for Commons select committees to split on party lines is destructive of their usefulness and influence. They will cease to carry conviction," concluded the *Times* editorial. "As for the people of those coral islands one hopes, and on the evidence believes, they have a happier time than the distant legislators with double vision."

Back in the Turks and Caicos, chief minister Saunders, like the *Times*, recognized the odour of partisan politics in the Foreign Affairs Committee report. But then again, he had more at stake. "They were out to make mischief over a carefully thought-out scheme," he told a British newspaper in a telephone interview from his Grand Turk office. Saunders also divulged

155

that he was not surprised by all the criticism because he had been aware since speaking with them in February 1980 that Labour MPs on the Foreign Affairs Committee were planning to use the issue of aid to the Turks and Caicos as a way of embarrassing the government. "They were using it then as a political football."

Saunders still wholeheartedly endorsed the Club Med project. "This is a business-like venture, a wise investment to make sure that these islands do not go on forever requiring aid from Britain," he said. "If the British government had done something like this before, maybe we would already have cut the aid strings."

Nicholas Ridley, the minister of state responsible for the Foreign Office, who had been asked to testify in mid-January 1981, provided an interesting insight into the whole affair. Ridley was asked about investing so much money in a tourism-related project rather than in other, more conventional forms of aid. "We all share the same objective, which is to get the economy of this group of islands to the point where it can, so to speak, stand on its own feet and then take off," he said. Later he elaborated on some of the problems inherent in foreign aid investment.

"There has been a long history of failure to find projects which developed into viable industries," the minister explained. "Those who have been engaged with it from the government and those in the ODA have all come to the conclusion over the years that agriculture does not give great potential nor does fishing. It became absolutely clear from the very great lack of natural advantages that there was no obvious alternative to tourism.

"The trouble has been, I think, over the past that no really viable and large-scale projects have come forward," he continued. "That is why we were particularly delighted when we succeeded in this negotiation with the Turks and Caicos government and the Club Med, and the Club Med decided to go ahead.

"I must say that the Turks and Caicos government have enthusiastically and quickly committed themselves to supporting very large numbers of possible speculative investments over the years without evaluating them," said Ridley. "If you live in groups of islands where there are virtually no facilities or industry, anything that appears on the horizon makes people rush to grab it; and, of course, few of these projects come to fruition because often they require aid from us which we have not granted because the projects were dicey themselves; and often on evaluation they turn out to be less attractive than at first sight.

"The relationship between the ODA and a dependency of this sort is that while they often suggest a number of projects, the final decision about which projects we should be prepared to finance and which projects we should not be prepared to finance rests with my Honourable Friend the Minister for Overseas Development," said Ridley, passing the buck to Neil Marten, the minister in question. "But, of course, we are obligated by our accountability to the House to make sure that decisions we take incurring British taxpayers' money are decisions which are based on good analyses and proper economic investigation."

Unfortunately for Club Med, the August 1981 uproar wasn't the end of it. The second scandal began in September 1982 when the Foreign Affairs Committee was "astounded" to learn from independent sources, not from the government's own Overseas Development Administration, that "Club Med by that date had effectively made no effort whatsoever to begin construction of the holiday village, which, according to the text of the agreement between the Club and the TCI [Turks and Caicos Islands] Government, 'shall be operating not later than 31 December 1982.' "

The Foreign Affairs Committee immediately decided to hold another inquiry. This time, however, it would be a much more wide-ranging investigation, including an examination of the ODA's role, the precise cost to the British taxpayer, the social and economic impact of the Provo airport, drug trafficking, and other related subjects. The committee also delved into "the behaviour of Club Med," planning a much more thorough look at the French vacation company's activities than it had taken on the previous go round.

The committee offered three reasons for investigating the

Club Med deal. They were: "our belief that a disproportionately large sum of money was to be used for a project on an island with a population of less than 1,000; our concern lest nearly all the infrastructure being provided on grant terms would be of little direct value to the islanders, but only to Club Med visitors; and our fear that there would be undesirable social and ecological consequences for the island of providing a number of hotel beds greater than the adult population."

In October, the ODA submitted a memorandum to the Foreign Affairs Committee, summarizing how much work had been done on Provo up to the end of August 1982 to lay the ground for the Club Med project. The bulk of the foreign aid money had been spent on roads and on the by now famous airport, the third in the Turks and Caicos to carry an "international" designation, an amazing transport capability for a place with only 10,000 people.

According to the ODA, the work on the airport and roads was approximately 70-per-cent complete and running only a few weeks behind schedule. The work on Provo was in the hands of a British firm, Johnston Construction, which had been awarded a $7.5-million contract in May 1981. Both the ODA and Johnston Construction anticipated that the airport would be fully operational by November and that the rest of the roads would be finished by January 1983 at the latest. In other words, the British-financed Turks and Caicos government had lived up to its end of the bargain.

As for the Club Med village, virtually no work had been done at the Grace Bay site, and the ODA was extremely pessimistic about the situation. In its memorandum, the ODA stated that "despite repeated assurances, both in writing and orally, it is clear that Club Med have no present intention of building a holiday village on the island of Providenciales." The ODA also made note of a baffling letter from Club Med's Gilbert Trigano to Neil Marten, the ODA's minister, claiming "that Club Med have 'fulfilled — even over-fulfilled' all their obligations, despite the absence of any progress towards the construction of the village."

What had gone wrong? Why hadn't Club Med started work

on the Provo village? The ODA pointed out that Club Med claimed to have discovered, after signing the original deal in February 1980, that the cost of construction was far greater than the original estimate of $12 million, thus making it impossible for the company to run a reasonably profitable operation.

On this point, the ODA said, "Club Med assert that the difference in cost arises from factors peculiar to the TCI," factors of which Club Med's own hotel construction experts were apparently unaware. To illustrate its assertion, the French holiday company pointed to the lack of building materials on Provo, the enormous cost of transport to the island, and the absence of housing for workers. The Turks and Caicos government was partly to blame, according to Club Med, because it wasn't providing electricity and water.

In a message to Trigano, ODA minister Marten rejected Club Med's claims. It was just too difficult to credit that the vacation company had not known about the conditions on Provo before committing itself to the project; the conditions must have been similar to those on Eleuthera in the Bahamas, where Club Med also operated a holiday village. As for the problems with electricity and water, it had been the ODA's understanding that Club Med was going to look after its own needs by installing a power plant for electricity and a desalination facility for water.

For once, the Foreign Affairs Committee agreed with the ODA. "Senior Club Med management had visited Providenciales before entering into the original agreement with the TCI Government and were therefore in a good position to judge the availability and likely cost of building materials," the committee said in its second report. "There is, moreover, a Club Med holiday village nearby, in the Bahamas, which are coral islands geographically similar to the TCI. We find the explanations for the Club's failure to proceed with the project implausible."

However, the Foreign Affairs Committee also criticized the development agency for its failure "to secure performance of the agreement."

To back its case, the committee presented a chronology of the contacts between the ODA and Club Med, beginning with the signing of the original agreement on February 5, 1980. It wasn't until October 5, 1981, 20 months later, that ODA minister Marten wrote to Gilbert Trigano expressing his worry at the delay in starting construction of the Provo village. Bearing in mind that the ODA had estimated that Club Med would have to start building between September and December of 1981 to finish the resort on time, the contacts at this time were vitally important. The October correspondence was followed by a further exchange of letters in November, but none of this prodded Club Med into action.

There was no further progress until a meeting between Marten and Trigano was scheduled for London on March 22, 1982. Norman Saunders, the chief minister of the Turks and Caicos, also attended the meeting, as did the soon to retire British-appointed governor, John Strong. However, once again Club Med gave no firm commitment about when it was going to start building.

On April 23, a month after the London meeting, Marten again wrote to Trigano, but this time he received no reply. Other letters followed through the summer, all to no avail. Finally, the exasperated ODA minister solicited the help of the French minister for development and co-operation. This seemed to get things moving again, and British Embassy officials in Paris met with representatives of Club Med at various times in July and August 1982. But still nothing of a concrete nature developed.

"We consider it extraordinary that no meeting was held between the Minister and the President of Club Med until more than two years after the date of the agreement, since it was clear as early as the end of September 1981 that Club Med was not fulfilling its part of the agreement," summed up the Foreign Affairs Committee. "The ODA appears to have pressed the matter more vigorously since March 1982, and even made representations to the French Government, but by that time it was clear that there was no possibility of completing the village by the prescribed date."

The ODA was also blasted for not informing the Foreign

Affairs Committee of Club Med's failure to begin construction. "We also find it astonishing that the ODA made no attempt to inform us that Club Med was not proceeding with the construction of the holiday village in accordance with the agreement," said the committee. "While the ODA cannot be expected to advise the Sub-Committee [the Overseas Development Sub-Committee, which was conducting the inquiry for the Foreign Affairs Committe] of all mishaps that occur in the administration of a £1,000 million aid programme, the Sub-Committee's interest in the TCI's problems should have been obvious and we consider that, in this matter, the ODA have been less than forthcoming and less helpful than they should have been in dealing with a Select Committee of the House of Commons."

All of this set the stage for Neil Marten, the minister responsible for the ODA, to testify before the Foreign Affairs Committee, which he did on December 9, 1982.

"Has the Government had further communications from Club Med in recent weeks?" asked Frank Hooley, the Foreign Affairs Committee chairman, in his first question to Marten.

"I have just had a letter from Mr. Trigano dated 22 November," replied Marten. "'I can only reiterate Club Méditerranée's desire to build the proposed tourist complex in Providenciales within the limits of a reasonable financial budget which would not definitively jeopardize the prospects of exploiting this centre,'" Marten read, explaining to the committee that the word "exploiting" in Trigano's terms probably meant profitability.

The letter continued, "I would remind you of the commitments which I undertook in the course of our conversation in London last March [1982], during which I confirmed that, instead of US$13 million, as initially agreed, I was prepared to consider a new investment budget of US$17 million." Trigano then revealed that one of the estimates Club Med had for building the Provo village was for $30 million, an amount of money that Club Med obviously felt was exorbitant.

"In the meantime, we have recently been approached by

Mowlem International," Trigano's letter went on to say. Mowlem was a business associated with Ghaith Pharaon, who was listed as the president of Saudi Mowlem Limited.

Club Med was clearly banking on getting a reasonable estimate from Mowlem. To this end, the holiday company had dispatched its technicians to London on November 3, 1982, "to work with Mowlem, giving the firm all the plans and specifications for the project in order to determine its exact cost." Mowlem had promised a tender by early December, and Trigano was quite optimistic. "I do not conceal the fact that I hold out great hopes for Mowlem's proposals," he confided to Marten.

Marten still had a lot of faith in Club Med. "I feel that they are trying to fulfil their part of the contract if they can get the price right. I would not wish to say anything which would disturb that intention as it is their intention to complete it and we hope they will go ahead and complete it."

Marten was then asked how long he planned to wait for Club Med to respond. After stumbling a bit, Marten calmly replied: "I think it is only courteous to wait a certain amount of time. I would expect to receive it [the letter] from them before the end of the year, and if we do not receive it I will chase them up," he said.

Marten was later quizzed about land speculation in the Turks and Caicos. Apparently it had been reported that this kind of wheeling and dealing was quite common in the islands. Marten was asked about "a well-known device to put up a project which then does not appear." After hedging for a moment, Marten replied, "That is life in the Caribbean. If one knows the Caribbean, this is happening all the time, that sort of thing."

The committee also asked what would happen when Club Med was technically in breach of its contract — on January 1, 1983, just a few weeks in the future.

"The Turks and Caicos Government," the minister carefully answered, "would consider the merits of putting it to arbitration for loss of income as a result of Club Med's failure to honour their side of the contract; and that would have to be judged in the light of chances of Club Med actually coming here and not putting them off by going to arbitration. That is a commercial judgement of theirs."

As he finished his testimony, Marten remarked, "I just wish I was not retiring from Parliament and this Committee could reassemble in three years' time and see what has happened."

A month later Marten retired as the minister responsible for the Overseas Development Administration. He was replaced by Timothy Raison, a tough-talking Conservative MP, who quickly arranged a discussion with Gilbert Trigano on January 21, 1983. Raison wanted to talk about the progress of the Club Med project and, unlike his predecessor, he didn't mince his words.

"He [Trigano] informed me that he is in active discussion with a number of contractors and assured me that a binding contract would be signed by 31 March [1983]," the new minister told Parliament three days later. "I made it clear that, unless a contract satisfactory to the Turks and Caicos Islands Government is signed by then, the Turks and Caicos Islands Government will initiate legal proceedings."

For reasons known only to its members, the Foreign Affairs Committee didn't wait until the March 31 deadline. Instead, the committee published its second report on February 21, precisely one month after Raison had delivered his ultimatum to Trigano.

The committee's second report was harsh, and none of the principal participants escaped criticism. In the 12 main conclusions, the ODA seemed to get the most blame. It was castigated for failing "to show sufficient determination in pressing Club Med to fulfil its side of the agreement" from 1980 to March 1982. The members of the ODA were also blamed for being "less candid and helpful than they might have been" about other reports and studies relevant to the economy of the Turks and Caicos, and for making the big mistake of taking "no action to inform the Sub-Committee of the total failure by Club Med to begin the construction of the holiday village."

The Foreign and Commonwealth Office, which had negotiated a significant part of the original agreement but was not a signing participant, was also bludgeoned by the Foreign Affairs Committee. The FCO was held "responsible for the ineffective nature of the agreement between Club Med and the TCI Government." And for future reference, just in case Club Med or some other big multinational company tried to cut a deal that involved using British aid money, the committee helpfully suggested that "agreements with transnational corporations involving the use of U.K. aid funds should contain more rigorous sanctions against default."

The committee recommended that if no binding contract to building the holiday village on Provo was signed by March 31, 1983, then "the TCI Government, with support from [the British Government], should invoke Clause 16 of their agreement or seek any other appropriate legal remedy, and also make it clear that they do not regard Club Med as a satisfactory partner in this enterprise."

Although it was never mentioned or discussed in the Foreign Affairs Committee's second report, it should be pointed out that the inquiry was initiated in the aftermath of Britain's 1982 war with Argentina over the Falkland Islands in the South Atlantic, a bloody conflict that came to an end on June 14, when the Argentinians surrendered. Two of the most devastating weapons in the Argentine arsenal were the French-built Super Étendard jet fighter and the terrifying Exocet missile, an ultra-deadly, water-skimming torpedo that was successfully used to attack and sink British ships and kill British sailors. Although France had immediately suspended all arms sales from the time of the invasion — as well as backing Great Britain diplomatically — just a few months after the British had defeated the Argentinians, in an act that reportedly angered British Prime Minister Margaret Thatcher, the French resumed sales of Super Étendards and Exocets to Argentina.

This created the extraordinary situation of having one partially French government–owned company, Club Méditerranée, involved in a deal that required millions of pounds of the British taxpayer's aid money, while at the same time another branch of the French government had permitted the resumption of arms sales to Argentina, weapons that could conceivably be used against British military personnel.

Typically, the real loser in this arrangement was the British public, which would have to pick up the bill. Not only were taxpayers paying for the infrastructure connected to the Club Med project, a deal that could potentially enrich the French government coffers, but they also had to cough up a staggering $1.6 billion for Britain's war with Argentina, a country that was being rearmed by France, presumably for more profit.

Meanwhile, Gilbert Trigano had finally managed to put together a construction deal to his liking. There was going to be a Club Med village on Provo after all, much to the chagrin, no doubt, of Club Med's critics and the anti-Conservative forces on the Foreign Affairs Committee.

On February 25, 1983, it was disclosed that Club Med had signed a letter of intent with Johnston Construction, the same British firm that had already been commissioned by the British government to build Provo's airport and the roads to the village site at Grace Bay. A month later, the French company awarded a $23-million construction contract to Johnston to build the resort. Gilbert Trigano did not sign the deal with Johnston until March 31, 1983, the very last day before the British government had said it would recommend legal action against Club Med.

There was one slight catch. The Provo village was not going to be as big as Club Med had originally indicated. Instead of a resort accommodating 650 GMs, the new, scaled-down version would be able to handle only 490 GMs, a loss of 160 beds. But everyone was so delighted, and probably so relieved, that the resort was finally going to become a reality, that no one bothered to point out that the Turks and Caicos government's already miserly annual income from the bed tax had been slashed even further.

On April 21, the day on which the contract with Johnston became binding, the British government received assurances in writing from Club Med that work would definitely start on the Provo village within four weeks. Six and a half weeks later, on June 6, Club Med's engineer's commencement order went into effect, and at long last, the construction was officially started. It was anticipated that the village would be fully operational by December 31, 1984.

The British government waited until after the building had commenced on Provo before formally responding in July to the Foreign Affairs Committee's second report. In response to the charge that the Overseas Development Administration had failed to show "sufficient determination" in making Club Med look after its end of the deal from 1980 to March 1982, the British government presented the following carefully worded version of the events.

> The agreement signed in February 1980 (to which Her Majesty's Government was not a party) stipulated that the Club Med village should be open by 31 December 1982. There was therefore a period of nearly three years for the design stage, for negotiations with contractors and for actual construction. It was not in fact until May 1981 that the contract to improve the airport and roads was ready to be awarded. Her Majesty's Government was aware from meetings between officials and Club Med representatives in November 1980 and again in July 1981 that Club Med had both the design of the village and negotiations with contractors in hand. Nevertheless, in May 1981, before the contract to improve the airport and roads was awarded, the then Minister of State had sought and obtained from Club Med a further assurance, in writing, that the village would be built. (It will be recollected that the airport had to be ready in September 1982, i.e., three months before the village.)

In other words, it was the view of the British government that it had done all one could reasonably expect, both legally and practically, in this important preliminary time-frame. In addition, Club Med had obviously spent a great deal of time and effort designing the holiday village and was negotiating with building contractors.

The government's response continues:

> At this time, it was known that, depending on the type of

166

construction, the village would take 12 to 18 months, i.e., an average of 15 months, to build. Any risk that the village could not be built and open for business by end December 1982 would only have become apparent by the end of September 1981.

As the British government next points out, the end-of-September date was very important and, in fact, it was well aware that the village might not open on time unless work started almost immediately. This was a critical, very sensitive time because it was in no one's interest to see the project collapse, a distinct possibility had a heavy-handed approach been taken at this crucial juncture.

As soon as the deadline of end September 1981 for construction to commence had passed, the then Minister for Overseas Development [Neil Marten] immediately wrote to Club Med, on October 5, to express his concern at the delay. On 5 November Club Med replied that it was still their intention to build. At this time, Club Med was in negotiation with a British contractor who confidently expected to be awarded a contract to build the village by the end of January 1982. As the aim of both the Turks and Caicos Islands Government (TCIG) and Her Majesty's Government was to get the village built — and in view of the repeatedly expressed intentions of Club Med — it was considered that further pressure on Club Med at this stage could prejudice the prospect of a valuable contract being awarded to a British firm. Immediately the end of January had passed, a further message was sent to Club Med and this led directly to a meeting of all concerned in London in March 1982, at which Club Med stated that they hoped to conclude negotiations to build the village "within a few weeks."

What was Club Med's reason for delaying the start of construction? One can only speculate that it might have stemmed from Club Med's own grossly inaccurate estimate of the building costs of Provo before the initial agreement was signed in February 1980. Naturally, any rise in costs from $12 or $13

167

million to $30 million would be of concern to the company. If Club Med had been forced to build what would have become a losing proposition, it would have done more damage to the future of tourism in the Turks and Caicos than not having the hotel built at all.

Moreover, the delay for a few months or even a couple of years wasn't as significant as many who opposed the project believed. The British government had indeed spent their tax-payers' money with no apparent return, but even if Club Med had pulled out of the deal (an unlikely event considering all the oral and written assurances it had made), Provo still had the benefit of a superb infrastructure that surely would have suited some other hotel chain.

As the British government made a point of highlighting in its response to the Foreign Affairs Committee: "It must be empha-sized that, through the whole of the period referred to, Club Med was not apparently in breach of the agreement of Febru-ary 1980."

The British government then dismissed the rest of the For-eign Affairs Committee's second report. "Together with other private sector developments now in progress or at the planning stage, the establishment of the Club Med village will justify the decision to make aid funds available for the development of the airport and roads." The final cost to the British taxpayer had risen from £4.69 million, the 1981 estimate, to £6.11 million, an increase the government claimed was brought about by the devaluation of the British pound against the U.S. dollar and by some runway surfacing problems at the famous Providenciales International Airport.

In December 1984 the 490-bed Turkoise village on Provo finally opened for business. Ballyhooed as the "Tahiti of the East Coast," with two- and three-storey pink bungalows, talcum beach, genuine French stemware and cutlery, and its very own submarine for checking out the coral reef, the resort had been completed at a cost of $26 million, $3 million more than Club Med had expected to spend in 1983.

Club Med's experienced public relations and marketing team went all out to promote the new village. The company sent out a press release that included a section on the design. "To keep a feeling of spaciousness throughout, the facilities at Club Med–Turkoise are being built to provide lots of elbow room, as if the Club were going to accommodate 700 instead of only 490 people," read the promo piece. The same release also offered an entertaining passage about why Club Med had decided to open a village in Provo. Club Med claimed that it chose the island because not only did it have no TV stations or crowds, but there "were also no roads and no airport, except for a private landing strip, until 1982 when the government, in its efforts to lure Club Med to the island of Providenciales (known as Provo), agreed to build a jet airport and a road to the 70-acre site selected for the village."

The resort received rave reviews from the GMs who stayed there. "Great! Wonderful! The best Club Med I've stayed at" is typical of the comments of those who have vacationed at Turkoise.

In March 1985, less than three months after the long-awaited opening of the Club Med village on Provo, Norman Saunders, the 41-year-old chief minister of the Turks and Caicos, was arrested by U.S. Drug Enforcement Administration agents in Miami after carelessly allowing himself to be videotaped stuffing his pants pockets with $20,000 in cash, supposedly the down payment on a $250,000-a-week bribe to let a weekly shipment of 800 kilograms (1,760 pounds) of cocaine pass unhindered through the Turks and Caicos Islands. Two other prominent politicians from the Turks and Caicos were also arrested. They were Stafford Missick, the mysterious 47-year-old, East German-educated minister of development, and Aulden "Smokey" Smith, the 33-year-old junior minister of works. They each picked up $5,000 apiece. A fourth man, a Canadian laundry-owner named André Fournier, was also arrested.

In July 1985, Saunders and the other government officials went on trial for the drug charges. With the overwhelming weight of the videotaped evidence, the defence had a hard case to make, and all three were convicted after eight hours of deliberation by the jury.

The conviction and subsequent sentencing of Norman Saunders, who had tried to evade prosecution by claiming diplomatic immunity because he was carrying a British diplomatic passport at the time of his arrest, set an interesting legal precedent in the United States. It marked the first time that a foreign government's top elected official had ever been criminally prosecuted.

The leadership of the islands passed to Nathaniel "Bops" Francis, the elderly deputy chief minister. However, in an investigation into a fire that destroyed the Government Buildings on Grand Turk, the British Foreign and Commonwealth Office discovered evidence of widespread corruption throughout the PNP, and the local government was replaced by an advisory council appointed from Britain.

CHAPTER SEVENTEEN

Inside Paradise: The GOs' Story

> "At Club Med, the only time you're not working is when you're asleep."
>
> John Nadeau, 1986

A fascinating band of free-spirited adventurers living life to its fullest, or an arrogant and selfish bunch of outcasts who can't cope with reality? Thoughtful, caring, and considerate, or just plain rude and manipulative? Sincere and straitlaced, or wild and crazy? Energetic and hard-working, or lazy beach bums? Gods of sex, or paid studs? Such are the range of perceptions about the GOs, Club Med's legendary cadre of employees.

The GOs generate such strong opinions among vacationers at Club Med villages because the GOs, more than any other factor, are the very essence of Club Med — a unique international army of workers that distinguish the French holiday company from other vacation enterprises.

"The magic ingredient of a Club Med vacation is our talented team of GOs," declares the company, proudly recognizing the contribution of the GOs to its success. "They serve as hosts, teachers, entertainers, friends."

John Nadeau, Alexandra Benko, Amy McDonald, and David Wright, four North Americans, have all worked for Club Med in the past five years. All have agreed to tell their stories, giving a rare and honest insight into the ups and downs, the highs and lows of working for the world's biggest and most famous vacation company.

Nadeau, an articulate fellow in his mid-20s, worked in the Club's traffic department, looking after the GMs' travel arrangements in the Bahamas, Mexico, and Tahiti at various intervals between 1983 and 1986. Benko, a lively woman in her late 20s, spent several seasons working in the boutiques at three different villages in the Bahamas and Mexico. The vivacious yet introspective 24-year-old McDonald worked as an aerobics instructor and in village night clubs in the Bahamas and Mexico. Wright, a cheerful 24-year-old tennis pro, taught his sport in the Dominican Republic and Mexico and was last seen headed for a new assignment at Club Med's Copper Mountain village in Colorado.

Although each had a clearly defined main role, all were very flexible and participated in a wide variety of activities while working for the Club. And as Nadeau clearly explained, "The only time you're not working is when you're asleep."

How did they get involved? "I approached Club Med directly," says the lean and physically fit Nadeau, who would live up to most people's stereotypical expectations of what a Club Med GO should look like. "There was a hole in my life. I was 22.

"I went in and they told me I had a good chance," he continues. "My background was in modelling, working, an entrepreneur ... a little bit of everything. I had a transportation background — my mother owned a travel agency. I'd been bonded because I had a real estate licence. So there was no real problem in hiring me because I covered all the bases."

Club Med, obviously impressed with the outgoing and confident Nadeau, offered him a position shortly after the interview. "Three weeks later, I was told I had to be in Eleuthera on Saturday," he remembers, mentioning that his starting salary was $400 a month. He recalls feeling somewhat taken aback by the experience.

What were Nadeau's specific duties? "I was hired as assistant traffic," he explains, listing his different responsibilities. "He's the person who takes care of the ins and outs of the guests. You have to take care of the airport operations, transportation to and from the airport, luggage, reconfirmation of airline tickets. You hold all the airline tickets. When people check out, they come and see you and pick up their airline tickets."

Unlike Nadeau, Amy McDonald was more or less recruited while vacationing at Club Med's Playa Blanca village in Mexico. "I got in with some of the GOs," says McDonald, discussing her initial contacts with the company. "They said: 'Why don't you stay for a while and work?'"

McDonald, who had picked up one of those fabled Mexican stomach ailments while on holiday, returned home for a couple of weeks to recover physically and ponder the Club Med offer. "I discussed it and decided it was something I should do," she says. "I was feeling very stifled and I love to travel. It was an escape in some ways. I was escaping from bad things. So I looked at it positively. I went because it was an offer I couldn't refuse. I did it because I knew it would make me better."

Alexandra Benko, who had been working as sales representative in the recession-racked computer industry, took a much more businesslike approach. "I thought it was time for a change," she says, summing up her reasons for contacting Club Med. "Number one, I wanted to travel. Number two, we had a recession and nobody was buying anything. A lot of companies were going bankrupt. The field was coming to a halt. Two or three years prior to that I went to Club Med for a vacation and I saw the life-style. So I applied to Club Med," Benko continues. She sometimes found it hard to shake old habits. "Because I had been working in a very professional field, I went into the interview in a business suit, a briefcase, etc. In the meantime, the other people were sitting in the lobby and they were very sporty, very fashionable. I was the complete opposite. But I had the interview and I had it in French. It was a heavy interview, but before I knew it I had the job."

David Wright, who candidly admits that he was not "bright" in school, also contacted Club Med directly to see if they would be interested in acquiring his services as a tennis instructor, but he confesses that he knew little or nothing about the company. "I'd heard of Club Med, but I didn't know what went on there," he says, relating that he was working as a squash pro at the time. "I'd never been there. I didn't know anything about it. I was always good with racquet sports. So I called them up and they said, 'Send us a résumé.'"

Why Club Med? "Because there was nothing else to do," says Wright bluntly. "You think about what you do in the city. You work eight hours a day and you go home. You sit down, you pull out a beer, and you do nothing."

Wright, like Nadeau, Benko, and McDonald, was paid a starting salary of $400 a month, including room and board and a few other small benefits; but money, they all say, was never an issue. "All of the GOs I ever knew got paid that," confirms McDonald. "It was a flat $400 a month."

And like so many other new GOs, Wright's first few days on the job at Club Med's Guaymas village in northern Mexico (now known as Sonora Bay) were filled with excess. "The first three weeks I was in the disco until three in the morning, partying every night," he admits, acknowledging that the wild nights couldn't last forever. "I suddenly realized, 'Hey, this is a lot of fun but take it in stride, because you've got six months.' So I laid off."

John Nadeau tells the same story. "The first week is a complete blur," he smiles, probably trying to forget the memory of the killer hangovers. "But then you realize that if you keep doing this, you're not going to last two months. I'm gonna die! I drink more than my dad now."

From a work standpoint, most on the outside rarely realize what a demanding schedule most of the GOs have. Indeed, some days are very long, beginning early in the morning and lasting well into the night. This is because in addition to their regularly assigned duties — such as Nadeau's in traffic, McDonald's in aerobics, and Benko's in the boutique — a GO is also expected to participate in all kinds of other activities ranging from the carnival-like arrival ceremonies to performing in the nightly stage show. The tennis instructor, Wright, detailed a typical GO's day.

"On an average day, I would wake up at eight," he begins.

"I'd teach at 8:30. We'd all go to the courts and one of the pros would do the stretching exercises. Then we'd go out and teach for about an hour and a half until 10:15. After that, we'd have breakfast with our students. We'd usually get out of there about 10:30 or 10:45. Then I'd go back and have a shower and get changed. Sometimes I went to the beach, sometimes I took a nap. Sometimes I just went to the pool to talk to people.

"There were pool games at noon," continues Wright, whose afternoon schedule at Guaymas generally started after a 12:30 lunch with the GMs. "Usually after lunch in this village, because we had so many shows, there would be a rehearsal at 1:15. We would usually rehearse for 45 minutes. Then I had two and a half hours off to do anything I wanted, and then we went back to the tennis courts and taught until 6:15. I then had an hour and a half before dinner."

Before carrying on with a description of his night-time activities, Wright explained that GOs in Guaymas sometimes had to take part in zany costumed entrances to the restaurant, yet another special Club Med touch to amuse the GMs. "You'd go to animation and come up with a theme," says Wright. "We did James Bond, for example. I was Bond and the guys dressed up as zombies, and we had flames and a fire. The tennis team would do it one night, then the water sports team, then the land team. Every different service would do a different one every night.

"After that, we'd have dinner from 7:30 till 9:00," he continues. "Then we had a show from 9:30 till 10:45. After that, either we had half an hour until another rehearsal, or you could go to the disco. It would depend on the time of the season. If it was the beginning, you'd have a lot of rehearsals. By the end of the season, we'd just run through it once. Then it was midnight and you could do whatever you wanted."

At first glance, it appears that Wright was scheduled for only three to four hours a day as a tennis instructor. Added to that were the few hours a day that he might have to spend either rehearsing or performing the nightly shows and his periodic participation in one of Club Med's restaurant entrances. From an outsider's point of view, it might look like a very easy schedule. However, Wright and his fellow GOs also ate most of their meals with the GMs and partied with them in the evening. All of this left very little free time for Wright. With only an hour or so in the morning and two or three hours in the afternoon to do as he pleased, he had almost no time for himself until he went to bed.

Amy McDonald, who was later transferred from the Playa Blanca village to Guaymas, was asked what would happen if a disgruntled GO refused to take part in all the extracurricular fun and games that were outside their normal working domain. "They would have gotten rid of you," she says matter-of-factly. "Participation was definitely a big part. You were expected to go to the night club even if you had to get up in the morning. It had to be done."

McDonald began teaching aerobics after she was shifted to Guaymas. She was later transferred to the Paradise Island village in the Bahamas. There, she was put to work in the village's lively night club, which stayed open until the wee hours of the morning. This made for long days, with no raise from her basic $400-a-month salary, let alone tips, which are taboo at all Club Med villages.

"When I worked the night club seven nights a week and I would serve $1,000 or $1,500 in drinks a night, I'd think, 'God, if I was at home I would make $100 or $150 a night,'" she says. "But I made this choice. The positive reasons for being there overtook that."

John Nadeau's work experience at Club Med was unusual. "I had the best of both worlds," he says. Destroying a few myths about Club Med, he explains: "People say that you can't bring your girlfriend to Club Med. I had my girlfriend at Club Med. People say that you can never leave a Club Med. I had dinner five nights a week outside of Club Med."

What qualified Nadeau for special treatment? "Because there is a way to do anything you want to do," he answers. "It's a matter of knowing how to deal with people."

According to Nadeau, his improved life at the French vacation company stemmed from his work in the traffic department, a vital cog of the Club Med operation that looks after the all-important land transfers, customs and immigration procedures, airline arrangements, and so forth. "In traffic, you're dealing with almost a $500,000 budget in six months," he says. "You have to know what you're doing or you can lose a company a great deal of money. And you are also on the public relations side, because you are the first and last impression everyone has of the company. You really have to have a crack operation."

As Nadeau tells it, he was doing such a good job for the traffic department at his first village in Eleuthera that he asked his *chef de village* if he could bring down his girlfriend, whom he had been forced to leave behind when he went to work for Club Med.

"Things were going my way. Things were going well," he explains. "So I asked the *chef de village* if I can bring this girl down. He said: 'Yeah, as long as you don't act as if you're married.'"

What was wrong with that? "The GMs want you to be ... not loose with them, but they want to be entertained, and if you are a couple then there is jealousy, and the guests will feel it," he responds. His girlfriend joined him in the Bahamas after he had been working for Club Med for only three months. She was hired as an au pair, a GO-like position that involves everything from being a hostess to looking after children. However, unlike the badly paid GOs who earned $400 a month, the au pairs were paid absolutely nothing, except for their room and board and the standard extras, an incomprehensible and exploitive way of doing things at a company that makes many millions of dollars in profits every year.

"It took about a month for her to fit in," he continues. "But then we were accused of being too much of a couple. When the *chef de village* found out that we wanted to go to another village together, he said, 'You are both great GOs. You're in all the shows. Everyone likes you. You're good motivators and have the team spirit. But you're always together, literally living your home life. You can't do that! So I'm giving you a month to work it out.'"

Did the *chef de village* mean they should end the relationship? "No, not end the relationship. Not at all," answers Nadeau, conceding that he and his girlfriend did their best not to act like a couple, a difficult and humiliating emotional process. "We ended up doing sort of what we wanted."

A few months later, everything apparently resolved, Nadeau and his girlfriend were transferred to the swinging Playa Blanca village on Mexico's west coast in the state of Jalisco. There she was no longer an au pair but a full-fledged GO at $400 a month, while Nadeau continued his work in the traffic department. While the domestic situation was temporarily resolved, Nadeau had to cope with the corrupt and extremely dangerous nature of life in Jalisco, a centre for drugs in Mexico.

Because of his responsibilities in traffic, Nadeau came in contact with the Mexican authorities, who could make things very difficult if things weren't done their way. "In Jalisco, you're constantly dealing in bribes with the customs officials and the police because it's one of the most corrupt states in Mexico," explains Nadeau. "In Manzanillo, I found myself in a room with a Colt .45 pointed at me. The guy pulled out his gun and put it on the table and said, 'I want 50 pesos a head for not searching bags, and I want 50 pesos a head to let people through immigration.' I went off saying, 'For $400 bucks a month, to have a guy pointing a gun at my head . . .'"

Nadeau cooperated with the Mexican authorities. "You pay, and it's in your Club Med budget. In the traffic budget," he specifies. "There are no questions asked. In Mexico, I found that as long as you had it running properly and people were happy and no one was getting stuck at customs, they didn't give a shit what you were doing."

Besides dealing with the Mexican authorities, Nadeau also had to contend with the ever-present threat of violence. On one occasion, he had to fend off an angry mob of taxi drivers. "They surrounded me and started poking me, and a guy pulled out a gun," says Nadeau.

"Believe me, I had my protection ring set up," says Nadeau. "If someone wanted to fuck around with me, I had enough friends. My bus company, my taxi company. I had friends in immigration and customs, anything I wanted I could get. It's just a system," he goes on. "I have a lot of people living off me. Okay, if you want to fuck with me, then fuck with me! Sure it's violent, but the guests didn't know!

"I had my hard times in Mexico," Nadeau sums up, adding that he still very much liked the country. "It was a challenge. It's a challenge that I miss. It's a beautiful country and there are so many things to see. I'll be back there eventually."

Despite the fact that Nadeau had virtually laid his life on the line for Club Med while working at Playa Blanca, the vacation company decided that it could no longer tolerate him and his girlfriend living and working as a couple. For the next season, they offered only Nadeau continuing employment.

"I quit after the second season in Mexico," says Nadeau, admitting that he was quite bitter and angry at Club Med's decision. "They didn't want to hire both of us. I was tired and said, 'Who needs this shit?' I worked my ass off and they won't even hire my girlfriend. Fuck 'em!"

But that wasn't the end of his association with Club Med. A while later, the vacation company had a change of heart and offered both Nadeau and his girlfriend jobs at the Moorea village in Tahiti, which was then in the midst of a multimillion-dollar renovation.

"They said, 'We'd like to hire you for Moorea,'" he recalls, pleased that he could once again work for the company in some semblance of normalcy. "We're keeping the position open for you for two weeks, and we'll give your girlfriend a job in the boutique. She's going with you," Nadeau remembers Club Med saying.

Although he still had two weeks to consider the Club Med offer, it was almost a foregone conclusion that he and his girlfriend would go to the South Pacific. Sadly, things started to unravel for Nadeau and his girlfriend at the Moorea village. "I had a very difficult season in Tahiti," he says sombrely. "I wound up working 16 hours a day. I was up every day at five-thirty. I had bad personnel. They couldn't keep up so I had to let them go and hire new personnel.

"She [Nadeau's girlfriend] didn't come out until about a

179

month later. We ended up splitting during the season and she went home. Things worked out, but at the expense of my health. I was very tired."

Despite the brutally long hours and unhappiness associated with the break-up of his relationship, Nadeau loved Tahiti. He especially adored the native Polynesians, many of whom were to become his close friends.

While in Tahiti, as Nadeau tells it, his tireless efforts had been noted by the powers-that-be in Club Med, and he was told that he was being seriously considered for promotion into the *chef de village* program, the dream of any career-minded GO. At least that was what Nadeau was led to believe by one of the company big shots in Los Angeles.

Soon after the successful reopening of the Moorea village, Nadeau was transferred to the Ixtapa resort in Mexico. Although he was earning more than the regular GO salary (albeit paid in Mexican pesos) and he had an expense account and a car, it was over for Nadeau. Nothing seemed to be happening about the recommendation that he be trained as a *chef de village*. "I called their bluff," he says with a touch of remorse. "I said: 'All right, I've had three excellent reports and on my last report in Tahiti it was recommended that I become a *chef de village*.'" When that failed to produce any results, he told them in no uncertain terms, "I'm done!" And he resigned after giving the company three weeks' notice. It was March 1986.

Were there any regrets about his decision to leave the company? "It's like a relationship," he explains, obviously still caring a great deal for Club Med. "When you leave it, after a while, you forget the bad things and you just remember the good times."

In Tahiti, Nadeau came to recognize the enormous clout of a *chef de village*. He remembers one occasion when he, as the GO responsible for making all the travel arrangements, booked his *chef de village* at Moorea on a flight from Los Angeles to Tahiti, a flight that was already packed to the rafters.

"I phoned my contacts at UTA," he recalls, throwing in that the airline employees had been partying at the Moorea village on numerous occasions. "I said, 'The *chef de village* is taking a flight. Can you take care of him?'"

To Nadeau's surprise, the *chef de village* wasn't just provided with a single seat on the crowded flight. Instead, he was given three seats on which to rest his weary bones. According to Nadeau, some fairly prominent passengers were shuffled around and made to sit elbow-to-chin just so the *chef de village* could stretch his legs on the flight. This, says Nadeau, shows Club Med's impressive "buying power" and ever vital "connections."

But this kind of pampered treatment is not unusual for *chefs de village*, remarks Nadeau. "Everyone sees the *chef de village* as the god of sex and sports," he says, commenting that a few he knew behaved as if they actually believed it.

"In the old days, the *chef de village* could do anything he wanted as long as the GMs had fun," he explains, telling a couple of wild stories about the "gods" who are in charge of a Club Med resort. "I've known a *chef de village* who went around the village shooting out the lights with a gun." Another *chef de village* hired a helicopter equipped with loudspeakers blaring the soundtrack from the movie *Apocalypse Now*. He would "attack another village, dropping free-drink vouchers down to the bar. Doing things that were completely crazy."

However, it wasn't all fun and games for the *chefs de village*, says Nadeau, who feels that Club Med is in a period of transition. "I think Club Med is trying to weed out the old school," he guesses, adding that times have changed and that what worked in the past isn't necessarily applicable today. "It's a different mentality."

Nadeau believes a few of the *chefs de village*, especially those from the "old school," are having a hard time adjusting to present-day realities. "These are people who are seeing a whole way of life go down the drain and become a business," he says sympathetically. All the years of endless partying and living up to an impossible image can take quite a toll, physically and emotionally. "These are people who have been drinking like crazy, or they're reformed alcoholics, or they still are alcoholics.

"At 35, some of them look 50," he goes on. "I've seen them

crying when they have a drink. They're saying, 'What do I do next? I have no place to go!' You can tell that a lot of the *chefs de village* are thinking, 'I just can't do this any more. It can't be this hard any more. I just can't do it.' In Club Med, people just see the glossy side of it. There is a glossy side to it, and at the same time there is a very sad side to it."

According to Nadeau, one of the great traumas for a veteran Club Med employee is to be transferred to the Paris offices to perform some menial and drab task, a difficult transition after the adventurous life they have been leading. "I've seen it in Paris," he says. "A guy has a five-by-five-foot office and he's in charge of buying towels or something. And he's not buying proper towels because he doesn't know how. He knows how to have fun and do sports."

Amy McDonald tells the story of how one *chef de village* started to experience emotional problems while still on the job. When she first went to Paradise Island in the Bahamas, everything was running smoothly. As is often the case, the *chef de village* had brought with him most of the members of the team that had been with him for the previous four seasons. "They were very tight," McDonald says. "They loved him and would do anything for him. It worked. It was a nice atmosphere. But that all changed and that's the reason I quit.

"His wife and children were at the Club, and he had a nervous breakdown," she continues, mentioning that alcoholism was probably the root of the problem. "His wife and children left him, and after that he fired most of the team. He fired everyone because he thought they were the reason his family left him.

"I think he was insane. And that's when I left Club Med. It wasn't that I wanted to leave the Club; I just couldn't work for this particular man. Head office found out everything. All of the GOs who had been fired or quit were given a reprieve. If they wanted to be hired back, they could be."

McDonald also found that her previous boss at the Guaymas village in Mexico was very difficult to work for. "He was very negative," she says. If a GM had written to complain of a real or imagined slight, he would berate his staff in long meetings that would sometimes last for two hours. "He'd bring up names. He'd shit on that person in front of everyone. There wasn't really a good side to the *chef de village* there. I didn't enjoy working for him at all. I didn't respect him."

Of course, it would be unfair and untrue to leave the impression that all of Club Med's *chefs de village* behave in a similar fashion. The vast majority are a committed group of hard-working professionals who run a good resort operation and handle the GOs in a fair and pleasant manner.

"My *chef de village* in Paradise Island was a beautiful man. His name was Michel. He was just fabulous," gushes Alexandra Benko, who couldn't say enough great things about the resort managers she worked for. "My *chef de village* in Playa Blanca was a very nice man too."

David Wright, who admits enjoying a "constructive" atmosphere when he is working, feels the *chef de village* should be an inspiration and driving force for the GOs, "a leader who is going to take charge and who everybody is going to like." The *chef de village* should "create an atmosphere and set an example. That's the way the village should be run."

John Nadeau offered some fascinating insights into the relationship between the GOs and the GMs. It was tough, he says, always to be on stage. "It's hard to be entertaining all the time," he points out. "You sit down at a table with seven people and every meal you're asked: 'How much money do you make? Where are you from? Do you like Club Med?' But what can you say — 'No, I think it sucks!'? Even if you think that, you can't say it."

Nadeau divulged that on occasion the GOs and the GMs were clearly at odds. "In the Bahamas, we used to have a weekly water polo game, GO men versus GM men," says Nadeau. "The GOs would end up with cuts on their faces. One guy was punched in the sternum. They just wanted to kill us!"

Why would the GMs suddenly become so violent? "Because we were everything they weren't to their wives," he speculates, raising the possibility of sexual jealousy among the more macho, image-conscious male GMs. "We had to stop the games because one of our divers was almost killed. He got an elbow in the solar plexus and sank to the bottom of the pool."

However, the GMs weren't always hostile to the GOs, according to Nadeau. Sometimes, especially if a GO had blabbed about some of his or her problems, the GMs might take it upon themselves to discuss it with the resort's manager, in an attempt to help. "He feels that he is going to be your lawyer, that happens often, and he might be in casual conversation with the *chef de village* the next day," says Nadeau. "You know, he'll say, 'I think you're treating John like a . . .'

"The GMs have paid $1,000 a week and they are not there to hear your problems," he sums up. "I've seen GMs' vacations ruined because they have infiltrated the GO circle and they saw the shit. They saw a GO getting stoned because he couldn't hack it. They saw the drunk GOs. They saw the GOs trying to pick up someone else's wife or a female GO trying to pick up someone else's husband. They saw the GO who was completely burned out because he's been doing it for 15 years."

Nadeau further illustrates his point by revealing the contents of some of the letters he received from GMs when he was working as a GO. "It's unbelievable the letters you get," he says, describing a picture that was mailed to him by one of the GMs. "You know, there is a picture of you standing next to the bar with a person who is sort of near you. It says, 'Meeting you was such a great opportunity. It changed my life. How can I become a GO?'

"You get letters from people pledging their love," he adds. "They don't see the work that is involved. Some GMs see the GO who gets burned out . . . who works his butt off trying to make it the way everyone thinks it is. When someone says, 'You guys don't work!' that's because we try to make it look as if we don't work. But we're on constant duty. A bad village is where the GOs are showing their flaws."

Nadeau also experienced some difficulty in adjusting to the constant turnover of GMs, a fact of life in any resort hotel but something many newcomers to the business aren't prepared for.

"We get to be really close and then they leave," he says sadly, revealing that an emotional transformation takes place after a while. "You're losing very good friends because it's one week of quality and compact time. That was very hard because I found myself lonely every Monday. Then a new group came in and I thought I'd fill that void with new people. But ten days later, they're gone.

"You just can't keep doing that! How long can your emotional system take this, week after week after week?" he asks. "You end up withdrawing a bit and you wind up dealing with people on a superficial level. You have fun with them, but you leave your heart out of it. Your heart at Club Med takes care of yours truly, that's all!" he concludes.

The effervescent Alexandra Benko didn't have a problem coping with lost friendships because, to her, it just didn't happen. "They don't disappear because you still have the friendship," she explains, pointing out that she often stayed in contact with the GMs long after their vacations. "I get more letters and packages from guests. I'd write to people and they would write back. Meeting these people was exciting because they were from different backgrounds, all facets of life. They were all very interesting. I learned so much about people, it was fabulous.

"I think when you live in a city, people are so busy. Work, work, work! They're in a bit of a race," she says, contrasting the hectic, pressure-packed life in urban North America with the calming ambience of Playa Blanca, her first Club Med village.

"In the Club Med environment you're locked away," Benko says of Playa Blanca. "You don't have television, you don't have radio, you don't have a telephone. You're completely secluded. There you have the time to meet people and to talk with them. You can talk about your feelings and really have the time to get to know somebody."

Perhaps the last word on the subject should go to the easy-going David Wright, who commented that he liked most of the GMs he met. "Very much so. I mean, there were always a couple of GMs that you'd want to kill, but you'd only have to put up with them for a week."

Not surprisingly, sex is often a big feature of the unusual relationship between the GOs and the GMs, sometimes a lusty crew, depending on the village, who take advantage of a Club Med holiday to live out their carnal fantasies. To put it crudely, there are more than a handful of GMs, male and female, married and single, who think that having sex with the GOs is just another component of their all-inclusive vacation.

Although most GOs are reluctant to have their names attached to anything concerning sex, almost all have a few wild stories, some of which defy belief. They range from the sordid Blow Job Olympics in Martinique to *chef de village*–inspired gang-bangs with some of the raunchier female GMs, who will allegedly take on five or six men, one after the other. Then there is the story of the accountant-like male GO who maintains a detailed log of his sexual conquests, a tally that at last count numbered 150 different women. As usual, it is virtually impossible to find anyone who will admit to participating in events like these.

Amy McDonald, a female GO with a ringside seat, was asked how promiscuous a holiday at Club Med really is. "That all depends on which particular club," she says straightforwardly. "Some are known as being very much more singles-oriented than others. Playa Blanca, Cancún, Martinique ... In Guaymas, the GMs were mainly from California. They were older and more sports-oriented. It wasn't really a party club at all."

Did the GMs expect a sexual encounter with a GO? "Not so much in Mexico," McDonald answers. "In Paradise Island, it was expected!" Her colleague John Nadeau agrees. "The wilder villages are the night-club villages," he explains. "The ones with no kids and where the night club can stay open quite late. That's where things happen, in the night club."

"I'm not a slut!" says David Wright, dismissing the suggestion that male GOs are a kind of stud service for horny female GMs. "A lot of people think a GO is a slut. I met a lot of nice girls. My relationships were very honest. They always used to come on to us."

Alexandra Benko, who, like McDonald, also worked at the Paradise Island village, had her own special way of dealing with the hordes of lecherous men that the village attracts. "I didn't see them," she confides, pointing out that she is not a drinker. "I didn't hang around the bar. I kept out of their way. So if there were any people who had wandering hands, I wasn't there."

How did other female GOs handle it? "I don't know," says Benko. "I have no idea how they dealt with it. I mean, you could sense when somebody had a little bit too much to drink. The security people would help them find their rooms."

The strong-willed Benko also turned down an opportunity to work at Club Med's notorious Buccaneer's Creek village in Martinique. "I was asked to go to Martinique and I refused," she reveals. "I didn't want to go because I'd heard stories. I'd heard from the guests that it was wild and crazy and I didn't want to be in an environment like that."

Interestingly, Benko, who was later sent to the Ixtapa village in Mexico instead of Martinique, felt that Club Med was not the free-wheeling sexual paradise many outsiders believed it to be. "I don't think it is," she declares. "I didn't see it. Maybe that's what you hear from people who went on vacation and wanted it to be that way and realized it's not. But why go home and say, 'Well, we sat around the beach.' So they make up stories to make it sound exciting."

Amy McDonald related that she just didn't meet that many men that she was attracted to. "I didn't meet very many interesting men," she confesses. "They were friendly and nice enough, but the type of man I'm interested in wouldn't go to Club Med on holiday. Club Med is for people who like to be very lazy and have everything scheduled. They don't want freedom. They wouldn't know what to do with it.

"The male GOs fucked their brains out," she elaborates. "But the women, the female GOs ... Speaking for myself, I can't sleep with just anybody. I get emotionally attached. I couldn't sleep with someone that was only going to be there for a week. I didn't need the hassle emotionally."

McDonald points out that the constant availability of sex-hungry female guests ensured that many of the women GOs were virtually ignored by the male GOs. "The male GOs select from not only the GO women, but also the GM women. They're willing! They want it! They push it! They ask for it!" she says. "Why not just fuck a woman that was going to come and go?

187

And that's what they did! I found that almost all the GO girls I worked with in my first season were celibate, myself included."

McDonald also divulged that it was not uncommon for younger female GMs, usually operating in pairs, to holiday at a Club Med village and work their way through the ranks of the male GOs. "There were often younger girls that would come down and work as a team."

According to McDonald, some GMs would have sexual encounters even if they were on vacation with their wives or husbands. "There were often times when they would bring their wife and would have a mistress while they were there. That happened a lot," says McDonald. "But there were often cases where it was the other way around. The women would have the affairs. He's taking tennis lessons or is out in the middle of the ocean while she's off screwing her brains out."

David Wright and John Nadeau added their own insights into the sexual shenanigans at Club Med. "If you come here to get laid, then you've really got a sad sex life back home as far as I'm concerned," says Wright, putting everything into perspective. "A lot of people would love to do what I'm doing. But a lot of other people, maybe because they're jealous, don't show much interest. They think that all we do is get fucked all the time which, in some cases, is true."

"It's just unbelievable!" remarks John Nadeau, rolling his eyes and confirming that there was never a shortage of available women. "There are more women looking for guys at Club Med than guys looking for women."

Nadeau wasn't entirely sympathetic to his women colleagues. "The female GOs you get are sporty, gung-ho. You have a lot more better-looking men GOs than women GOs," he laughs, playing the chauvinist. "It was a funny thing, you know — the female GOs who are getting it slim down. The ones who aren't get fat during the season. Whereas the guys," he chuckles, "have less self-respect."

Nadeau was asked about the prevalence of homosexuality at Club Med. A gay GM had disclosed that while on holiday at the Eleuthera village, he had found more than willing partners among the male GOs. "If you're a GM, you might land on a homosexual village. There are some that will follow a homosexual *chef de village*. Of course, he has his cronies."

Amy McDonald was a little more direct. "I found that most of the people who were higher up in the company were not gay, but bisexual. Especially the Europeans, much more so than the Americans. If anything it made it better. I get along very well with gay men."

The laid-back David Wright hadn't noticed. "It's a difficult question because you wouldn't even know if guys are gay," he says. He denied that homosexuality had anything to do with career advancement at Club Med, as has been alleged by other GOs in the past. "You don't have to kiss ass that way," he insists.

Alexandra Benko quit after her fourth season of working for Club Med. "I just wasn't interested any more," she confesses, relating how her friends back home had kept her abreast of the improving economic climate. "They said that things were 'wonderful' at home. There are job opportunities."

Although she is hesitant to discuss it, money and security were becoming important to her. She also admits that she had not received any kind of a raise from Club Med, but didn't consider it really significant. "I don't think anyone else got a raise either," she says. "I don't think the men got a raise. Everybody got paid the same."

Benko indicated that there were much more important things in life than working for Club Med. "I couldn't start a family," she says warmly, raising an issue that must haunt many of the company's GOs. "I couldn't go and have children and take care of my husband because Club Med is a seven-day-a-week job. I think it's short-term, unless you don't want to get married and don't want to have children."

Had she ever considered trying to carve out a career at Club Med? "I don't know if I wanted to pursue a career in that area. I couldn't see any growth. I was a manager. I wanted more. I'm the type of individual that wants more. I want bigger and better things in my life."

However, Benko remains extraordinarily positive about her

experiences at Club Med. "I would tell people that it is a wonderful learning experience," she says from the bottom of her heart. "I'd advise a lot of people to do it."

Alexandra Benko had no problems adjusting to the realities of everyday life after leaving Club Med. But for others, like Amy McDonald and John Nadeau, and for many more young men and women who have had the unique experience of working as a GO, it was an emotionally trying time, an interlude somewhat akin to de-programming. Club Med was an important and all-consuming part of their lives.

While finding a good job didn't seem to pose much of a problem for McDonald and Nadeau, they experienced some difficulty in psychologically letting go of the Club Med experience. McDonald, for example, still finds it awkward to have a meaningful discussion about what happened.

"It's very difficult to talk about," she candidly admits. "People don't understand. Some people don't like to talk about it because it's like talking about your family.

"When you first leave, you talk about it a lot. It's like a drug that gets in your body. You have to stay completely away from it or you'll want it back again. There's a lot of bullshit there.

"When I left the Club, I found that I needed a lot of people around me," she sums up. "I understand people, I always did, but now it's even more so. At the same time, when it comes to personal things, like letting go and becoming very close to someone, I'm having a hard time. The problem with my relationship now is that I can't get close."

On a more upbeat note, McDonald was asked about the funnier side of Club Med. "Every week, we would have a GM show where the GMs would do what GOs did," she answers, a patented Club Med grin sweeping across her face. "They'd act crazy and it would be like the night of their life. It's hard to believe, and it's pathetic in a way. There are so many people out there who work all year for a one-week vacation and then they have one night where they all go crazy and live out their fantasies. I used to find it funny. I realized, of course, that I was doing the same thing every single day."

190

"Club Med has opened my eyes to the world," says John Nadeau. "The highs were seeing things that I never would have been able to see. Going into a culture that is foreign to your own, to live in it and experience it. I've met people from so many different cultures. Some GOs, though," he adds as an afterthought, "will spend an entire season and never step outside of the gates. Personally, I said I'm going to make the most of it. I'm going to meet people. I'm going to make business contacts."

On the other hand, Nadeau was disappointed by the emotional manipulation. "At Club Med you have to be void of emotion," he says bluntly. "You're allowed to show that you're happy, but you can never show you're sad. You become callous.

"If you have a relationship, you're not allowed to show it," he continues. "If you have a problem in your family, you leave because guests cannot see that. I can understand that, but it's so hard. The old GOs have been able to do that."

He expanded on why he had left the company. "Not being respected," he says slowly, indicating that there were some Club Med employees who would never change their ways. "Being the victim of some people, who thought that becoming a GO in 1955 made them smart now.

"I was lonely. I'd split up with my girlfriend and we'd done the villages together. I missed the emotion. I'm an emotional person and I missed being able to express that."

Because he still thinks a great deal about the company, Nadeau was asked how Club Med could make the experience better for the GOs. Not surprisingly, he believes the company should make more of a commitment to its employees, financially and in career terms, if it doesn't want to wind up with a major human resource problem, especially in North America.

"They should start giving you the security of a better job, better lodging. They should start respecting you," he says matter-of-factly, focusing once more on the abusive conduct of some *chefs de village*. "The old chefs would call you dirt and shit on you. Nobody gave me shit in front of the guests, but you'd get *chefs de village* who would do that because they are so frustrated with their lives.

191

"Club Med loves to distinguish itself from Sheraton. They'd say, 'Hey, if you don't like it here, go and work at Sheraton,'" he says, suggesting that many at Club Med believe that working for Sheraton is somewhat like labouring in a soulless holiday factory or prison.

Nadeau also feels that the more independent North Americans, who grew up differently from their European counterparts, are not as likely to go along with the paternalistic nature of working for Club Med. In other words, he's afraid that Club Med will lose some very good employees because of the company's inability to change with the times; that, in effect, was what caused him to leave the company. "What's going to happen to Club Med if all the good people leave?" he asks sincerely, sounding as if he wished he was still working for the company. "I'm scared to see the human resource problem at Club Med. It's not easy to find good GOs any more who understand the company.

"They have to start watching their ass because their advertising isn't what they're delivering," he gloomily concludes. "Hats off to their advertising, they're creating a dream. It's time to step back and look at what they had and what they have. To no longer say, 'You're supposed to be having fun here.' They have a terrific product, one of the greatest products in the world, but . . ."

Amy McDonald sees it somewhat the same way. "The first mistake is to try and have a career with the company," she says, focusing on the cultural and economic differences between Europeans and North Americans. "This is quite a generalization, but Europeans don't have the opportunities that we have here. And because Club Med has been a part of the European lifestyle, especially in France, it's more accepted to have a career in Club Med.

"Americans have a whole different attitude," she says, describing the difference in priorities. "They are much more money-oriented. They're younger and they got into it for much the same reasons that I did — to have a good time or to become a better person. They give it a time limit.

"For me, I gave myself a certain amount of time and I

realized I would leave after that," she says, summarizing her views. "My life had to go on. I had to come back to the real world."

Steve Renard, president of Canada-based Renard International Hospitality Consultants, one of the world's leading hotel executive-recruitment companies, was queried about Club Med. As an expert in the field, dealing with most of the major chains constantly, and as someone who has "enjoyed" a Club Med vacation, he is in a unique position to give a detached, professional assessment of the French holiday company's employees.

"They are the lowest level," he says bluntly, not at all impressed with the competence of the company's fabled GOs. "Most GOs who are working there are doing it because they enjoy the facilities and they use the facilities. They're waterskiers or they love the women. They are down there more for pleasure than they are for business.

"The corporate people are good, but generally the people who run their clubs are pretty near the bottom. They aren't looking for sophisticated food, therefore the culinary people are not sophisticated. They are not offering the highest quality of housekeeping, the highest quality of anything. They make it very *au naturel*. It's very blatant. If you look at their rooms and beds and everything, it's yechhh!"

While Renard is negative about some aspects of Club Med's operation, he acknowledges that it is "a very profitable company. It was the initiator of the all-inclusive vacation, which is far more profitable than a visitor or guest thinks."

Why is an all-inclusive holiday, which includes airfare, accommodation, transfers, and meals for one set price, more profitable than regular holidays? "Because [the guests] think, 'Well, I can get as much as I want,'" he replies. But it's not a deal: "You're paying up front for everything."

Renard is also impressed with Club Med's marketing. "Excellent. They're the best," he says without hesitation. "They market an image. They market an aura. They market an experience, they don't market a product."

Does Renard International get many Club Med employees

who are looking for work elsewhere? "Some, but not many," answers Renard, attributing the lack of veteran Club Med people among his clientele to their unconventional backgrounds; they aren't always suited to work for another company. "The reason is that their hotel experience is different from most. Some of them don't come through a hotel school. They just come through the GO ranks. A lot of them are professionals, but it is a lethargic type of professional that works for Club Med."

When told that the average GO's salary is a dismal $400 a month, Renard was slightly taken aback. "That's very low. Extremely low. Ridiculously low, especially for expatriates." When reminded Club Med also includes room and board as part of the deal, Renard was still unimpressed. "So what! They all do. It's standard."

But despite all this, Renard confessed that he had a terrific time when he stayed at Club Med. "I enjoyed the Club. I had a good time," he remarks, sounding a lot like a typical GM. "I enjoyed myself because you don't look at it as a normal hotel. Everybody wears togas or sheets or whatever. People who go there expecting à la carte food with French waiters and tuxedos . . ." He leaves the rest unsaid.

"You're not there to be impressed," he concludes. "I saw it for what it was, and it was basically an unrestricted whorization of 'let's have fun and away we go.' It was fine because it allowed somebody not to think, to be told what to do, where to eat and what to eat. Fine!"

Renard, who has staffed London's famed Dorchester Hotel and the renowned Bel Air in Los Angeles, was asked how Club Med rates against other resort hotels. "Two or three stars," he responds, recognizing that comparisons of this sort are not easy. "It would probably rate with the holiday camps in England. They may think they are better, and perhaps for what they are, they are five stars. But as you rate them against a normal resort that has a gourmet dining room, bars, and so forth, they'd probably rate two or three stars."

CHAPTER EIGHTEEN

Club Med Forever

"We offer a concept: we have our own special philosophy, which you like or you don't like. We started out with young singles, but we have matured as they have matured, as they've grown older and had children. We have gone through a gradual evolution, and what we need to do now is not so much change our image as erase the misperceptions — to better explain what we are."

Serge Trigano, 1985

Contrary to what a few diehards believe, Club Med is changing. Alas, the days of living down a wild reputation, whether deserved or not, seem destined to fade like a Caribbean sunset. Although this moderating move will undoubtedly disappoint some of the more casually minded GMs, there is simply too much at stake not to change, namely the increased growth of the company and the hundreds of millions of dollars pledged for future expansion.

"Initially the Club did attract the young escapist, a hedonist, even 25 years ago," Serge Trigano admitted to *Marketing and Media Decisions*, an American trade publication, in 1985, just a short time before he left New York to assume command of the Club Méditerranée's vast and financially important Europe, Africa and Middle East zone in Paris. "But the first people who came grew up, got married, and returned. They love the concept, which is a spirit, a way of life."

Trigano suggested that the establishment of Club Med in America was a way of testing North American reactions to the Club Med concept. "By locating Club Med Inc. in the U.S., the money market, we were able to see what reservations people had about the Club, those who said, 'Yes, it is a good formula, but not for me.' It was basically an image problem because the Club itself is the same as it was four years ago."

Is it only an "image problem," as Serge Trigano states? While that may indeed be an accurate appraisal for most of Club Med's operations, there are simply too many stories about the feverish happenings at some Club Med villages to be ignored.

"It happens," explained Club Med executive Jacques Ganin, in an interview with *Financial World*, remarking on the high incidence of sexual encounters at Club Med villages. "Single people get together everywhere. How can we stop it? Currently, at least 50 per cent of our members are married; 58 per cent are between 30 and 60 years of age. We have to change the wrong image that people have."

While Ganin either conveniently sidestepped the question or wasn't asked about the married people who behave like singles when on vacation at Club Med, the eradication of the "wrong image" is not going to be easy. Lauren Ritter, an American travel consultant, summed up the situation in an interview with the *New York Times*. "There are enough clubs that cater to families and couples," she said. "But some still have that swinging reputation."

Club Med didn't seem to be worried about the issue until after Club Med Inc. had gone public on the New York Stock Exchange, an event that spawned all kinds of articles and stories in the American media, downplaying the company's steamy reputation. Apparently, American leisure industry analysts — who, of course, worked for many of the brokerage houses that were selling the Club Med issue — felt that this was an obstacle to the company's continuing success. In other words, they were concerned that the conservative American investor might not go for the concept on a long-term basis.

In addition to the effort to moderate the image of Club Med among the U.S. public, there was also plenty of investment hype from the Wall Street crowd. "I don't think there is any competition," gushed Barry Gluck, a vice-president at Rooney Pace. "I think the uniqueness of the concept is part of the value. There is an economic value, too, because what Club Med offers would cost you 50 to 100 per cent more if you went to a hotel. I think we're dealing with a $40 to $50 stock here."

Even Joseph Townsend, Club Med Inc.'s rarely quoted treasurer, got into the act by boasting to *Financial World*: "We are more profitable than a hotel," supporting an observation made by hotel executive-recruitment expert Steve Renard. "We offer a lifestyle, not a room," Townsend carried on, breaking down some of the reasons for the company's success. "We measure by the bed, not the room, and all our guests pay full price. All our packages are pre-paid. This gives us a positive cash-flow and decreases our interest expense. We are not destination-oriented, so if one of our villages is overbooked, we can offer the vacationer an alternative location."

In any event, Club Med cannot be accused of not making every effort to revamp the public's perception. In May 1985 the French holiday company opened its St. George's Cove village in Bermuda, a place not generally associated with wild, uninhibited behaviour.

"It's very conservative," says Colin Rickards, formerly the publisher of the Caribbean *Business News*, commenting on Bermuda's tranquil reputation. "For example, it was the only place in the world where Holiday Inn wasn't allowed to have one of those great garish signs. You can't rent cars there. Tourism is so critical to their economy that they control it very, very carefully."

Unlike the Bahamas, Barbados, and numerous other Caribbean hot spots, Rickards explained, Bermuda for many years wouldn't permit anything as tacky as charter holidays, fearing that the upscale and dignified delights of the island would be spoiled by swarms of middle-class tourists. So it really came as no surprise when Club Med's plans to revive the failing Bermuda Beach Hotel, a 341-room albatross that had been operated by Loews, ran into local opposition from a few members of Bermuda's conservative establishment. However, cooler heads prevailed and the St. George's village opened, providing the pretty mid-Atlantic island with plenty of publicity, an important consideration in the fiercely competitive vacation industry. But though the situation in Bermuda was happily resolved, Club Med was encountering other problems on different fronts.

In the southern French province of Alpes-Maritimes, the holiday company's plans to build a 1,000-bed village at Opio ran into a snag when an outraged local environment group, the Association de Protection de l'Environnement de Châteauneuf-de-Grasse (APEC), got a regional court in Nice to issue an injunction preventing the construction of the FF200-million project. Reacting to this legal obstacle, Gilbert Trigano promised a fight all the way to the Conseil d'État, France's Supreme Court.

Apparently, APEC disapproved of some aspects of Club Med's proposed design and was concerned about future expansion plans for the project. However, the matter was resolved in March 1986, after more than two years of delays, when Club Med agreed to construct the resort's buildings in a manner befitting the architecture of the region and gave a written promise that it would not expand the village without prior approval from APEC. In addition, the vacation company agreed to participate in a new environmental protection association. With the dispute at last resolved, construction of the Opio village was given the go-ahead, with an anticipated completion date of 1987 or early 1988.

Besides legal wrangling with the APEC, Club Med was also having its problems in an American courtroom. In March 1985 a U.S. court awarded Wayne Duarte, a 26-year-old from San José, California, more than $8 million in damages stemming from a swimming pool accident in August 1983 at Club Med's Cancún village in Mexico, a tragedy that left Duarte paralyzed for life from the neck down.

Duarte's case was based on the disturbing evidence that there wasn't enough water in the resort's pool when the accident occurred. The disaster probably could have been averted had there been better underwater lighting and depth markings. According to his attorneys, James Boccardo and John McDonald, the multi-million-dollar judgement was a record of sorts, the largest ever against Club Med for a personal injury claim.

A month later, a mob of about 120 workers at the ritzy Laromme Hotel in the southern Israeli resort of Eilat, which had recently been leased by Club Med to become its Coral Beach village, barricaded themselves in the rooms and threatened to burn the hotel down unless the lease with the French vacation company was scrapped. A week earlier, there had been a wildcat strike at the Laromme, a labour action that resulted in several of the workers being fired. The occupation was initiated when the lay-off notices weren't rescinded.

"We will not let a single French worker in here. We will burn down the hotel," a disgusted Aryeh Snir, spokesperson for the workers, told the Associated Press, adding that the occupiers wouldn't get out until the fired workers were reinstated. According to an executive of the company that owns the Laromme Hotel, Amram Aharoni, the workers were fired because they went ahead with the wildcat walk-out even though they were already aware that only 10 jobs would be lost in the Club Med take-over. But in spite of the chaos, the hotel eventually opened.

Meanwhile, in the disputed Moroccan-occupied Western Sahara in North Africa, a phosphate-rich former Spanish colony once known as the Spanish Sahara, Club Med put itself in a difficult position by agreeing to operate a tourist complex, including the El Parador Hotel, in El Aaiun, the former capital. The troubles had begun when Spain ceded her former colony to Morocco and Mauritania in 1975, a corrupt political settlement that completely ignored the needs of the local people. This led to the formation of the Polisario Front, an Algerian-backed guerrilla army that has now been fighting a war of independence for over 10 years, mostly against the Moroccans who overran 70,000 square miles of the former Spanish colony in 1976 and have been at war to keep it ever since.

Despite Morocco's claims to the contrary, the situation today in the Western Sahara remains very tense. While vast numbers of Moroccan soldiers control the main cities, the surrounding desert areas are a virtual no man's land in the hands of Polisario. Furthermore, to protect the population centres under its control, such as El Aaiun, the Moroccans have built a wall similar to the Maginot Line, a form of defence that is useless against a committed enemy, as history has proved time and time again.

This was the hornet's nest in which Club Med had agreed to set up shop, a business decision that enraged the Polisario Front. At a press conference in Paris, Bashir Mustafa Sayed, Polisario's second in command, didn't pull any punches. He threatened to destroy the Club Med facilities in El Aaiun (although he pledged to try not to harm any civilians who happened to be there at the time).

Club Med brushed off the Polisario threat, claiming that the Moroccan wall was protection enough. But that didn't satisfy all the sceptics, who were well aware that the Polisario Front was one of the fiercest and most committed of guerrilla groups and that their threats were not idle.

That Club Med would want to operate a resort in the Western Sahara is incomprehensible. If Polisario did carry out its threat, hundreds of tourists might be killed or maimed in the attack. It just doesn't make any sense.

"The agreement is unprecedented," said Radio France International, summing up Club Med's decision to go into the hostile territory. "It is the first time that a French firm has set up a business in a disputed territory which is not recognized on an international level."

Club Med's Cefalu village on the northern coast of Sicily was robbed by a gang of armed bandits on September 12, 1985. Although this was not the first time that a Club Med village in Italy has been victimized in a stick-up, this robbery was a little different. This time the crooks, who numbered five or six, cruised into the resort by boat. After landing, the gang made its way to the club's office where, at gunpoint, they forced the resort's employees to hand over the loot, which was later estimated at $76,000 in cash and 600 passports.

A week after the Cefalu robbery, on September 19, Club

Med was dealt another blow, in the form of a devastating earthquake in Mexico that killed at least 20,000 and seriously displaced hundreds of thousands of others.

Although most of the dead and injured were in Mexico City, the country's densely populated capital, the powerful quake's tremors were felt over a large part of the nation. In fact, the epicentre was close to Mexico's Pacific coast resort of Ixtapa, the site of a Club Med village. The complex was forced to close for a short period of time in the chaotic aftermath. Luckily, the damage was minimal, a cracked swimming pool being one of the structural casualties; but numerous other hotels in Ixtapa didn't fare nearly so well.

A side effect of the Mexican quake, which was accompanied by an avalanche of negative publicity in the American media, was that Club Med Inc.'s shares on the New York Stock Exchange dropped more than 20 per cent in less than two weeks. Some investors, queasy about Club Med's substantial holdings in Mexico and too lazy to find out the details, simply bailed out.

"Club Med has been under heavy selling pressure lately due to concern over Mexico," explained Dan Lee, an analyst with Drexel Burnham Lambert. "Club Med has five [*sic*] villages in Mexico that contribute over half of the company's annual income. One of these, Ixtapa, is located almost directly over the epicenter of the recent earthquake. Damage to the facility was apparently not serious, consisting largely of a crack in the swimming pool.

"However, due to the disruption of transportation to and from the village and negative publicity about the area, Club Med has opted to close the facility until November 15," Lee continued. "Fortunately, this is Club Med's off-season, and we expect the temporary closing at Ixtapa to have little or no impact on earnings. Thus, the unwarranted 22 per cent decline in the price of the stock is creating, in our view, an excellent buying opportunity."

In April, a few months before the deadly earthquake, Club Med had been involved in something billed as "The Battle of the Network Stars" at its Ixtapa village. In this publicity stunt, a variety of television stars were put through their paces in such events as carrying surfboards and paddleboards through the waves, relay races, volleyball, mixed-doubles tennis, and the ever-popular tug-o'-war between the stars. This nonsense was presumably organized to promote tourism to Ixtapa. The "stars" of the winning team were paid an amazing $20,000 a head, while second-place contestants picked up only $12,500 per team member. As for the last-place finishers, they had to make do with only $8,000 per person.

At about the same time, Club Med acquired the problem-plagued 256-room Halcyon Days resort on the Caribbean island of St. Lucia, the last remaining major asset of the Court Line Holiday Company, which had been in liquidation since 1974.

The French vacation company's take-over of Halcyon Days, which had been closed for almost a year, was hailed by St. Lucia's political leaders. "The publicity that St. Lucia will receive from the international group will be a major boost, not just to the tourism industry but to the fortunes of Vieux Fort as well," enthused John Compton, the island's prime minister. Peter Bergasse, the head of the island's tourist board, was similarly enthusiastic, describing the deal as "the best thing that could have happened to St. Lucia at this time."

While Club Med's move into St. Lucia seemed to fit the traditional expansion program, the holiday company's intriguing involvement in Vienna's City Club resort centre was anything but routine. Opened in 1986 in conjunction with El Dorado Hotel and Sportpark of Austria and Switzerland, the City Club venture is radically different from anything Club Med has previously participated in and is arguably one of the most exciting hotel concepts to come along in years.

Brilliantly conceived as a cold-weather alternative to the tropical getaway, appealing to both the tourism and commercial sectors of the travel market, the five-star City Club facility offers a complete range of features not normally associated with Club Med. These include luxurious guest rooms, 24-hour-a-day room service, direct-dial telephones, radios, remote control 11-channel televisions, mini-bars, and international newspapers — an atypical offering of creature comforts that are bound to leave some of the older Club Med GMs gasping in disbelief, especially those who recall the company's slogan of being an "antidote to civilization."

The City Club, which is located about 20 minutes from downtown Vienna, also features full-service gourmet restaurants and bars, hairdressing salon, concierge, boutiques, and Telex services for the busy executive. To wind down, there is a fully equipped sports complex with a superb American Fitness Center gymnasium, four indoor tennis courts, archery and driving ranges, Jacuzzis, and an immense Turkish bath and sauna, one of the largest saunas in Europe. All of this is linked to an eye-catching 120-foot-high glass pyramid, the centrepiece of the City Club resort. Inside the pyramid, where the temperature is maintained at a soothing tropical level, is a gargantuan 2,700-square-metre swimming pool enhanced by an artificial wave-maker.

If the Vienna City Club catches on, it might be a sign of things to come from Club Med. It could be that Club Med has finally found an appropriately exotic formula that is workable in the heart of big cities.

Club Med's capacity for corporate innovation was recognized in a 1985 study by the U.S. consulting firm of Arthur D. Little. The study, entitled *From Vision to Reality*, examined 28 multinational firms and how they coped with the management of innovation.

Ironically, in light of Club Med's past labour difficulties, the company was lauded for its clever handling of employees. Club Med follows a policy known as "nomadism," which involves constant staff rotation. Employees are shifted from village to village every six months. Arthur D. Little observed that this was an important driving force for innovation.

The study also commended Gilbert Trigano for not relying on traditional hiring criteria in recruiting employees and praised Club Med's staff training programs.

The year 1986 got off to a questionable start with the broadcast in the United States of *Club Med*, an unsuccessful two-hour made-for-TV movie. Produced by industry giant Lorimar-

Telepictures, which is responsible for hit TV series like *Dallas*, *Knots Landing*, and *Falcon Crest* as well as countless other successful programs, the Club Med movie was sort of a cross between *Love Boat* and *Fantasy Island*. Shot in Mexico at Club Med's quake-rattled Ixtapa village in December 1985, the movie was aired just a few weeks later on January 19, on ABC-TV. According to a press release from Lorimar, it marked the first time in the company's history that "world-renowned Club Med has allowed a production company to film inside one of its resort villages."

A month after the movie was aired, an explosive device went off at the French vacation company's Santa Giulia village near Porto Vecchio in southern Corsica, the scene of numerous other outrages against the holiday company in the past. Fortunately, the blast occurred in the winter season when the village was closed, and there were no injuries. Once again, the local authorities suspected the Front de Libération Nationale de la Corse (FLNC), who were complaining that Club Med was a symbol of "touristic colonization." The same night, the attackers also set fire to 15 luxury houses in Porto Vecchio, causing about $200,000 in damages.

Meanwhile, in the troubled Caribbean nation of Haiti, where the regime of Baby Doc Duvalier was already crumbling, Club Med's Magic Isle village was reeling from loss of business; eventually the company was forced to close the resort until the political chaos subsided, late in 1986.

In south Florida, the holiday company announced in April its plans to take over the luxurious Sandpiper Bay resort on the tranquil shores of the St. Lucie River in Port St. Lucie, about a two-hour drive north of Miami on Florida's Treasure Coast. The acquisition of the Sandpiper Bay resort, a 1,000-acre property with a 45-hole golf course, 19 tennis courts, five swimming pools, a sailing school and marina, a fitness centre, and numerous other amenities, was Club Med's biggest gamble to date in the United States, a country that had not yet had a large Club Med village. There had been only a couple of failed attempts in Hawaii and California and the small Copper Mountain facility in Colorado.

"It is our first village in this part of the world where we have our very own golf courses, excellent facilities for both tennis buffs and sailors, along with something for practically every age and interest group," said Jacques Giraud, president of Club Med Inc. "We plan to keep it fun, with an international flavor and that very special 'something' characteristic of Club Meds everywhere."

Initially some of the locals in Port St. Lucie were sceptical about Club Med acquiring the Sandpiper Bay resort. Many had negative preconceptions about the French company. Charles Bigge, president of the quiet community's chamber of commerce, wondered why Club Med, with its reputation for attracting "swingers," would want to locate in sleepy Port St. Lucie, a resort not famous for an unabashed, Las Vegas–like life-style.

"We definitely don't have any nude beaches around here, unless they start their own," he told the *Miami Herald*, adding that he was surprised when he found out about Club Med's interest. "I was shocked when I heard. How they selected our fine city, I don't know. I guess they'll probably send their more tranquil guests here."

Another group of local residents were concerned that after the take-over Club Med was going to restrict access to guests only. Some, who enjoyed playing on the Sandpiper's championship golf course and tennis courts, quickly formed the Ad Hoc Committee to Save Sandpiper, afraid that they would not be allowed to use the facilities, one of the reasons many of them had purchased homes in the area in the first place.

"We're worked up about the fact that access might be limited if Club Med buys the Sandpiper, " said Will Roberts, an organizer of the committee. "They create an enclave, a world of their own where you don't need a car, you don't need to leave to eat, you don't even need money in your pocket.

"Our concern is that in creating their own little world they will withdraw the amenities which are a reason we came here," he summed up, pointing out that denying access to the resort would "reduce the value of our homes." Although Roberts had no evidence indicating that Club Med intended to restrict entry

205

to the resort, he suggested that legal action would be considered if that should turn out to be the case.

Club Med moved quickly to dispel the fears of the local residents. "The public will still be able to call and make reservations for dinner in the restaurant, just as they do now," said a company spokesperson. She also pointed out that existing members of the Sandpiper Bay golf and tennis club would be allowed to use the facilities. "We want to keep them," she said of the current members.

On April 29, 12 days after the deal was formally announced, Club Med's president, Jacques Giraud, visited Port St. Lucie to talk to the local residents at a meeting that put to rest their fears.

"We do want to belong to this community," Giraud told the assembled throng. "If we can bring you some happiness . . . it will mean we have succeeded." At the meeting, Giraud also promised that Club Med would keep the golf course and tennis courts open to the local residents. He also displayed a sense of humour when one of the locals grilled him about the prospects of anything happening in the next three or four years that would cause Club Med not to live up to its word. After thinking for a moment or two, he dead-panned in a French accent, "Hurricane," a remark that brought the house down.

To help dispel a few myths about the company, Club Med representatives put on a slide show about the activities of the company. They also displayed drawings and sketches of the proposed renovation and additions to the Sandpiper Bay resort, actions that indicated a sincere attempt by Club Med to work with the locals and not against them.

"This is the first time the new management has come to us like this and answered our questions," enthused Ed Gaudette, a long-time Port St. Lucie area resident. "It looks so encouraging and the spirit in which it has been given is terrific. We welcome them to Sandpiper Bay."

With the natives no longer restless, Club Med began an expensive $10-million renovation program for the Sandpiper Bay resort a short time later. The village was eventually opened in mid-March 1987.

Club Med also completed a $2-million renovation of its recently acquired St. Lucia village in 1986. There the company did a lot of work on the swimming pool area as well as constructing a brand new night club and disco, an entertainment centre that "will differ from most other discos."

The design for the new disco shows clearly that Club Med is tring to appeal to the older tourist market. "This one is divided into two separate sections," explains Club Med. "One side will be for people who want to relax in big easychairs and talk. Yes. Talk in a disco. Not shout! The other section is geared to those who want to dance the night away and will feature state-of-the-art sound and light equipment." With the work finished in just a few months, the St. Lucia village was reopened in time for Christmas 1986.

Also coming on stream in 1986 was Club Med's 700-bed Nusa Dua village on the island of Bali in Indonesia. The 35-acre resort, located about 15 minutes from the international airport at the southern end of the island, is an exotic complex featuring everything from an ancient temple to a Balinese theatre, where exhibitions of traditional dances will be held.

Elsewhere, Club Med also opened the exquisite five-star Hotel da Balaia in southern Portugal, a 40-acre jewel located just a few miles from the thriving Algarve resort of Albufeira.

In November, Club Med tried something a little out of the ordinary in the North American zone by organizing a women's issues theme week at its Punta Cana village in the Dominican Republic. Entitled "Women of Today, Looking Toward Tomorrow," the seminar program included lectures on such wide-ranging topics as health and nutrition, skin care, financial planning, and, of course, sex.

A few of the speakers scheduled to participate at the Punta Cana seminar included nutrition expert and author Gayle Black, whose theories include a diet based on astrology and motivation; Valerie Salembier, a vice-president of advertising for *USA Today*; Liz Schorr, a skin-care specialist whose clients reportedly include actors Paul Newman and Dustin Hoffman; Shirley Zussman and Carol Botwin, two sex psychologists; and Andrew Walkins, an accountant.

In another attempt to get away from its singles-only image, Club Med set up "Mini-Clubs" at about 30 of the company's vacation villages around the world. Designed exclusively for kids 2 to 11 years of age, the specially equipped Mini-Clubs feature virtually everything that could possibly amuse the younger set. Staffing the centres are a hard-working team of GOs who are the subject of universal praise from the parents, who can now finally take a break themselves while on holiday.

Open from nine in the morning to nine at night every day, the Mini-Clubs generally operate within their own special corners of the Club Med villages. Children's activities include supervised swimming, tennis, sailing, arts and crafts, games, and countless other organized diversions. Some, like the Mini-Clubs at Punta Cana, Eleuthera, and Ixtapa, also feature computer workshops for children; other villages, like St. Lucia, have a Circus School, a very popular facility with both children and adults, where Club Med's experts teach kids to use a trapeze, juggle, or bounce up and down on a trampoline.

Going a step further, Club Med has also introduced a "Baby Club" at a few of its resort villages. Baby Clubs are for toddlers between the ages of four months and one year. Open from nine to six, the clubs, which are thus far located at Paradise Island, Leysin, Zinal, and Don Miguel villages, have well-trained staffs, including pediatricians and baby nutritionists. Facilities for parents include diaper changing, 24-hour-a-day bottle-warmers, napping supervision, and entertaining, designed to appeal to new mothers and fathers.

Besides catering to the special needs of children and babies, Club Med is also experimenting with an idea called "Kids of the World" at its Copper Mountain village in Colorado. Kids of the World provides a longer-stay, summer camp–like holiday for children between the ages of 8 and 13. Reflecting the internationalism of Club Med, it is anticipated that many of the children who participate will come from nations all over the world, to learn a little about one another and the United States.

In France, Club Med also operates Kids' Clubs and Juniors' Clubs, two other special programs that cater to French children on school holiday. The activities offered include such things as organized sports tournaments, picnics, and hiking, all in addition to Club Med's usual full roster of games.

But kids aren't the only ones getting special treatment at Club Med. For adults, especially at European and African villages, Club Med organizes tournaments for golf, bridge, tennis, and Scrabble enthusiasts. For the really fit, there is even a gruelling marathon that has been scheduled for the Pontresina village in Switzerland.

On the corporate front, Club Med is forging ahead full-steam with its increasingly popular Rent-A-Village program, a combination leisure-convention package that allows a major corporation to take over an entire Club Med village for a few days or more. With Club Med offering such a diverse variety of resorts and locales and more and more big companies expressing an interest in the idea, the Rent-A-Village program can't help but expand in the future. And as Gilbert Trigano told *Time* magazine, "we make a special effort for corporations. They are especially precious to us."

Renault, Sony, Pizza Hut, Nikon, and Harley Davidson are just a few of the corporations that have rented their very own Club Med village.

With the corporate Rent-A-Village program, the facilities for children, and the City Club venture, Club Med has obviously taken very seriously the need to innovate in order to stay competitive in the modern world of vacations and travel. However, the original concept has not been swept away, as numerous Club Med villages, still run along the lines laid down nearly four decades ago by Gérard Blitz, will testify. These villages are still what most people associate with the name "Club Med." In the eyes of the public, Blitz's vision has stood the test of time.

The Garden of Earthly Delights

"At Club Med, you can relax in your own way. At your own pace. In your own time. Because at Club Med, you have the freedom to choose your own version of the perfect vacation."

Club Med, 1987

I am not a veteran Club Med GM. In fact, my first visit to a Club Med village, other than one lazy day at Cancún a few years ago, did not take place until spring 1987, when I spent a week at the new Sandpiper resort in Florida, a vast, 1,000-acre complex near Port St. Lucie.

Why Sandpiper instead of a more exotic Club Med village in Europe, the Far East, or the South Pacific? First, I wanted to stay at what the company refers to as a "family" village, a place that is perhaps more representative of the direction in which Club Med is heading than the reputedly raunchy Buccaneer's Creek in Martinique or other more singles-oriented resorts operated by the company. Second, I thought it might be interesting to see how a traditionally French vacation company would fit — culturally and competitively — in Florida, one of America's most popular tourist destinations.

What was it like? Well, as a novice, I found it definitely different from any other kind of vacation I had previously taken. The old, often-repeated axiom that Club Med is a "summer camp for adults" is true to a certain degree at Sandpiper, which, in all fairness, wasn't entirely finished at the time of my stay and was still muddling through the opening stages. It occurred to me that when you charge as much for a holiday as Club Med does — in my case, Cdn$1,205 for a one-week "land only" package that included a mandatory $30 for Club Med membership, but not the airfare or transport to and from the airport in West Palm Beach — the facility should be fully operational. It apparently did not occur to Club Med.

As I was travelling alone and was aware of the company's policy of doubling up singles, I expected to be accommodated with a complete stranger. Luckily, I was not forced to confront that ordeal, as it was nearing the end of the winter season in Florida and there were apparently a lot of empty rooms at the Sandpiper village. Thus, I was provided with private accommodations in Egret Lodge, a pinkish three-storey building just the other side of the restaurant and a stone's throw from the marina.

My room, a spacious and amply furnished unit complete with a twin bed, a sitting area, a tiny safe, a soap golf ball, and a small balcony, was better than I had anticipated. However, the view was less than spectacular, mainly offering a clear view of the heavy landscaping work being done at the rear of what was scheduled to become the Flamingo Lodge, another three-storey wing of rooms.

The first thing many GMs do after checking in is to use their personalized Club Med credit cards, issued on arrival, to buy beads, the currency of preference at all the company's vacation villages. The beads, which are sold in bags ranging from $10 to $30 (plus 5 per cent tax), are plastic; they interlock and come in three colours — yellow, orange, and white. Each is branded with the Club Med trident, the symbol of the company. The yellow beads are worth 80 cents apiece, and the orange and white beads are worth 40 cents and 20 cents respectively.

Why beads instead of cash or credit cards or simply signing the bill, the norm at most other resort hotels? Beads, it seems, are supposed to alleviate the holidayer of the vacation-ruining chore of worrying about money. It's a great idea, except that beads can have the same surrealistic effect that casino chips can have on a degenerate gambler, who, after a while, has absolutely no understanding of how much cash is evaporating. As Club Med explains: "To pay is easy: bar beads, simple, practical and fun."

Although they can be spent in the disco, an unscientific survey indicated that most GMs blow their bags of beads at the poolside bar, an airy, tropical enclave that serves as the unofficial hub of the Sandpiper village. Because the beads are purchased in advance of consumption and are non-refundable (left-over beads can be used on a future Club Med holiday), the GMs are paying up front for their drinking, as they are for everything else, whether they use it or not. This is the exact opposite of how things are done in most other hotels.

I asked one of the senior GOs why Club Med insisted on using beads. "We don't want anyone handling cash," she said matter-of-factly, hinting at the strictly supervised cash control systems.

Fortunately, the cost of imbibing at Club Med is reasonable. A Johnnie Walker Red and water, for example, is three yellow beads and one orange bead ($2.80), while a more exotic cocktail, like a mai tai or a piña colada, is only four yellow beads and one orange bead ($3.60).

"Where are you from?" asks almost every GO that you bump into on your first day at Sandpiper, a verbal ice-breaker that is no doubt intended to make new arrivals feel welcome and more at ease. However, it has a somewhat different effect because of the repetition, sounding programmed and reeking of insincerity. It is almost amusing to hear the same question, always accompanied by a patented Club Med smile, about ten times in a couple of hours.

"Where are you from?" asks a female GO for the umpteenth time, doing her best to look as if she is really interested in your answer.

"Borneo," I replied.

"Never heard of it," she said, shrugging her shoulders. "Is that in the United States?"

Each day at Sandpiper seemed to have a different GO question. On day two I was asked "What did you do today?" at least half a dozen times. On day three, it was "Did you play tennis?" or "Did you play golf?" and so on. All of which gave rise to barroom speculation that there was probably a mysterious Club Med person, dubbed the *chef de conversation*, who spent all of his or her time dreaming up the question of the day for the GOs to ask the GMs.

An initial suspect was Jill, a good-humoured, attractive, more mature GO who appeared to work out of the Welcome Lodge, where all new arrivals are greeted at Sandpiper. Soon to become known as the *chef de laughs* or the Ed McMahon of Club Med, she had the uncanny ability to explode into riotous laughter within 60 seconds of joining any GM's conversation, no matter how banal.

Mercifully, Jill's boundless enthusiasm was offset by the less feverish presence of Dr. Cocktail, a pleasant young man who worked as a bartender. While he didn't have the gift of the gab, he did have the skills to deal deftly with a pocketful of pushy New Yorkers who always seemed to be shouting and shrieking at the bar and trying desperately to draw attention to themselves. For this mob, who quickly became known as "the Oil of Olay crowd," Dr. Cocktail would prepare vicious drinks like a Turquoise Terrorist, a tropical concoction spiked with Blue Curaçao to give it that special colour and disguise the potent effects.

"We kindly ask you not to sunbathe topless," implores Club Med in a pamphlet distributed to all GMs at Sandpiper. While there is no nude beach at Sandpiper or, in fact, any beach at all, save a tiny strip of sand near the restaurant, it really doesn't matter. Club Med has more than made up for the absence with a dazzling assortment of swimming pools sprinkled throughout the grounds. They are beautifully maintained, with varying depths suitable for all categories of swimmers, so the idea of a dip in the ocean never really arises.

But for those who insist, Club Med runs a shuttle bus to nearby Jensen Beach, an expansive strip of sand with rolling surf.

In addition to the magnificent swimming pools, the Sandpiper village offers a wide assortment of recreational diversions, as everyone has come to expect from Club Med. Sailing, waterskiing, aerobics, bicycling, weight-training, tennis, golf, and lots more. It's all there, and included in the cost of the holiday, with the notable exception of golf. Those without clubs and who haven't pre-purchased the golf package must cough up $18.90 for green fees, $15.75 for golf clubs, and $8.93 for the mandatory golf cart. All of which adds up to $43.58 for one round, a tidy sum that is not included in the all-inclusive Club Med vacation.

The GMs can play on three courses, totalling 45 holes, at Sandpiper. Two courses, the 18-hole "Saints" and the 9-hole "Wilderness," are located approximately 10 minutes from the resort; the "Sinners," another 18-hole course, is situated near Sandpiper's volleyball court. Lastly, there is a 9-hole pitch-and-putt course near the arrival area that is ideal for beginners and is available for play at no cost to the GMs. Visitors should take seriously the "Beware of Alligators" signs that are placed near the water hazards — two or three ponds where, if you look carefully, you can spot one of the mostly docile reptiles.

On one sunny and extremely hot afternoon — the temperature was in the low 90s — a golf tournament was organized for the GMs, whether or not they had any experience in the game. I played with one American and two Frenchmen, neither of whom spoke English. We all struggled along in a new language — part-French, part-English, and all gibberish.

The other GMs at Sandpiper were a diverse group. As befits Club Med's status as an international vacation company, there were quite a few Americans along with Canadians, Latin Americans, and a fairly strong contingent from Europe. Most of the Europeans were from France and a number had brought the entire family. Almost all had planned a day or two at Disneyworld and Epcot, Florida's two leading tourist attractions.

Because of the language differences, the GMs socialized with their own kind — French-speaking with French-speaking, English-speaking with English-speaking. There was little opportunity for any sort of "cultural exchange."

I found the much-trumpeted Club Med cuisine to be nothing special. The food at Club Med's Sandpiper village is usually served as a buffet, a labour-saving and cost-effective method of feeding the masses that I feel doesn't really belong, for all meals, at a high-priced resort hotel.

The breakfasts at Sandpiper were mostly standard morning fare accompanied by a good choice of fruits, yoghurts, and juices. There was also a first-rate selection of croissants, sweet rolls, and freshly baked breads.

Lunch, which was served between noon and 1:45, was the best meal of the day. Informal, professional, and perfectly suited for the resort's ambience, the midday feast usually offered a dazzling array of choices ranging from grilled meats and fish to fresh oysters and clams, salads, fruits, and very good cheeses.

However, while the lunches at Sandpiper were enjoyable, the dinners were almost always disappointing. They started with a buffet of appetizers, soups, salads, and so on. The highlight of the meal was supposed to be the main course, which was to be delivered to your table by one of the pleasant local staff.

But it didn't always work out that way. To begin with, the main course was usually lukewarm, tasting as if it had been languishing in a steam table for hours and had been prepared by a chef who was cooking with less than prime ingredients. For example, on my first night, the featured selection was a chicken leg that was rubbery and greasy. A couple of nights later, it was a thinly sliced slab of meat, probably beef, that was so tough that no one at our table could down more than a couple of mouthfuls.

There were other problems. One night, the kitchen ran out of Alfredo sauce for the green fettucine, but that development didn't stop the serving chef from continuing to dish it out. When it was explained that dry fettucine can be a little chewy if not downright bland, the chef, a young Frenchman in his mid-20s, just shrugged his shoulders and muttered that there wasn't any more and there was nothing he could do about it. Many of the GMs were too hungry to care and ate the pasta without sauce anyway.

Besides the mediocre food, the service at night was simply atrocious. On one memorable occasion, diners at the same table were served at varying intervals, sometimes as long as 15 minutes apart. The dirty dishes, glasses, and ashtrays were allowed to pile up, an unpleasant situation that was eventually remedied when some of the guests cleared away the dishes themselves and grabbed clean ashtrays from other tables.

Dinner or, in fact, any meal at Sandpiper, is not an intimate affair. The company's policy is to seat all the GMs at tables for eight, which, of course, can have its advantages or disadvantages, depending on who you're dining with. Sometimes it can be quite entertaining, at other times it can be dull, or even unpleasant.

Usually a few empty places at a table would be filled by GOs, who never seemed to have any time for themselves, even at meals. Although they were always polite and could be counted on to fill in any lapses in the conversation, the GOs rarely provided very interesting company. Because of their cult-like, isolated life-style, they didn't have much to talk about, except their experiences at Club Med. Even on that subject, they mostly expressed their views like androids in clichés that could have been out of the pages of any Club Med brochure.

After dinner, which was typically washed down with several bottles of good French wine, most of the GMs shuffled over to the theatre to watch the show, an everyday feature of a Club Med holiday. There, the GMs were once again entertained by the GOs, who performed in anything from comedy sketches and musicals to lip-sync contests, the latter being adjudicated by an international panel of enthusiastic GMs.

One evening, the show moved outside to the pool area, where the GOs took part in a fiery stage production that climaxed with the word "SANDPIPER" lighting up the warm Florida night, a corny touch that generated a standing ovation from many of the GMs.

Following the show, at around eleven, the village's fairly large disco opened for business. Situated just a few steps from the main swimming pool, the disco seemed at first impression to be mostly for the enjoyment of the ever-present GOs, who crowded around the bar and seriously outnumbered the GMs every night I was there. The imbalance can probably be explained by the fact that many families were vacationing at Sandpiper; as for the GOs, they more or less had to put in an appearance, lest the powers-that-be in management accuse them of having a negative attitude.

There appeared to be little sexual interplay between the GOs and GMs; if there was, it was remarkably well concealed. One GM, an attractive Frenchman, had travelled to Sandpiper with a Canadian girl, whom he had met while on an earlier holiday at Club Med's Magic Isle village in Haiti. Although they had probably both envisioned a continuation of their affair, it just didn't work out that way. While he was out for a good time, she seemed to be much more introspective and displayed all the signs of a woman who had seriously miscalculated the true nature of the relationship. Predictably, this all-too-familiar scenario ended up with him discreetly taking up with one of the more attractive GOs, while she spent much of her time alone.

Another European GM, a beautiful girl in her early 20s, appeared to be having a good time working her way through the ranks of the male GOs. There were also a couple of girls from New York who seemed to be dallying with the hired help. Apart from these exceptions, however, the general rule seemed to be that the GMs and GOs slept apart.

There were all kinds of stories running through the Sandpiper village following the unexpected arrival of a number of GMs from the celebrated Turkoise resort in the little-known Turks and Caicos Islands in the Caribbean. These GMs had had their vacation spoiled by an ugly incident that "may have been racially related," according to Stanley Williams, police commissioner of the British-ruled islands.

The incident began on Easter weekend when one of Turkoise's local black employees, apparently outraged by a Club Med policy banning the resident islanders from using the resort's facilities, entered the resort and started smashing up the bar and kitchen. Throwing liquor bottles, breaking glasses, and causing general chaos, he reportedly generated about $1,000 in damages before order was restored by a Club Med GO. The staff member allegedly beat up the local man who was not only injured in the mêlée but also subsequently jailed.

The arrest of one of their own didn't sit well with the other islanders, many of whom also worked at the Club Med village, mostly in menial positions. Shortly after, when word of the brawl had spread throughout the island, mobs of locals started congregating at the Turkoise resort and at the police station where their fellow islander was being held.

The situation escalated when a crowd of about 50 islanders, their anger enflamed by a sign that read "No Blacks Allowed into the Club," invaded the holiday compound, disrupting everything and scaring the daylights out of many of the approximately 375 GMs, most of them from North America and Europe, who hadn't really counted on a race riot as a component of their vacation. Later the mob's occupation turned into a full-blown wildcat strike by most of the Turkoise resort's 200 local employees, who demanded more money, improved working conditions, and the termination of what they referred to as Club Med's "racial" practices. Not surprisingly, the tense situation made the day-to-day operation of the vacation village impossible and Club Med was forced to close the resort indefinitely. Most GMs, who had seen their holidays go down the drain, were either refunded their money or transferred to other hotels; a few were transferred to the Sandpiper village in Florida.

John Cortina, a 23-year-old GM from Miami, told the *Toronto Sun* that the guests were "so scared and panicked after the incident that most just wanted to go home." The paper summed up the explosive situation by saying, "Tensions run so deep at the Club Med resort here that a race riot could erupt at any time."

Paul Vinyard, a GO at the Club Med resort, also told the *Sun* that the village might be closed for a year, blaming the incident on the shortage of police on the island. "It was a very serious incident that could have been prevented had there been more police officers on the island," he said, pointing out that there were only four cops stationed on Providenciales, the island where the Turkoise village is located. "It looks like we'll be closed for a long time."

Club Med makes a big deal out of not having any clocks in its vacation villages. The theory is that no one should have to worry about the time on holiday. But after spending a week at Sandpiper, I found that it was definitely wise to wear a watch. I didn't, and consequently I spent a lot of time constantly asking people for the time.

For example, tennis lessons start at 8:00 or 9:00 in the morning, a sensible time because of the Florida heat. Low-impact aerobics are similarly scheduled for 10:00; water exercises began at 11:00. And so on, right through the day.

Meals are also served at specified hours. Breakfast is from 7:00 to 10:00. A late breakfast, presumably for those GMs who have slept in or have a hangover, runs from 10:00 to 11:30. Lunch is slotted from noon to 1:45 and dinner from 7:45 to 8:45. Dinner at the "La Paloma" Mexican restaurant, an additional dining facility in the Sandpiper complex, was scheduled for 7:30 to 8:45. However, I am unable to describe what it was like. It never opened during my stay.

In addition to the recreational activities and meals, virtually all of Sandpiper's administrative departments also work on a rigid schedule. For example, the traffic office, where GMs confirm flight reservations and transfers to the airport, is open from 9:00 to noon and from 4:30 to 7:00. Similarly, Sandpiper's other facilities, like the bank, boutique, bazaar, laundry, and infirmary, only operate at designated times.

Did I enjoy my week at Club Med? Would I consider spending another vacation frolicking as a GM? I am still undecided. I honestly can't make up my mind if I liked it or not. Certainly there were some aspects I could do without, like the awful dinners and the non-stop, party-line propaganda of most of the GOs. However, there were some very positive elements. As advertised, Club Med does deliver on its promise of a laid-back ambience. No one twists your arm to do anything. It really can be as hectic or as lazy as you choose to make it. My rotten tennis game did improve marginally after several hours of flailing away on Sandpiper's excellent courts. I also played in a tennis tournament and had a round of golf — something I really didn't imagine I would do before I grabbed the plane.

What about my fellow GMs? While I did enjoy the company of several guests, the vast majority were just not the sort of people I would normally socialize with at home. Not because they were morons incapable of independent thought, a common perception of the Club Med clientele held mainly by those who have never vacationed at a Club Med village. Rather, it probably had more to do with different life-styles and interests.

If I had a family, Club Med would definitely be on the top of my list as a vacation destination, especially if I had younger children. I simply can't imagine any other hotel or resort doing a better job of looking after kids. From 8:00 in the morning to 9:00 at night, the children in the Mini-Club are taken care of by a dedicated team of GOs, who not only obviously enjoy their work but also have the creativity to dream up new and interesting ways to amuse them.

Obviously, Club Med isn't for everyone. Villages such as Sandpiper provide a standardized format that isn't to everyone's taste. However, the Club Med formula evidently appeals to sufficient numbers of holidayers to make the company extremely successful in a very competitive field. This ability to satisfy thousands of people from a large number of different countries is what will keep Club Med expanding into the next century.

INDEX

223